QUEST

HARPER & ROW, PUBLISHERS, New York

Cambridge, Hagerstown, Philadelphia, San Francisco

London, Mexico City, São Paulo, Sydney

1817

QUEST

The Life of Elisabeth Kübler-Ross

by Derek Gill

with an Epilogue by Elisabeth Kübler-Ross

All the events in this biography are real. However, the names of some individuals and certain details about their lives have been changed in order to protect their identity.

FIRST EDITION

Designer: Gloria Adelson

Library of Congress Cataloging in Publication Data

Gill, Derek L   T
    Quest: the life of Elisabeth Kübler-Ross.
    1. Kübler-Ross, Elisabeth. 2. Psychiatrists—United States—Biography. 3. Death—Psychological aspects. I. Title.
RC339.52.K83G53   616.89′0092′4[B]   78-19823
ISBN 0-06-011543-2

80 81 82 83 84 10 9 8 7 6 5 4 3 2 1

297816

Contents

Illustrations follow page 208.

Introduction

In September 1976 I was at a birthday party at a house near San Diego, California, when I was approached by a young woman who said, "Mr. Gill, I think your next biography should be on the life of Elisabeth Kübler-Ross."

My normal response would have been a noncommittal smile; for writers are often offered such unsolicited advice. However, on this occasion my jaw dropped in surprise, for not twenty-four hours earlier I had seen the name of Dr. Kübler-Ross for the first time—at least, in any context that made impact on memory.

In my dentist's reception room the previous afternoon I had been riffling through a copy of a popular magazine and lighted upon an interview with Dr. Kübler-Ross. The simplicity and originality of her replies to the interviewer's questions on the subject of death had so intrigued me that I ripped the four pages of the illustrated feature from the magazine (guiltily albeit) and stuffed them into my coat pocket.

That night in bed I reread the feature twice more, and still would have found it hard to explain my excitement. I don't suppose that I have pondered more than the average man upon the mystery of death, nor, having soldiered for five war years, have I been sheltered from mortality.

But here was a scientist and philosopher whose answers to questions about life and death seemed to have a compelling ring.

One picture of her in the journal showed a plain bespectacled middle-aged woman, casually dressed in a loose windbreaker and pants. Against the backdrop of a handsome house, she was accompanied by her two teenage children and the family's St. Bernard. An adjoining paragraph quoted her as saying that because of her work with the dying she was quite ready to let go of everything of value. "I know that to see a winter sunset or to watch a pheasant family stroll the lawn are infinitely more important than material things."

A pheasant family on the lawn, indeed! How engaging that anyone could be so stirred by such a sight as to prefer the glimpse to the option of treasure and high honors.

She was quoted too on her views of life after death: "Whoever you most loved in life who preceded you in death is there to help you make the transition. . . . The important thing is that you don't go through it [death] alone. It is wonderful to be able to assure parents of dying children. 'Don't worry. There will be someone waiting to take care of your child.' "

What caught me, of course, was that this was a scientist talking. From the pulpit one had heard often enough rhetorical promises of resurrection and assurances of heaven. Yet even as a young child I had doubted that a beloved grandfather had "gone to a beautiful place." I had looked up at the relative who had given me this assurance and had asked, "Then why is everybody crying?"

But that was a long time ago, and I was speaking of a birthday reception of comparatively recent date, and of how I was taken off guard by a statement by a young woman whom I had not previously met. Naturally I asked her what had made her come up with the idea. She murmured something about having read my books and having heard Dr. Kübler-Ross speak and, if I remember her phrase, that "there seemed to be a sort of symbiosis."

"Symbiosis" is one of those biological words that send the layman to his dictionary. It tripped easily off the young woman's tongue because, as she now told me, she was a newly graduated physician.

In any event, while driving to my home in Los Angeles I gave little thought either to the coincidence of coming across an unusual name twice within so short a spell, or to the young physician's suggestion of some link between my craft and the life of Elisabeth Kübler-Ross. Indeed, the suggestion would surely have faded quickly from my mind had I not, on reaching my hearth, received a phone call from a friend who had, she said, just bought me a ticket for a Kübler-Ross lecture!

Three times within one cycle of the sun the name of Kübler-Ross had been impressed upon me.

I went to the lecture in the cavernous auditorium of the University of California at Long Beach. As one of an audience of 3,000 and from the twenty-fourth row I first saw Elisabeth (for so we shall now call her). What struck me as she walked to the podium was how small she was. Not a quarter of an inch taller than five feet and weighing almost exactly a hundred pounds, she was wearing a hand-embroidered, peasant blouse, fawn corduroy pants and roman sandals.

From the moment she started to speak in her soft German-accented voice until, three hours later, she returned the hand-held microphone to its stand, she so captured the audience that an occasional cough or a sneeze somewhere behind me sounded like gunfire.

"Today," she began, "we will talk about life. We will talk about death. And we will talk about love. All are really different facets of the same thing."

Every now and then she turned about and stepped toward a blackboard where she chalked up salient points, but mostly she sat on the corner of a table swinging a sandaled foot.

Her delivery was devoid both of rhetoric and flamboyant gesture. She spoke, in fact, with such simplicity and clarity that a child of perhaps ten or eleven who was sitting alongside me never took his eyes off the stage. Nor did the scientist friend who had bought my ticket.

For the first two-thirds of her address she spoke of her work and of the care of the dying. I surmised from the busy note taking that many in the audience were professionals of the healing arts. Then she spoke of death itself and of life after death. For the first time there was a stirring in the audience, like the shadowed movement in a wheat field touched by sudden wind.

My scientist friend was among those who became restless as Elisabeth moved across the border from medical and social issues to an area generally reserved for theologians. I had not up to this point used my shorthand (Elisabeth had asked that tape recorders not be used), but now I did, for this was what I had come to hear.

With some editing, here is a sample of what she said: "Mrs. Schwarz, one of my patients, had been in intensive care fifteen times in my hospital in Chicago. In one of her hospitalizations she was put into a private room, where she sensed she was very close to death. One part of her mind wanted to lean back on the pillows, but the other part needed to make it through her new crisis because of her family. Suddenly she was aware of herself floating out of her body. She was surprised to see her corpse. Then from her elevated position a few feet above her own body she watched a resuscitation team dash into the room and attempt to revive her. She frantically tried to tell the team to relax and take it easy, but the team could not perceive or hear her. Mrs. Schwarz heard herself declared dead, but three and a half hours later she made a comeback and she lived for another eighteen months.

"Since then I've had hundreds of cases of people who have had similar out-of-body experiences. They all relate the same sort of thing. They are fully aware of shedding their physical body, like a butterfly coming out of a cocoon. We now have overwhelming evidence that death is a transition into a higher state of consciousness. It's like putting away your winter coat because you don't need it anymore.

"Of my patients who have had this experience none are ever again afraid to die. Many of the patients have spoken of the peace they experienced—beautiful, indescribable peace, no pain, no anxiety. They speak of the higher understanding that comes to all at the transition. They tell us that all that matters is how much you have loved, how much you have cared; and if you know these things, as I now know them, then you cannot possibly be afraid of death."

Elisabeth gave a number of examples of people known to her who had had experiences similar to that of Mrs. Schwarz. Then she added, "Only if you keep an open mind, and learn to get in touch in silence with the voice within, will you know that death does not exist, and that everything in life has positive purpose."

My own reaction to Elisabeth's address was a mixture of fascination and incredulity. I was determined to meet her, but after the lecture it was impossible to get near her, for she was surrounded by an adulatory mob. Not knowing that she received 3,000 letters a month, I wrote to her to ask for an interview. Only later did I learn from Elisabeth that my letter had slipped to the floor from a pile on her secretary's desk. In the ordinary way, the secretary would have answered the letter herself, and negatively, because Elisabeth is deluged by similar requests for personal interviews and gives priority to the dying. However, she picked the letter up herself and was "guided," as she put it, to see me.

Her reply to me read, "Will be in Fresno, California, to lecture on February 17 [1977]. I can see you at five o'clock for 30 minutes." That was all.

My wife and I traveled to Fresno and we easily found the lecture hall—actually the biggest theater in town. There were only two vacant seats right at the back wall. Once again I was held spellbound. When the lecture ended, I was about to push my way through the crowd now shouldering its way to the exits when I distinctly heard a voice saying, "Tell her you're a friend of Viktor Frankl."

Assuming the voice was my wife's, I turned to her and asked, "Why should I tell her that?"

She arched her eyebrows, and I repeated the question. "Why do you feel that I should tell Dr. Kübler-Ross that I'm a friend of Viktor Frankl?"

"What are you talking about?" she said.

I felt a bit shaken; but if I was to catch Elisabeth, there was no time to seek an explanation of this mystery. Certainly there was no one else within range who could possibly have known that I had recently collaborated in writing a book on the noted Viennese psychiatrist.

When I finally reached Elisabeth on the stage and reminded her of our appointment, she shook her head. She was sorry that she would not have time to see me after all. She had to go straight to a dying patient at the local hospital. I would surely understand.

In fact, I was more than disappointed. I was angry. I curtly told her that I had traveled more than 250 miles for the promised thirty minutes of her time. She apologized again and was turning away when I remembered the inexplicable voice at the back of the theater.

"By the way," I said, "I'm a personal friend of Viktor Frankl."

I might just as well have fired a gun. She snapped back her head and pulled me by my shirt-sleeve to the side of the stage. The previous day, she explained, she had had her first meeting with Frankl, whom she had greatly admired all her life. She studied me with new interest. When I told her that I would be flying to Chicago in a couple of weeks and that I would be near her home, she invited me to pick her up by car after a lecture she was scheduled to give at Stevens Point, Wisconsin, two weeks hence. There would be plenty of time for uninterrupted dialogue.

What an unforgettable six-hour drive that was! The Wisconsin countryside was in the grip of winter. Shortly after we had set out from Stevens Point, Elisabeth insisted I pull the car to the side of the highway to watch a blood-red sun setting over a frozen lake and stark woodlands. She finger-touched her lips for silence. I watched her in profile. For some minutes she seemed to be in a distant place, savoring vibrations of light and color. She had looked tired as she got into the car, but now the lines of fatigue around her eyes vanished. She laughed, combed fingers through short hair beginning to gray, and said, "There, now, my energy's quite restored. Let's go."

We drove through the twilight in silence, and then as darkness settled she started to speak of her life, her dreams and her struggle. When she talked of her mystical experiences, my mind hovered between outright incredulity and a genuine desire to believe.

What I certainly accepted, though, was that I was in the enviable company of a unique person, a woman of profound compassion, exceptional courage and determination. She was also uncomfortably disconcerting. In the months ahead I was to discover that she was so rocklike in her convictions—convictions that I could not always support—that we had many clashes. Indeed, there were times when we regretted having set out on the task of writing her story. Then there were times when I believed (and still do) that destiny, the stars in their courses and the moon—what you will—played a part in this project.

Yes, certainly the moon, because on that memorable journey through the winter's night the biggest moon I've ever seen suddenly lifted above the horizon. It so entirely filled the windshield of the car that I was almost blinded. I murmured something about atmospheric conditions and reflective snow creating the phenomenon.

Elisabeth would have none of that. "What nonsense!" she exclaimed. "It's a celestial blessing on our working together!" She laughed and then, quoting Shakespeare, chided me to find "tongues in trees, books in the running brooks, sermons in stones and good in every thing."

Working together! She had read my mind and had known before my asking that I wanted to write her life story.

I have worked very closely with Elisabeth and have traveled many thousands of miles in order to record her story. Yet, as her biographer, I'm obliged to confess that I still do not really know her.

Oh, I acknowledge her genius as a physician and communicator. I can give testimony to her selflessness and generosity. I've seen her as a beautiful soul, childlike in her simplicity. Yet she remains for me an incredibly complex character, a woman of fascinating mystery.

ACKNOWLEDGMENTS

I am deeply grateful to Cass Canfield,
Ann Harris and Corona Machemer for their
encouragement and professional help during
the three years this book took to be written.

QUEST

1

The First Earth Day

IN THE LATE AFTERNOON of July 8, 1926, all appeared normal in the delivery room of a maternity hospital in Zurich, Switzerland. The fair-haired woman on the table was in the final stages of labor and being given sibilant encouragement by a buxom, motherly obstetrician. At the door of the room stood a tall powerfully built man, his arms akimbo and his emotions under control as he waited out the last minutes of the birth of what he most keenly hoped would be a daughter.

It was not the first time that Emma and Ernst Kübler had experienced the birth of a child; but their son, Ernst, was now six years old. Memory of the earlier occasion had dimmed.

From the hour in which his wife had told him she was pregnant once again, Mr. Kübler had quite persuaded himself that his second child would be a daughter—a girl strong in limb but with alabaster skin; a daughter to whom in due time he would introduce his beloved mountains; a daughter who would possess all the graces of the drawing room, yet would revel in the outdoor life and have his passion for

1

glacier, lake, forest, skiing and trekking the high trails. Mr. Kübler was a romantic.

The delivery-room drama moved to a climax. The obstetrician cupped her hands to receive the infant now struggling to escape the birth canal. A moment more, and a child was born.

It was the smallest baby the veteran doctor had ever delivered. The infant, surprisingly crying with life, was not much longer than the doctor's hands. It weighed exactly two pounds.

The doctor forced a smile to conceal alarm. Speaking over her shoulder to the figure at the door, she reflected cheerfully, "Yes, it's a daughter you have, Mr. Kübler—the daughter you wanted."

But on being shown the tiny shriveled baby, Mr. Kübler made no effort to hide disappointment. He barely heard his wife wearily murmur that she was "quite sure there's more to come." He retreated to an outer room where he dutifully telephoned his mother with the news.

Emma Kübler was right. She was shortly delivered of a second child—a two-pound replica of the first. Mr. Kübler returned to the telephone to announce the girl twins; but by the time he was back in the delivery room once more, a third child had been born. The third baby girl weighed a healthy six pounds.

The obstetrician, a self-styled clairvoyant, held up the plump last-born, who was to be christened Emma (but who would be known as Eva), and told Mrs. Kübler, "This one will always be closest to her mother's heart, just as she was in the womb."

She held up the second-born, who was to be named Erika, and declared, "This one will be frail, and she will be her father's child."

Then she lifted up the firstborn. "But this one—ah, this one will be an independent spirit. This one will be a pathfinder, just as she was at her birth."

The firstborn triplet was named Elisabeth.

Zurich's newspapers recorded the rare birth of triplets to the wife of a prominent citizen. The papers reported that Mr. Kübler was assistant director of the city's leading office supply company, a part-time teacher at a technical college and an official tourist guide for Swiss visitors to Belgium, Hungary and Austria. His favorite pastimes were hiking, mountain climbing and skiing. He was a member of the exclu-

2

sive Zurich Ski Club and he had recently been accorded the special honor of custodianship of the Furlegi Mountain ski chalet.

Press reports added that Mrs. Kübler was recovering well from her ordeal, that the biggest of the triplets, the non-identical, was also doing well, but there was "some concern" over the welfare of the tiny identical twins.

In fact, the identical twins were battling for life. But their special benediction was that they had chosen a most unusually dedicated mother. Mrs. Kübler spent only a few days in the hospital before deciding to take the babies home, where she herself could give them round-the-clock care. Aside from the obstetrician, who recognized the strength of Mrs. Kübler's resolve, members of the hospital staff held out little hope for Elisabeth and Erika.

Indeed, the petal mouth of Elisabeth was so small that initially she could not take direct nourishment from her mother's breasts. For the first month of her life she was fed maternal milk every two hours from a doll's bottle.

For nine months after giving birth to her three daughters, Mrs. Kübler never went to bed, nursing her three babies every three hours day and night. She slept for short spells on a Victorian chaise longue in a makeshift nursery in the Kübler home in Zurich.

Like balloons given a first puff of breath, the wrinkled skin of the babies slowly began to fill out. Craftsmen friends of Mr. Kübler hand-carved a unique three-bed cradle. Elisabeth and Erika shared one end of a three-place baby carriage, and plump Eva occupied the other. The routine of the triplets being wheeled out into the streets and parks inevitably attracted sightseers—not to Mrs. Kübler's displeasure and, when he accompanied them, to Mr. Kübler's expressed pride and delight.

Mr. and Mrs. Kübler were a handsome couple whose personalities were in sharp contrast. He was the extrovert who tackled work and recreation with equal and enormous vigor. He was close to being a stereotype of an upper-middle-class Swiss-German. Boasting an ancestry he traced back four centuries, he was stolid, strong, conservative, and he reflected the reliability and rugged independence of his heritage. There was a no-nonsense look about Mr. Kübler, whether he was standing broad-shouldered behind his office desk or striding

3

jut-jawed up a mountain trail. His big frame matched the mountains. He possessed a rich, vibrant bass voice that bespoke authority and which he exercised with singing at the family piano. His brown eyes could glint with anger, but as readily sparkle with high humor. His was a predictable personality. There was for him a right and there was a wrong, a white and a black, and only rarely any gray areas in between. He was a natural leader and organizer, methodical, not intuitive but logical in his approach to challenges and problems. When he took risks—as he often did when mountain climbing—they were carefully calculated. Yet he was not drawn to the beaten path and the known way. If the trails were new, he would carefully test the strength of his rope before setting out. He loved to travel. In the days when travel was still something of an adventure he explored a number of countries in Europe, including Austria, Hungary and Belgium (where, he declared, he found his favorite people). When entertaining at home, which he most thoroughly enjoyed doing for a wide variety of friends and business acquaintances, Mr. Kübler was a stickler for etiquette. He had an excellent wine cellar. When the wine had flowed, his parties could be boisterous with song and laughter.

Mrs. Kübler had married before ever taking up a profession. Although only a couple of inches over five feet, she was far from being frail. She too was familiar with mountain trails and she was an advanced skier. She seldom used makeup on her small tanned face. Her voice was soft, melodic, rarely raised. She had a good figure and small practical hands that wrought magic in her kitchen. She sewed and knitted exquisitely, and indeed had all the acceptable assets of a Swiss-German homemaker. Mr. Kübler's income was large enough to allow his wife to engage a servant. On several occasions she did employ a maid or housekeeper, but none could measure up to the skills and efficiency she demanded. It was, she told her friends, less stressful to do all the housework herself—even when she had to cope with newborn triplets. Mrs. Kübler enjoyed dancing and the opera, and she delighted in the outdoor life, but her contentment stemmed essentially from a strong sense of self-worth as a housewife and mother. She was proud of her reputation as a cook, proud of her spotless home, of her immaculately dressed children, proud of a garden that produced all the fruit and vegetables the household needed.

From the outset the Kübler triplets were identically dressed, from pink-ribboned socks to pink-ribboned bonnets. Before they left the playpen, Elisabeth's long struggle for identity had begun.

Eva, who from her birth always looked like an elder, was, with her mother's neat features, the beautiful child that Mr. Kübler had envisioned. Aware of her physical advantage, she was soon the most physically assertive of the trio. She would, for example, grab food away from placid Erika. But always she had to contend with Elisabeth. If Eva snatched half a banana from Erika, Elisabeth would snatch it back again and return it to her passive identical twin.

Photographs of the family taken when the triplets were one year old disclose this early diversity of character. Eva and Erika are often seen beaming at the camera—Eva coquettishly, Erika dutifully—but the third infant seems to be uninterested in posing. Where Elisabeth is not trying to climb out of the playpen, her eyes are focused on something in the middle distance. Her fist is often clenched, her body alert. Occasionally a fourth figure is shown in these early photographs. Seven-year-old Ernst's scowl is resentfully deep. The young boy had, of course, been demoted from his place of prime parental attention by the arrival of the triplets. Visitors to the Kübler home almost invariably brought only three gifts—three pairs of slippers, perhaps, three dolls, three boxes of candy. It was rare indeed when a more sensitive visitor included a separate gift for schoolboy Ernst, the now uncelebrated son of the household.

Despite the identical twins' different personalities, even Mrs. Kübler could not tell who was Erika and who Elisabeth. In fact, Erika's first memory is of being bathed twice within ten minutes by her father. Elisabeth wryly reflects that she has no recollection of this incident. Elisabeth's first memories encompass a fairy-book bedroom with frilled polka-dot red curtains, in which the furnishings included identical potties bearing flower designs and a closet filled with identical clothes. Even the sheets, pillowcases and handkerchiefs bore identical hand-embroidered initials. The trio were almost never identified by name. They were simply called the "triplets." It occurred to no one that even infant triplets possessed their own thumbprints.

Family friends, relatives and the community at large treated the triplets more like rare zoo animals than like children. Strange faces peered into the baby carriage. Strange hands poked, stroked and patted. Enormous billboard pictures of the little girls advertised to train commuters that the famous Kübler triplets were washed exclusively in Palmolive soap or were being reared on Ovomaltine. This commercial exploitation, sanctioned by Mr. Kübler, who was motivated by pride, not need, was rewarded by occasional crates of soap and processed food.

The three little girls were expected to perform uniformly. Trigger-happy with his camera, Mr. Kübler typically would order his daughters to sit on their potties at the same time in his pursuit of another wallet photograph to amuse his friends.

Meanwhile, Mrs. Kübler uncomplainingly worked eighteen hours a day, seven days a week, on chores that included the hand-washing of perhaps sixty diapers a day. The diapers were hung on a clothesline on the roof of the Zurich home, the fluttering squares signaling to the neighborhood a household of unusual fertility and domestic industry.

Aside from the notoriety of their birth, the first years of the triplets' lives were not marked by notable events. Elisabeth recalls only a blur of memories—picnics, birthday cakes, periods in bed with head colds, visits to the shoe store for larger shoes, bedtime stories, days of snow and ice, languid days of high summer, playing in the park, bloodied knees, squirrels and squabbling, a brother who was tall and wise and enviably independent, a father who thrilled them with piggy-back rides, a mother whose soft lips kissed them good night.

But it was a memorable day in their fourth year when Mr. Kübler decided that his developing family needed a bigger home and country air. In the village of Meilen, half an hour along the lakeside railroad from Zurich, he rented a timbered green-painted three-storied house surrounded by meadows and vineyards.

Entrance to the home was made through what had originally been designed as an open coach house. The ground floor comprised a living room, dining room and kitchen; and above these were three bedrooms, one of which was occupied by Mr. and Mrs. Kübler and the second by the triplets. One of two large rooms in the attic was Ernst's bedroom and the boy's private lair. The second room was occupied by a maid on the rare occasions when a maid was employed, or by visiting relatives. The space between the two rooms in the attic was used for storage.

Elisabeth remembers the attic as the most exciting part of the Green House (as the family was to call it). On infrequent but memorable occasions Ernst would invite her to visit his room to examine his treasures—notably a stamp collection. From a grandmother Ernst had inherited heavy antique furniture, including an enormous chest of drawers with secret compartments. He allowed Elisabeth to touch hidden latches. A panel would suddenly slide away as thrillingly as the entrance to Ali Baba's cave. The drawer was likely to contain strange foreign coins or medallions, perhaps some ski-club or mountain-climbing trophies won by the family. For a few moments Ernst would permit Elisabeth to hold these treasures in sticky hands before they were returned to their secret places behind the sliding panels. These shared moments created a conspiratorial bond between Elisabeth and Ernst, who otherwise was a distant if admired figure in her young childhood.

There was more treasure than this in the attic. In the area between the two large rooms the triplets kept their large dollhouse, filled with miniature pieces of furniture, many of which were made by Elisabeth and her sisters.

On wet or frozen days the girls whiled away many hours weaving tiny mats for the dollhouse drawing room or making miniature clay flowerpots for its chalet-type balconies. If they wearied of this pastime, there was always the huge chest of drawers where Mrs. Kübler stored old clothes and linen. The attic was a place of make-believe and often the only place where Elisabeth could be alone.

In their own bedroom the triplets' cradle had given way to three neat half-size beds. In the bedroom closet the clothes were naturally several sizes larger, but still the same in design and color. Chintz-curtained windows led to a balcony which looked over a sweep of vineyards to the mountains and the lake.

Established long ago as a farming village, Meilen had grown and prospered with the advent of railroads. In spite of some modern buildings and a main street, the village retained a rustic picture-postcard charm. Most of the inhabitants knew each other—if not intimately, then on nodding acquaintanceship. Meilen was a perfect place to rear young children. And to raise a family successfully was considered the prime responsibility of Swiss-German parents of the upper middle class.

Mr. Kübler's career advanced, but in spite of increased business activities he found or made time for hiking, climbing or skiing, according to the season. On weekends, when the family was at home, the house was frequently filled with visitors, including a considerable tribe of relatives and sporting friends. For the pleasure and pride of their parents the triplets were always paraded, always deluged with gifts and the oil of flattery.

Few relatives stand out in Elisabeth's early memories. A widowed maternal grandmother was one of the more frequent visitors. She was very frail and nearly blind, and Elisabeth was touched by this old lady who softly and inexplicably protested that her life was useless—inexplicably, because she was much loved and respected.

Elisabeth also has a special memory of an uncle whom she never actually saw. The ghost of Uncle Herman often seemed to be around. He actually died by his own hand before the triplets were born, but the story was told of how Uncle Herman, unhappily married, had gone one night to a famous Zurich restaurant where he had asked the orchestra to play "Ave Maria." When he had heard the song, he had walked out into the night and committed suicide. After she heard this story, "Ave Maria" held particular meaning for Elisabeth, and Uncle Herman seemed to be close to her shoulder.

There were lively aunts and other older relatives with their grown-up talk, and if one or another played the piano or an accordion he was given special marks of approval. But the figures silhouetted against the years of early childhood are the neighbors' children with whom the triplets played, and the English lady who owned a bakery in the village and who was free with gifts of pastry and candy, and Rösy, who was a maid for a short spell, a simple country girl with a lovely singing voice. When their mother was out shopping or their parents were at the opera, the triplets would bribe Rösy to sing ballads by offering to help her sweep and dust the rooms or wash dishes.

The world was at peace, and the most peaceful country in the world was Switzerland. Timeless snow-capped mountains towered above pastoral valleys. The season changed in eternal rhythm. In winter behind the frosted windows apple-cheeked children were taught that God was in His heaven benignly protecting those who believed in Him. In spring the cherry trees exploded into pink blossom. In flower-perfumed summer the purest air was filled with the sounds of hay cutters and cowbells, the murmur of bees and children's laughter. In the fall grape pickers with leathered faces shouldered their wicker baskets and plucked abundant harvests from the vineyards.

Each year was highlighted by festivals, and the first of these was Christmas. The Swiss Santa Claus is but a distant cousin of the benevolent character familiar to children in the English-speaking world. He arrives on Santa Claus Day, always December 6, and he knows exactly how a child has behaved in the preceding twelve months, so he is greeted with ambivalent feelings of excitement and apprehension. Like his American counterpart, he conceals an avuncular or paternal chin behind cotton wool. He can recall with embarrassing clarity the details of a child's shortcomings—an untidy bedroom, bad school reports, ill manners and similar waywardness.

Elisabeth remembers this public declaration and admission of sins as a purging experience. Santa carries a whip, not often used, but symbolic of deserved punishment. He also carries a burlap bag full of fruit, nuts and candy, symbolic of reward and forgiveness.

The nineteen-day period between Santa Claus Day and Christmas is sacred. Freed of guilt and worry, and occupied with making gifts for family and friends, the Swiss child lives in a state of euphoria. Far from being a season of overindulgence, the Swiss Christmas has strong spiritual overtones.

Another festival in which Elisabeth delighted was Rabenliechtli, which is somewhat similar to Halloween. She and her sisters and all the children would don gruesome masks and carry lanterns carved out of a large turnip. Swiss legend has it that when nights lengthen in the fall, the masks and lanterns keep evil spirits at bay.

The end of winter is marked by the cheerful festival of Sechseläuten. Each year the children were taken to Zurich for this holiday, and the church bells pealed out as they marched behind an enormous snowman made of cotton waste and firecrackers. For these parades the triplets wore their special Biedermeier costumes with long pantalettes and skirts that revealed a provocative touch of lace. At the conclusion of the Sechseläuten parade, the snowman was symbolically burned by men dressed as Bedouins who rode their horses wildly around the bonfire. On the following day the triplets joined other young children in searching for the first wildflowers of the spring.

Every workaday morning of the year Mr. Kübler left home at eight o'clock and caught the train to Zurich. Mrs. Kübler fed the triplets and saw Ernst off to school. The family met again for lunch. When their father returned in the evening, he usually had time to romp with his daughters before packing them off to bed. Once they were in bed, Mrs. Kübler read them good-night stories, including, of course, the many adventures of Heidi.

Attached to Elisabeth's earliest memories are her recollections of her hopes, yearnings, imaginings and, as she now puts it, "strange beckonings." She was, for instance, irrationally excited by a picture book of life in an African village. The four-year-old child saw herself and her sisters as African children, their ebony skins glistening under a tropical sun. She could hear the throb of drums, taste exotic fruit.

She named her imaginary country Higaland and, by pouting her lips, spoke the ancient musical Higaland language. Eva soon learned this language, but Erika, who had difficulty pouting her lips, spoke a different dialect. Erika, it was mutually agreed, lived in the adjacent but friendly country of Popplesland, whose tongue could also be spoken by Mr. Kübler. Only Mrs. Kübler and Ernst seemed unable to comprehend these African tongues.

Adults' inability to tell Elisabeth and Erika apart was, even at this age, a puzzle and an annoyance. The identical twins knew they were different. They thought differently. They acted and reacted differently. Constantly seeking ways to help adults recognize her, Elisabeth started to display special identifications. Thus, if the clothing of the twins was the same (as it almost always was), Elisabeth would rip an ornamental button or ribbons from her dress. She respected anyone who called her by her own name.

By now Mr. Kübler had no difficulty in telling who was Erika and who Elisabeth, for the one daughter was always more active and more rebellious. Because Elisabeth was never still and, as her father phrased it, "always hopping from branch to branch," he gave her the pet name Meisli—"Little Sparrow." To placid Erika he gave the name Augedächli, "Eyelid," because he often found her daydreaming, her eyes half closed. Augedächli was a name that also implied closeness of relationship—the closeness of the lid to the eye. Erika was be-

10

coming, as had been predicted by the obstetrician, "her father's child."

A few weeks after her fifth birthday Elisabeth's hunger for African adventures was briefly satisfied when a group of Africans visited Zurich on a cultural exchange program which included construction of a replica of an African village in Zurich's zoo. Elisabeth smuggled herself aboard a train and somehow found her way to the zoo, where she met and talked with genuine Africans. Very dark-skinned and colorfully robed, the visitors were from West Africa, but for Elisabeth they were from someplace close to God.

While her parents and neighbors were frantically looking for the lost child in Meilen, the little girl sat at the feet of the tall Africans who played their drums especially for her. She felt completely at home in their company, and was more puzzled than pained when she was found late that evening by an alerted Zurich relative, brought home and spanked.

From that day, she put aside her collection of white dolls and announced to the family that she would not again play with a doll unless it was a black one. Her prediction was to be soon and dramatically fulfilled.

Shortly after the zoo incident, Elisabeth caught a cold which developed into pleurisy and then pneumonia. Mr. Kübler was away in the mountains when the child's fever soared. For the first time in her life Elisabeth was removed from the bedroom she shared with her sisters and put into the large bed in the second-floor guest bedroom.

On the second day of her illness her fever continued to rise, and that night in a spell of delirium she wandered outside the house, perhaps to cool her flushed skin with air sweeping down from the mountains. Her mother found her and carried her back to bed; Elisabeth recalls her mother's frantic telephoned pleading to a physician who refused to make a house call.

Mrs. Kübler then called a neighbor who owned a car. The neighbor immediately agreed to drive the sick child to the children's hospital in Zurich.

Although a tight, rasping cough stabbed her chest, Elisabeth was enthralled by the journey through the night, by the lights and the sounds of the city. She had a feeling of being special because she was separated from her sisters and had the undivided attention of her

11

mother. She was an individual, not just a triplet, not a collective noun; at least not for a while.

Her euphoria did not last. At the hospital she was weighed and labeled as if she were a package on a post office counter. All around her were strangers in starched white coats, strangers who prodded her and slid cold instruments over her hot skin. No one spoke to her. No one asked her questions. She couldn't understand why her mother was told to leave the room.

Elisabeth was to carry into her adult and professional life a vivid recollection of her first experience in a hospital. As a physician herself she was to lecture medical students and nursing associations on the "dehumanizing" procedures so common in emergency rooms, speaking often of that "utterly confused little patient who was treated as a thing."

The little girl was put to bed in a two-bed glass-enclosed isolation room—"a big fishbowl," as Elisabeth remembers it—whose second occupant was another very sick little girl. The other child, two years older than Elisabeth, appeared to be almost translucent, her face as pale as her pillowcase—"an angel without wings," Elisabeth recalls.

Neither Elisabeth nor her dying room companion was able to talk much, but because of their common frailty and their loneliness they shared an extraordinarily intimate communion, sustained by wan smiles and empathetic looks.

After a number of uncounted high-fevered days and restless nights, the thread to life of her ward companion quietly broke. Elisabeth found no deep trauma in the death. To the five-year-old it was as if the older child, a trail companion for a brief spell, had chosen her own pathway and followed it. The two young girls had smiled and parted, each taking the route of her choice—the one to a peaceful shadowed valley where there are no more hurts, no tears, no more painful struggling to breathe. But Elisabeth chose the steeply inclined, sharp-pebbled pathway to life.

There was no doubt in Elisabeth's mind that she would live, just as, without words spoken, without apparent trepidation, the other child had known of death's approach. The only sign of fear, Elisabeth recalls, was in the eyes and gestures of the masked figures who came into the isolation ward to feed and wash and otherwise minister to the

12

small patients, and in the eyes of her parents, who visited from time to time and waved from the other side of the glass partition.

In the long and critical weeks that followed there were several periods when pain and exhaustion almost enticed Elisabeth to follow the path of her friend. There were times when she saw her parents through blurred eyes, as if in a dream—just familiar faces and figures standing behind the glass partition, unable to talk to her. No one explained to her why her parents could not draw close, why she could not be held and hugged by those she loved. She could not understand either why the expressions of Mr. and Mrs. Kübler were so sad.

One innocent sickbed activity that helped Elisabeth occupy the endless stretch of hours was to peel dead skin from her fevered lips. However, the cantankerous senior physician caught her at this pastime and he immediately ordered that her hands be strapped to the iron bed. When she was denied this one small contact with her own body, her sense of isolation and abandonment increased. Her flesh continued to waste.

One morning she listened apathetically to a huddle of physicians standing in a horseshoe around her bed. Her eyes followed them to the door, where they discussed diagnosis and prognosis. She comprehended enough of the adult exchange to realize that her recovery depended upon her father giving her some of his own blood. It was all a mystery, but an exciting one.

In the 1930s transfusion procedures were still primitive. Transfusions were given with the aid of a hand pump that resembled a coffee grinder. When Mr. Kübler entered her hospital room, he told his daughter with a deep familiar laugh that she was now sure to get well quickly because he was going to give her some of his own "Gypsy blood."

Elisabeth had no idea what was happening to her body. She had barely the strength to turn her head. But it was wonderfully comforting to have her father lying close beside her. Now everything had to be all right, even when without explanation a technician jabbed her stick-thin arm several times to find a vein. Eventually tubes were connected, and the technician turned the handle of the coffee grinder.

Mr. Kübler had once read the triplets a story about Gypsies. So she could picture her father now—she could picture both of them—sitting under the stars against a colorful wagon. Gypsies traveled to faraway places. They laughed a lot and they loved music. Now that the Gypsy blood was in her own veins, she would soon leave the iron bed and the fish tank. Surely soon she would feel once more the sun upon her face.

The coffee grinder was disconnected. Mr. Kübler got up and held his daughter's hands. The grin remained, the love was certain. Then he gave her a promise. On the day she was ready to leave the hospital she would have the thing she wanted more than anything else in the world. He himself would bring her a black doll, even if he had to travel to darkest Africa to find it.

As if it were a lifeline, Elisabeth seized her father's promise. She had never had a present that had differed in color, shape, touch or smell from gifts given simultaneously to her sisters. Now there was the best of all possible reasons to get well.

The fever began to subside. The racking cough spasms eased and stopped. Her blistered lips healed. The day arrived when her doctors approved of her discharge from the hospital. For the first time in six weeks she was taken out of the goldfish bowl and put into a small dressing room.

She heard again the deep familiar voice outside the room, and a moment later the door opened. Her father was standing there, a giant with the broadest smile. Mr. Kübler held a small suitcase containing Elisabeth's clothes. He placed this case on a chair within her reach. Inside the case, he told her, was the special gift he had promised her, but she herself would have to open the case. She managed to release the latch, but her arms were too weak to raise the lid. Mr. Kübler watched and shook his head. No, he wasn't going to help her. If she wanted something that badly, she could certainly find the strength. Sweating and summoning all her energy, she made a fresh attempt. Slowly, inch by inch, she pushed back the lid. There it was! A black doll in a rag dress and with fuzzy hair lay within. The tears came now, tears that splashed onto the ebony porcelain face as she clasped the doll to her breast.

Through the remainder of her young childhood the black doll was her most treasured possession; naturally it understood the musical language of Higaland!

Elisabeth had to learn to walk again. Her father carried her up-

14

stairs in the Green House, where she was put to bed in the guest bedroom on the second floor. Its window could be opened to a south-facing balcony, sun-splashed and bright with geraniums. Her sisters were not at home to greet her, because they had started kindergarten while Elisabeth had been in the hospital, but the reunion later that afternoon was breathless with stories, plans and excitement.

The black doll never left Elisabeth's pillow. For the first time in her life she possessed something that was uniquely her own. No matter three identical beds in the next room; no matter a closet filled with identical clothes; no matter that grown-ups called her Erika as often as they called her by her real name. A doll with fuzzy black hair and a rag dress was an outward and highly visible insignia of her individuality.

Elisabeth, she now knew, was Elisabeth, and not anybody else in the world.

2

Memories of Childhood

MRS. KÜBLER'S NOURISHING MEALS contributed to Elisabeth's convalescence. So did the late summer sunshine. Each morning she sat on a chair on the balcony and soaked up the warmth of late August and September. Prayers for her recovery were said in the village's two churches and in the kindergarten. One morning Eva and Erika, with their class teacher, "Aunt" Bürkli, and all twenty-five children in the kindergarten arrived on the lawn under the balcony and sang for the invalid.

From the balcony too she watched the grape pickers, lean and weathered peasants, gathering the harvest in adjacent vineyards. They shouted greetings to the little girl, who waved back to them. Before the leaves on the vines had withered, Elisabeth was allowed to explore the outdoors once again. Her long sickness had made her content with her own company. Yet she never felt she was quite alone. Rabbits no longer ran for cover at her approach and birds no longer took instantly to wing. In the vineyards and the meadows she found relief from the robust noisiness of the family circle. When she was late for supper, her sisters or Ernst knew just where to find her.

A few days before the first snowflakes swept down from the mountains, Elisabeth was strong enough to go to school. The kindergarten, middle school and senior class were enclosed in one compound near the railroad station. The ten-minute walk to school was either through the vineyards or, on the slightly longer route, by way of the village main street.

Elisabeth adored the kindergarten teacher, Aunt Bürkli, who appeared to the child to be about a hundred years old, although in fact she was in her thirties, and not only because she never confused Elisabeth and Erika. Aunt Bürkli gave Elisabeth a very special welcome and introduced her to the creative joys of finger painting, modeling with sand and playing simple musical instruments. Meilen's kindergarten was no prison for an independent spirit.

Memories of childhood are rarely slotted chronologically and, looking back upon her pre-adolescent years, Elisabeth now speaks of her early memories as "views from different windows." One vista is of her home and village life, the family circle and festivals. A second view is of the mountains in all seasons, for the mountains helped to build her physically and, in a special way, contributed to the development of her philosophy. The third window of her mind frames her school, and through it she sees the teachers whose skills and personalities gave a first polish to the intellectual facet of her character.

The figure dominating the vista memories of her home is her father. He was the absolute master, his word was law, his decisions final. Any child who broke the rules was summoned to face him across his desk in a book-lined den. Should the offense be serious—such as talking back to an adult—the standard punishment was a spanking on the buttocks with a carpet beater made from woven cane. Because Elisabeth was more rebellious than her sisters, her small bottom received at least three times more thwacks than were given to them. For lesser offenses, such as quarreling or leaving muddy footprints on a carpet, the punishment was usually confinement for several hours in a bedroom or in the coal cellar.

Elisabeth did not mind the spankings. What deeply wounded her pride was being ordered to collect the carpet beater from the cupboard under the stairs. This was, she remembers, like a condemned villain being ordered to build his own gallows. The lesser punishments Elisabeth actually enjoyed, for during these spells of isolation she created fantasy worlds to play in.

Mrs. Kübler rarely chastised her children physically, but her terse warning, "Just you wait till Papa comes back from the office," was as meaningful as the sound of a hanging judge clearing his throat.

Mr. Kübler's disciplining of Ernst might have been taken as a caution by the very young triplets of how their father expected model behavior and that the sense of responsibility shown by his children would increase with their years. Before a soccer game, for instance—and Ernst was to develop into a skilled player—the boy's boots and uniform were given a military inspection by Mr. Kübler. He was not allowed to leave the house if his clothes or equipment did not pass muster. To save Ernst from her father's wrath, Elisabeth herself often polished his boots to a toecap shine.

While there was no sharp division between the tender years of paternal tolerance of waywardness and the beginning of sterner attitudes, the triplets were, by the age of six, left in no doubt that their father was to be obeyed, even when his rulings seemed to be illogical or downright unfair.

Still, if Mr. Kübler's level, penetrating gaze could wilt a recalcitrant child long before he reached for the carpet beater, he was never angry long. Justice, as he saw it, having been served, he was the benevolent and loving father once more, ready with a joke or a song.

In his workaday routine, Mr. Kübler was as precise as a Swiss watch. He took the same train every morning from Meilen's station and arrived half an hour later at his Zurich office. He returned for lunch every day, arriving home at about the same time as the children returned from school. Only meetings of the Zurich Ski Club or a lecture at the technical college would delay his punctual return home in the evening.

The happiest familial moments in the Kübler home were spent around the piano, where Mr. Kübler led the family singing with his robust voice. He enormously enjoyed singing Swiss traditional songs and contemporary ballads. When a musical soiree came to an end, almost invariably with his favorite song, "Always," it was time for the triplets to scamper upstairs to bed.

At the risk of their fearing him, Mr. Kübler was determined that his daughters would grow up to be physically strong and emotionally independent. Elisabeth remembers vividly one blazing summer's afternoon when the family went to the lake and her father characteristically decided that it was time his six-year-old daughters learned to swim. The girls were happily building sandcastles when he ordered them to follow him to the end of a boat jetty. There, without warning, he pushed Eva into ten feet of water. Before she had surfaced and before Elisabeth and Erika had had time to express alarm, he threw them into the water too.

Standing on the pier and laughing, Mr. Kübler watched his daughters dog-paddle to the shallows. He was of course ready to jump in himself and do some lifesaving, but he rightly guessed that the girls would discover how to keep afloat. Nonetheless, after their sink-or-swim experience, it was a long time before the triplets again went to the lake with their father, who himself found little enjoyment in swimming.

By their ninth birthday, some physical differences between Elisabeth and Erika were beginning to be noticed. Erika, the dreamer, possessed only a fraction of the physical energy of her sister, which was why Elisabeth and Eva were the closer physical companions. Elisabeth burned off her calories running, scaling trees and climbing barn roofs (she was the first in her class to climb a rope to the ceiling of her school gymnasium) while lethargic Erika added extra pounds.

Paradoxically, because Elisabeth was so wiry and seemingly less developed than Erika, at about this time her mother took her to a Zurich physician for a complete physical. Mrs. Kübler's main worry was that Elisabeth did not eat enough, and this in a society where a good appetite and good health were synonymous. The physician took her pulse and stethoscoped her chest. He prescribed a course of vitamins and gave instructions that Elisabeth was to take a half hour's rest before her evening meal. It would have been easier to have trained a puppy to be still. After a week or so, Mrs. Kübler gave up attempting to make Elisabeth lie down before supper, and Mr. Kübler resumed dishing out mini-portions to the eldest of his triplets. The vitamin tablets were abandoned too.

Shortly before the triplets celebrated their tenth birthday, Mr. Kübler bought a fifteen-room house on the higher elevation of Meilen. With its sweeping views of village, lake and mountains, the "Big House" was home for the remainder of the triplets' childhood. The new house stood on two acres of ground, nearly half of which was a vegetable garden, the remainder mostly lawn and flowerbeds. There were fifty acres of vineyards on three sides of the house and a well-known hilltop restaurant on the fourth.

The cellar was divided into six rooms, which included separate storage spaces for canned fruits and vegetables, coal and unused furniture. Mr. Kübler stored his wine in the cellar, and one of the busiest areas was Mrs. Kübler's laundry room, equipped with washtub and wringer. There was still plenty of space to spare for Elisabeth's animal hospital and later her laboratory adjacent to a large garage.

The principal rooms on the main floor were a dining room, living room and kitchen. The house had six bedrooms, the triplets sharing one of the bigger ones. Ernst, now sixteen and going to commercial school in Zurich, again had his own lair. There were two guest bedrooms and an attic room set aside for a maid or housekeeper, when employed. A little sewing room nestled behind the living room.

The triplets, and Ernst when he was home, were allocated specific chores, and their domestic work had to measure up to their mother's demanding standards. Elisabeth's main duty was the care of the garden. It was at the Big House that she developed "green fingers." In fact, tending the vegetable garden, which supplied most of the household's vegetable needs throughout the year, and cutting the grass with the help of her father did not seem like chores at all. She took her turn at the washtub and wringer and, because it was the part of the house she loved best, she was responsible for cleaning out the cellar. All three girls helped with the wash-up after meals.

Now there was much more room for hospitality. On weekends when the family was not away in the mountains, the house was rarely without visitors; if not relatives, then her father's widening circle of sporting and international friends.

Mrs. Kübler reveled in her reputation as a hostess. She gave as much care to her table setting as she did to her cooking. Wine glasses were given a diamond polish, her porcelain was the best obtainable and the snow-white hand-embroidered table linen was starched to the sheen of silk.

From a very young age the triplets were invited to participate in the welcome given to guests. If it was a dinner party, they wore special party dresses. One or the other of their parents would formally introduce them, and they learned the art of accepting compliments with grace.

When their bedtime came, they would linger on the stairs or, on summer nights, watch their parents and the guests from bedroom windows. They enjoyed the aroma of cigars and listening to the clink of brandy glasses. They listened too, absorbed by the conversation, often political. When foreign guests were in the home, the conversation usually turned to the growing might and menace of Germany. It was at one of these formal dinners at home that Elisabeth first heard talk of the persecution of Jews and of refugees slipping across the Swiss border.

However, Mr. Kübler was an expert at balancing issues of moment with conviviality. Suddenly his deep-throated laugh would ring out, and the guests would be invited to gather round the piano. He was never happier than when he had persuaded a group to give renditions of popular ballads. Sitting on the stairs and hugging her thin legs, Elisabeth would add her small voice to the mixed chorus below, and she picked up a considerable repertoire of songs, Swiss traditional and international.

If one of the guests had brought an accordion with him, or if Ernst could be cajoled into playing, a dinner party was likely to conclude with dancing. Rugs were rolled back and furniture pushed to the side of the room. Then as Mr. and Mrs. Kübler set the pace for waltz or tango, Elisabeth, if she was still awake, would embrace an imaginary dance partner in the kitchen or in the hall and dance herself into a glow of excitement. Eva might join her, but Erika was likely to have been long asleep.

Family sing-songs remained a tradition on evenings when there was no formal party, with Eva now more frequently at the piano. In

21

addition, from time to time, often on a wet weekend, Mr. Kübler would summon the children for parlor games demanding intellectual acumen. A favorite took the form of a general knowledge test. The triplets (Ernst disdained the junior rivalry) would be asked to write down, for instance, as many names of trees as they could remember. The next round would be the number of wildflowers they could recall, or the names of Swiss towns with populations of over 20,000, or the names of glaciers. With proper ceremony, the winner was presented with a prize, usually a bar of chocolate or a pastry.

Mr. Kübler accepted as a prime paternal duty the intellectual stimulation of his children. He encouraged them to read, to browse through magazines, and thus to gain some comprehension of current events beyond the gossip of the village. The answers to the questions he asked in the general knowledge games usually had to be acquired extramurally and not in the classroom, so Elisabeth and her sisters were painlessly introduced to library research. He delighted in debate too, and often deliberately baited the children with an outrageous opinion. He would, for instance, opine (with tongue in cheek) that all thieves should have their hands lopped off.

Elisabeth rose to the bait every time. If the discussion was on crime and punishment, she was the criminal's first advocate. With the passion of a Portia she argued that there always had to be a logical reason for a crime. A thief stole because he was hungry. He shouldn't go to jail, but be fed and taught right from wrong. If she had her way, the jails would soon be empty.

Mr. Kübler would shrug his shoulders and laughingly call her a "Pestalozzi" after a Swiss hero who in the late eighteenth century established schools for impoverished and orphaned children, demonstrating that with care and sound education a child from the most wretched of environments could develop into a responsible citizen. In the modern Swiss idiom a Pestalozzi is defender of the downtrodden. Mr. Kübler could hardly have given his daughter a higher compliment. Elisabeth sensed this. She would much rather be called a Pestalozzi than a Meisli, and soon the new nickname replaced the old one.

For Elisabeth, the special advantage of the Big House was her greatly increased opportunity to be alone, to develop interests and find activities that her sisters had no desire to share. She converted one room in the basement into a menagerie and animal hospital for birds with broken wings and fallen fledglings needing special care. Of course, she had a shoebox in which caterpillars wove chrysalises and miraculously metamorphosed into butterflies; and, of course, there were the life cycles of beetles to be studied. But her hospital sometimes had exotic patients, including grass snakes wounded by the mowing machine.

In the basement, too, in a room hidden under the staircase, Elisabeth had her first laboratory. Built as a darkroom for photography by the original owner of the house, it had a sink and running water, and shelves all along one wall for chemicals. Here Elisabeth spent much of her free time, especially in winter when the weather was cold or wet. Although she occasionally had an accident when the chemicals did not react the way she anticipated, her parents did not interfere. No one else ever entered the room. In this very special, to her almost sacred, place, Elisabeth synthesized pharmacological chemicals such as pyramidon and aspirin. She received her first award in science for this work, in a contest when she was thirteen years old.

An adored pet of Elisabeth's childhood was Chiquito, a very small monkey with permanently startled eyes, brought from Africa by a friend of her father's. She fed Chiquito tidbits smuggled from the kitchen and dining-room table, and soon the pet's favorite perch was Elisabeth's shoulder.

One day she took Chiquito to the village bakery to introduce him to the cheerful English woman who ran the establishment and who was much in favor among village children for her generosity with cookies. The novelty of the monkey attracted a small crowd, which frightened the animal, who leaped from Elisabeth's shoulder into the display window. Pandemonium reigned as Chiquito evaded attempts to recapture him, jumping from a shelf of cream-topped pastries to a newly iced birthday cake. Cookies and bread rolls were hurled about like shrapnel. Within minutes half the village turned up to see a chase that Charlie Chaplin might well have contrived on film!

That night Elisabeth waited with some trepidation for her father's summons and a punishment to fit the heinous crime. The bakery lady surely had submitted a bill to cripple the family budget. Strangely, however, no paternal summons was issued. Indeed, no mention was

23

made of the incident at the family table or even when she dutifully kissed her father good night.

Next morning she returned to the bakery and pleaded with the owner to send the account for damage to her father, because, as she explained, she could no longer endure waiting for his punishment. But the cheerful pastry cook laughed a big rolling laugh and thanked Elisabeth for her "happiest and most profitable" day. The shop, she explained, had been filled for the first time since it had opened. Almost everyone had bought wares carrying imprints of a "lucky monkey's paw."

The escapade of Chiquito, whose life was sadly short, was the main topic of discussion in Meilen for a week.

From the time the family arrived at the Big House until the time Elisabeth left it, her favorite sanctuary was a rock outcrop beyond an adjacent meadow. The place was completely concealed by scrub and trees. No one else, not even Erika or Eva, knew of this secret place, which could only be approached by crawling through a tunnel of blackberry bushes and wild roses. The penalty for any intruder was likely to be a severe skin laceration.

After penetrating the natural fortification, Elisabeth scrambled to the flattened top of the tallest rock, where, unseen except by the wildlife, she performed her own sun dances, extolling the "Spirit of Heaven" in the manner of American Indians. Elisabeth is unable to recall having read any book of Indian lore; it just seemed natural to her to hail with arms outstretched the life-giving energy, in a dance very similar to ancient Indian ceremonies.

Shafts of the setting sun would pierce the foliage and light up the small animated face, brown as a walnut through the summer, as she murmured her prayers. The rabbits that were witness to her primitive routine, the squirrels and occasional grass snakes, soon got used to their visitor and lost their natural timidity.

Suddenly a bell would ring out from the church tower down the hill, or a distant train would huff from the lakeside track. Elisabeth would be aware once more of time's passing, obliged to return from her sun worshipping to the family table where her father would be frowning disapproval of unpunctuality.

Although Elisabeth was not conscious of strain between herself and her father, as she grew older she became increasingly aware of being the "odd one out" in the family. The special ties between her mother and Eva and between Erika and her father were not flaunted, and Elisabeth's feelings of rejection were subtle, but they were painful. As far back as she could remember, Eva had had a priority claim to her mother's lap, and her father's lap seemed to be reserved for Erika.

Hurt though she often was by parental preferences, real or imagined, Elisabeth tightened her jaw and tried to convince herself that she didn't really need a lap. She was the independent member of the trio; she was the strongest; she could go it alone. She pretended that the hand holding, the caress, the snuggling on a parental shoulder, were not needed. It was self-delusion, of course. But she smothered yearning and jealousy. She bit her lips and held back her tears. To beg for a lap, to protest or to cry would have been to reveal a character frailty that she wasn't prepared to admit to herself, let alone to her family.

If her parents had been trained in child psychology, or if they had been more sensitive or less busy, they might have noticed that the increasingly independent spirit of the firstborn of their triplets camouflaged a heart that longed for the physical expression of love. Elisabeth's unguarded expression of rejection might have been observed when Mr. Kübler hoisted Erika to his shoulder or Mrs. Kübler pressed Eva's blond head to her breast.

Elisabeth had her circle of friends, but none was intimate, none close enough for the sharing of her deepest feelings. Her best friend was Klara, a plain-looking girl who was the daughter of a widowed cleaning woman. Klara was probably the poorest child in the village. She lived in a building that had once been the jailhouse. The bleakness of the tiny rooms was not much relieved by the few sticks of furniture. But although Elisabeth shared some secrets with Klara, as well as candy and clothes, her friend was never introduced to the secret sanctuary of the Sundance Rock.

She was eight when she found one outlet for her love. Half a dozen domesticated rabbits became dearer to her than any other living creature.

It is a common practice among the thrifty Swiss to rear rabbits to supplement the diet, so when she first approached her parents to ask them if she could take in a pair of baby rabbits they offered no objec-

25

tion. She would have to look after them herself, of course, feed them every day and keep their hutch clean.

She built the hutch out of chicken wire and old lumber, and fed her pets newly cut grass. Indeed, she now had a special incentive for cutting the lawn. The rabbits grew rapidly and proverbially multiplied. Each was known and named, and loved without reserve. When people misunderstood her, she could go to the hutch and bury her face in the fur of the warm and undemanding creatures. In the company of the rabbits she could shed tears she refused to shed at the family hearth or in the shared bedroom.

But one shadow hovered over her love for her rabbits. Because he enjoyed a change of menu, her father from time to time would order Elisabeth to take one of the pets to the village butcher to be slaughtered. Numb from horror over her role as executioner's aide, she was obliged to select one of her dearest friends for sacrifice. The agonizing choice made, she carried the rabbit down the village street. Every beat of the condemned creature's heart turned a knife in her own.

One day only Blackie was left in the hutch, Blackie beloved above the others. She could not conceive that her father would demand the execution of Blackie. But he did, across the breakfast table.

Elisabeth did not protest. To do so would be futile. Nor did she cry—not then, not in front of her father. After breakfast she walked slowly to the rabbit hutch. Blackie, full of trust, did not have to be coaxed outside. Elisabeth placed the rabbit on the lawn and tried in vain to persuade it to escape. She shouted and clapped her hands, but Blackie returned to her arms.

She carried it to the village butcher, a huge man with a coarse red face. He grunted as he seized Blackie roughly by the ears and told the girl to wait outside.

A few minutes later the butcher in his blood-stained apron reappeared and held out a paper sack. It was a pity, he said, as if talking of the weather, that Elisabeth had not waited a few more days. The rabbit was going to have babies.

Holding the warm paper sack in front of her, Elisabeth walked back up the hill.

That evening Mr. Kübler, oblivious of the agony he had caused, shrugged indifferently when Elisabeth declined a helping of rabbit

26

stew. Not until she was in her late teens did she eat meat again.

Through a child's eyes she saw her father's insensitivity as thriftiness carried to brutal callousness, for her father was well enough off to be able to afford a roast every day of the week. From the day of Blackie's execution, Elisabeth could not tolerate anyone who exhibited a streak of parsimony, and the division between herself and her father began to widen, until it was to become a gulf of open rebellion.

Elisabeth's childhood included three very different experiences with death, each of which was to exert a profound influence on her life's choices and her thought. The first was the pastel experience of mortality at age five, when the child with whom she had shared her hospital room died. The second occurred when she was in the first grade.

A new physician had come to Meilen with his family, which included a daughter Elisabeth's age. As was typical in a Swiss village at the time, the newcomers—"city people"—were received with a "wait-and-see" attitude by adults and children. One day, after the strangers had been in town a few months, the news spread through the village that Susy, Elisabeth's classmate, was seriously ill. Soon the curtains of the child's room, which her schoolmates passed by every day on their way to and from school, were closed. Susy, the children were told, could no longer tolerate the light.

Step by step, day after day, Susy died a slow death of meningitis, becoming paralyzed, deaf, blind. Each step in the progression of the illness was announced to the frightened village population, and the children talked of all that happened among themselves. They were quite aware of the fears of their parents—that one of their children might contract the dreadful disease; and that Susy might not die, but would exist as a "vegetable"—although they did not share them.

Elisabeth remembers vividly the day the news of Susy's death spread through the village—the sorrow, the relief that it was over, the regret that the family had been so alone in its suffering. The children, who every day had sent flowers they had picked in the meadows, were at the funeral to say goodbye. And months after Susy's death they often hoped to wake up with a sore throat so they could go to the new doctor, not because they liked doctors, but, Elisabeth believes, from an instinctive desire to show their trust in him, no more a stranger.

A few years after this, Elisabeth had her third intimate experience

27

with death, this time the death of an adult. A farmer friend of the family, a man in the prime of life, and the father of children in her class at school, met with a fatal accident. Elisabeth knew the farm well. It was adjacent to the village. She had often gone there with her mother to buy fruit and potatoes, or to help pick apples in season.

One autumn afternoon the farmer fell from an apple tree and was rushed to the hospital with a broken neck. Aware he was dying, he insisted on being taken home, and he sent for his friends, the Kübler family among them.

By the time the Küblers arrived, the dying man had already communed with his own children. He had called them to the deathbed and had talked quietly about the lessons he had learned from life and about eternal truths as he saw them. He had then asked each of his children in turn to share the burdens of running the farm, and he had made it very clear that he did not want the land to be divided after his death.

When the three Kübler girls went into the dying man's bedroom, in spite of his obvious pain he greeted them by name and then asked if they would take special care of his own young children.

Elisabeth recalls a room filled with wildflowers gathered from the meadows. She remembers too a sense of love and peace and orderliness. Through the window the dying man could look out upon the fields whose hay harvest he had reaped through many seasons. He could see too the fruit trees he had planted and hear the cowbells of the cattle he had raised.

The tableau was encompassed by sorrow, naturally, but not by despondency, not despair.

On the following day the farmer died and the grieving family invited the Kübler girls to view the body laid out on the bed. It made a profound impression on Elisabeth and stirred within her unarticulated questions about man's mortality. She was conscious too of something she was only able to speak about later. Essentially it was a sense of a life's completion, of a man who, though dying in his prime, had left behind no unfinished business.

Instead of sharing these thoughts, she pondered them alone. There were answers to questions, she felt, that one had to find out by oneself.

28

3

Mountains and Mentors

THE SECOND OF ELISABETH'S "memory windows" of her early childhood has a glorious vista. The richest of her recollections are backdropped by mountains—mountains in all seasons.

The triplets were only two when their father first took them to the cabin on Furlegi, of which he was honorary custodian. A chalet-type construction built of strong timber to withstand the storms, the cabin could sleep twenty-eight people on straw mattresses. The sisters usually slept in the loft. A large tiled stove provided heat, hot water and cooking facilities.

A hard climb above the village of Amden on Amden Mountain, the cabin was reached by taking the train to Weesen, and then the bus around hairpin bends up to the village. Far below was Switzerland's deepest lake, Wallensee—dark, brooding, perilous with currents. Above the village towered the three dentine peaks of Leistkamm.

On weekends and on vacations, Swiss city dwellers trek to the mountains with the same ritual enjoyment as Scandinavians go to their summer houses and Bostonians to the Cape Cod beaches. Elisa-

29

beth remembers that the farmers who lived on the high slopes were hardy folk and mostly poor, but they were the friends and provisioners of the people who regularly came up from the valleys below. There were no class distinctions on the slopes, and no matter the attraction of skiing or climbing, time was always made for visiting, for adult talk over steaming cups of chocolate or coffee, for children's games in the hayloft.

Time almost stood still during visits to Furlegi. The majesty of the peaks, their sense of eternity, slowed the calendar and clock. Up in the mountains too Mr. Kübler's personality seemed to change. When he shouldered his skis or laced up his climbing boots, he revealed a humility and a quality of caring he often concealed at home.

Elisabeth remembers her father when he was in the mountains as a mentor of endless patience. He would, for example, take his daughters far off the trail to show them one small rare flower growing in a niche of barren rock. He had known since his own childhood exactly where to find the flower in a place that to the unobservant eye seemed utter desolation. Without preaching or pomposity, and in simple ways, he introduced the children to the wonders of nature—primary lessons upon which Elisabeth was to build her own creed.

Coinciding with school holidays, Mr. Kübler always took a vacation in midsummer. Starting when the triplets were seven years old, and each year until they had completed school, he expected one or more of the girls to accompany him to the mountains. Elisabeth's memories of these vacations blend into a montage. August was blueberry season. Perhaps nowhere in the world do blueberries grow more abundantly and lusciously than on the slopes of Amden. In the cabin or in farmhouse kitchens, huge china bowls of blueberries were topped with fresh cream—a meal for mountain men, princes and indeed the gods themselves!

The children were encouraged to help herd the cows for milking and then to carry the still-warm milk to a barn where they assisted in making cheese and butter.

On summer evenings when the work was done, some of the farmers played Alpine horns and harmonicas, others yodeled, with the cheerful or melancholy sounds echoing back from the cliffs.

Then at sunset the cabin's kerosene lamps were lit. The tiled wood-burning stove crackled. The air was filled with the smells of stew and strong tobacco. For by evening the rugged mountain men, the climbers of the peaks, had returned for shelter. The climbers were a special breed of strong-legged men, their hands and faces burned to the color of walnut. Their party might include a banker, a lawyer, a farmer, a railroad engineer—it mattered not. What bound them together was that they loved mountains with a passion that other men devote to women or to finding gold.

Sitting on her straw mattress and hugging her knees, Elisabeth watched the returned climbers with awe, and listened to the stories they swapped of their adventures, of crevasse and chimney. By dawn next day the men were gone, and if Elisabeth had risen early enough she would see small dots far up the slopes, and she would understand, even with a young child's mind, the seductive challenge of pitting one's strength and courage against the neutral might of nature.

The other seasons in the mountains had their own special charms and thrills. In winter, skiing was, of course, the pastime; and along with most of her countrymen Elisabeth cannot remember learning to ski, because skiing for the Swiss is almost as natural as walking. In spring the snow line edged upward, the cattle too. Suddenly the lower slopes exploded into color, undulating carpets of wildflowers. Not far from the cabin was a marshy area where flowers grew in such profusion as to defy a palette. This flowered marsh was Elisabeth's Persian carpet and special sanctuary. Here she would lie down and send her thoughts floating upward to the clouds caressing the peaks of Leistkamm. Here she wished she could stay forever.

But her wishes could not stop the movement of the sun, the stretch of shadows. Back at the cabin she had her duties. Each child was allocated special jobs. As Furlegi's honorary custodian, Mr. Kübler saw to this. Elisabeth's main chore was to fill with water from a creek the big copper tank alongside the tiled stove. When this was done, she had to stir the pots and otherwise help cook meals for mountain-hungry stomachs.

Then there were the hikes, usually in the summer, sometimes in the spring and fall. They were always carefully planned. Maps were spread across the dining-room table, trails penciled in, rest camps too. Sometimes the whole family trekked along the mountain trails. In later childhood Elisabeth and Eva would be their father's companions. Ernst had his own friends and pastimes, and Erika was beginning to show a physical frailty that would increasingly curb her outdoor activities.

Elisabeth never felt closer to her father than when she was with him in the mountains, whether they were accompanied by her siblings or whether they were alone together, as they often were.

On the family hikes in high summer, Mr. Kübler was sensitive to the short strides of his daughters. They started slowly, perhaps only four hours' walking on the first day. But as sinews stretched, as the ache of muscle eased, and as rucksacks seemed to lighten, the hours of walking lengthened. At night they stopped at different mountain cabins, pleased with their conquest of fatigue. By the end of a week's hiking, Elisabeth and Eva were ready for a twelve-hour trek.

Elisabeth was never afraid with her father, not even when (at the age of eleven, she believes) she fell through a crevasse on Hufi Glacier. Suddenly the snow gave way, and she was hanging by a rope, the top of her head ten feet beneath the snow line. Below her was darkness and death. The outside of one leg was scraped of skin from knee to hip. It was intensely cold. Looking up, she could see that her rope had been cut half through by a razor-sharp edge of ice, and that in fact her life was supported by a few threads of twine. But her father was up there in the sunlight. That was all she needed to know. Completely trusting, she waited for a loop of fresh rope to be lowered down to her. Mr. Kübler's instructions were terse and clear. She grasped the loop firmly, and a few moments later her father pulled her to safety.

Even as he bound up her wounded leg he told her what she, child though she was, should do in the event that his 220 pounds should fall into a crevasse. Mr. Kübler was ready to trust his life to a child who weighed seventy pounds and whose head barely reached his chest.

Although, when at home, her relationship with her father became increasingly strained, Elisabeth thinks of him as one of her most influential teachers, and his image often moves in the third "window" of her childhood memories—her recollections of her schooling. Of course, Mr. Kübler's instruction was extramural; what he imparted

32

more than knowledge was self-discipline and self-reliance, in addition to a love of nature.

Neither her one year in kindergarten nor her first three years in grade school are deeply etched in Elisabeth's memory—essentially, she assumes, because the routine of school life was so foreign to her maverick nature. It wasn't that she hated school. She accepted school as part of life. The confinement of classroom walls had to be tolerated with the same sort of resignation as head colds and dreary sermons. There were bright moments, of course, and later there were school subjects that really captured her zest.

In the Swiss junior educational system a teacher stays with one class for three years. At best, this system allows the relationship between student and teacher to become almost familial. Weaknesses and strengths are recognized and understood at deeper levels than normally found in American schools. Unfortunately, from the age of six to nine the triplets were assigned to the class of Mr. K, a sarcastic middle-aged man who later made no secret of his admiration of Adolf Hitler. Of course, when in the charge of Mr. K, the children were too young to be much interested in the gathering political storm beyond the Swiss frontier, but in any case there was a more personal reason for Elisabeth's dulled memory of grade school and her dismissal of Mr. K as a significant figure in her pre-adolescent years. He could not—or could not be bothered to—differentiate between Erika and Elisabeth (although it must be admitted that by continuing to dress them alike Mrs. Kübler was not helpful to people who found difficulty in telling the identical twins apart).

Elisabeth was an average student during her time in Mr. K's class. If she didn't achieve the scholastic excellence of which she was capable, it was probably because she was rarely if ever challenged and because her own work was so often confused with Erika's.

As in every other facet of their personalities, Erika was academically a mirror-image twin. In those school subjects in which Erika excelled—languages and grammar, for example—Elisabeth found little to excite her. In subjects in which Erika was weaker, including mathematics and history, Elisabeth was a natural scholar.

However, as often as not, when Elisabeth gained good class marks,

33

or deserved them, she was given only average credit. When protests were of no avail—at least in Mr. K's classroom—she decided to conserve her energy and to coast. Anyway, she found homework so easy that she was usually able to complete it while walking home from school, more often and by preference, alone.

School hours were from eight to five, five days a week, and from eight till noon on Saturdays. At the end of the school day Elisabeth was the first out of the classroom. Outdoors was another word for liberty.

After leaving Mr. K behind, Elisabeth had another "rather forgettable" class teacher in her junior school. But then, in what was known as the Second School (the classrooms were on the same campus as the Junior School), her mentors become sharp-focused. In the Second School different teachers taught different subjects, and one of these special teachers was Mr. Walter Weber, who taught history and French.

Although in his French classes Mr. Weber carried ennui from the blackboard to the desk at the back of the room where Elisabeth struggled with irregular verbs, as a teacher of history he had no peer. His skill stemmed from his ability to re-enact great events as if they were yesterday's news and he an eyewitness.

In describing a major battle, for instance, he stood on a chair and played the role of a general commanding a bloodied field. He would become so vicariously involved in the ebb and flow of the fortunes of war that it seemed to Elisabeth she could hear the sound of gunfire and see soldiers fall from mortal wounds. Hannibal's elephants recrossed the Alps in a Meilen classroom, cities were sacked by Attila the Hun, and in the chancellories politicians redrafted the maps of Europe and the East.

So involved did Mr. Weber become in relating the stories of great deeds and heroic men that real tears rolled down his florid cheeks. So deeply imprinted were the tales on the mind of Elisabeth (in history lessons she always sat in the front) that she was capable of instant recall. Reviewing for history tests was never needed.

Although she didn't recognize the bonus at the time, the history lessons laid the foundations of Elisabeth's talent for public speaking.

Mr. Weber showed her how to present facts in such a way that an audience could visualize the action.

Yet in his French class Mr. Weber's zest so dipped and drained that Elisabeth passionately hated her country's second language. Throughout her school career, French was the only subject in which she failed.

Mr. Weber did not understand that the cause of Elisabeth's failure was his pedagogy, and one day, more than usually irritated by her lack of concentration, he marched her to the blackboard and berated her in front of the class. This student, he shouted, was so indolent that she would never learn a foreign language. The girl's face flushed, not in shame but in rebellious anger at the judgmental prognostication. As was often to be the case, Elisabeth was to confound her critic.

Ten years later, when she returned to Meilen from doing relief work in Europe, she was invited by a grizzled Mr. Weber to speak to the class about her experiences. The children asked her how she was able to communicate in so many foreign countries. The question was a gift, and with glee she told the class of Mr. Weber's gloomy prediction. At the age of twenty-one she could speak eight languages, several fluently. The children laughed as Mr. Weber shuffled his feet. But Elisabeth then turned to the teacher. Her motivation in becoming an exceptional linguist, she said, was given impetus first when the blushing child in front of the blackboard resolved to expose her teacher as a false prophet.

Another favorite teacher during these years was Mr. Otto Wegmann, who had a profound influence on Elisabeth's life. Mr. Wegmann was not an intellectual, nor did he have the talents of Mr. Weber in the history class, but he embodied all that was best in the Swiss-German character.

Elisabeth saw him as an avuncular figure: loyal, honorable, understanding, self-disciplined and completely reliable. He taught her chemistry, physics, mathematics and physical training—subjects for which she (though not Erika) had a natural bent. Mr. Wegmann possessed the attribute of stimulating the mind rather than instructing. He asked provocative questions more often than he provided answers. In the physics class he would typically throw out questions such as

Why is the sky blue? The children reached for their books and the quest was on.

While she was in his class, Elisabeth did not consciously compare Mr. Wegmann with her father, but retrospectively she sees the two men sharing many of the same qualities, particularly a sense of honor, stern self-discipline and passionate patriotism. She was, however, beginning to see the flaws in her father's personality, notably his stubbornness and his aggressive refusal to listen to the other side in a dispute. She didn't, of course, realize that she was her father's child and that her own stubbornness and aggressive sense of justice, for example, would cause her much pain. But in Mr. Wegmann she saw no fault. He was a genuine hero.

However, the village pastor who gave the class compulsory religious training was no hero. Elisabeth loathed him, loathed with childish vehemence a man who attempted to instill spiritual truths through fear and physical force. The pastor had a coarse mottled face, black unruly hair and a habit of plucking nervously at the buttons of his coat with large fleshy hands. He had sired eight children, all of whom, it seems to Elisabeth now, would have qualified psychologically for the battered-child syndrome.

A hell-fire preacher on Sundays, the pastor relished his limited authority in the village, and especially the trepidation he created in his confirmation classes, which the triplets were obliged to attend.

Elisabeth was not alone in being repelled by a man who, within moments of unctuously interpreting the benedictions of the Sermon on the Mount, could conduct himself as the village lout. He broke a dozen rulers a month on the hands of his charges. He was the polar opposite of the popular conception of a selfless man of the cloth.

With a temper that could flare over even a small or imagined injustice, Elisabeth's clash with the pastor was inevitable. Her short fuse was lit when one afternoon the pastor interrupted a prayer by suddenly lunging forward and seizing the blond braids of Eva's hair and the hair of a friend in the next seat. He accused the girls of whispering during devotion and, without waiting for their answers, crashed their heads together.

It was, in fact, another girl in the row behind who had whispered, but it was Elisabeth who reacted. Impetuously she hurled her prayer book straight at the pastor's face. A stunned silence lasted perhaps ten seconds. Then Elisabeth ran to the classroom door, where she fired her Parthian shot. She would rather be crucified, she shouted, than spend another minute in the pastor's class. She stood awhile outside the door, panting, trembling and realizing what she had done.

The one-child rebellion in the village school was a big scandal in the peaceful village of Meilen. At home that evening Eva and Erika talked of the incident in hushed voices, but Mr. Kübler simply demanded the facts. Although they had not expressed their feelings, her parents themselves had very little use for the pastor, whose uncouthness they readily recognized. At this time, too, neither of her parents was a regular churchgoer, and there had been little discussion of religion within the household. Mr. Kübler reserved judgment over the confirmation class incident but he warned Elisabeth that there would surely be repercussions.

Indeed there were. The school board was summoned to an emergency meeting. The pastor demanded Elisabeth's immediate expulsion from the school. However, it was the noble Mr. Wegmann who came to her aid. What he said about the pastor was not recorded, but he did successfully appeal to the school board to take no action against Elisabeth until the young girl had had a chance to defend her behavior.

A message was sent to Elisabeth to appear before the board, which met in one of the classrooms. Her knees knocked but her voice was steady as she related the pastor's brutalities, not only when she had been provoked to throw the prayer book, but a long series of outrages against the children. Board members listened to her in silence before they dismissed her to consider their verdict.

The night was moonlit as she walked back home, and stars glittered in a crystal sky. The consternation that had weighed upon her was lifted as she wondered at the majesty and mystery of the universe. She felt a strange sense of peace. The pastor's teaching of hell and damnation seemed to her petty and far removed from the glory all about her. It didn't really matter what the school board decided. At least she had stood up for what she had believed to be right. She had no sense of guilt.

A couple of days later Mr. Kübler was notified by the school board that Elisabeth and her sisters were to be given official dispensation from further religious instruction by the village pastor. It was recommended, however, that the girls continue religious instruction under the guidance of a suitable clergyman.

Erika and Eva continued their confirmation classes under the tutelage of a well-known theologian, the Reverend Karl Zimmermann, in Zurich. The girls traveled to Zurich once a week to attend these classes. But Elisabeth didn't join them. Mr. and Mrs. Kübler apparently realized that Elisabeth's quest for spiritual truths was not likely to be helped by formal denominational instruction.

Shortly before Erika and Eva were to be confirmed, however, Pastor Zimmermann sent for Elisabeth and took her into his office. He told her that he had had a vivid dream in which he had confirmed the three Kübler girls. He asked Elisabeth whether she would not contribute to the fulfillment of his dream. It was an unexpected request. She was confused by it, and flattered too. Eventually she replied that until she saw people practice the faith they talked about she did not see any reason for being associated with a church. Without her passion the response would have sounded self-righteous and smug, but Pastor Zimmermann understood the girl's protest. A wise and kindly man, he made no attempt to defend dogma or ritual. He reminded her that intolerance of hypocrisy had been demonstrated by Christ and suggested that perhaps Elisabeth had a deeper understanding than many adults of a basic religious precept. What mattered, he added quietly, was not what people claimed to be their belief but how they lived. The young girl was impressed, and eventually she nodded her head. All right, she said, she would be confirmed along with her sisters, but only if it was clearly understood between them that her confirmation would not be a commitment to a denominational church. Her agreement would be a sort of personal gift to the Reverend Karl Zimmermann.

It is the practice in Swiss Protestant churches to allocate one special Biblical verse to each confirmand. Because the Kübler girls were triplets, Pastor Zimmermann allocated one special verse to be shared among the girls. The words were taken from St. Paul's Epistle to the Corinthians: "And now abideth faith, hope, love, these three; but the greatest of these is love."

As the pastor placed his hands on the head of each of the triplets, who wore traditional black confirmation dresses, he gave to each a word for her life guidance, as he put it. To Eva he gave Faith, to Erika he gave Hope and to Elisabeth he gave the word Love.

At the time, the ritual held no deep meaning for Elisabeth beyond being a happy family affair which pleased her parents, her sisters and, particularly, the Reverend Karl Zimmermann. She had no precise interpretation of the word "love." Surely love was being in the sunshine, she thought. Love was the elation felt on a ski slope or when climbing a mountain. Love was the feeling experienced when giving a gift or rendering a service or caring for a bird with a broken wing, finding the first wildflower in springtime. Love was linked to the excitement and joy of Christmastime. Love was the feeling you had for your parents, brother and sisters. Weren't love and happiness almost the same thing?

There would be time when she was more grown up to think about these things. However, in Switzerland children of twelve and thirteen are considered to be mature enough to be thinking about careers. At this age, when they are in the equivalent of the sixth grade, they are required to write essays on the careers they would prefer.

Elisabeth had thought often of what she wanted to be when she grew up. Africa, with its heroic figures of Livingstone and Albert Schweitzer, still had a powerful pull; but her teachers had urged her to focus on her academic strengths. It was the nearer future that should concern her now. In her six years of school she had begun to recognize that her bent was for science.

In Switzerland an early understanding of intellectual strengths and manual skills is important, because on entering his teens a child's education reaches a significant crossroad. By the equivalent of America's ninth grade, a student is channeled into an apprenticeship at secondary school or, more rarely and usually if the family is well off, sent on to the higher education (gymnasium) demanded by the professions.

Even girls expecting to be saleswomen or seamstresses and boys aiming to be garage mechanics decide on their apprenticeship at the age of twelve or thirteen. The gain is a nationally high standard of skill and stewardship among both blue- and white-collar workers. The three or four years of apprenticeship engender genuine respect for artisans; for in a real sense everyone in Switzerland, including the shop counter assistant and garage mechanic, is a professional.

Along with the other children in her sixth-year class Elisabeth wrote a composition on what she hoped to be in her adult life. She titled it "My Dream of What I Could Be."

Her first aspiration was to be "a researcher and explorer of unknown frontiers of human knowledge." She went on to clarify and wrote, "I want to study life. I want to study the nature of man, the nature of animals and the nature of plant life."

She still visualized herself as she had in young childhood, wearing tropical clothes and journeying through steaming and exotic jungles to discover lakes unmarked on the map. She saw herself playing with Pygmies or riding with Bedouins across desert sands. Her heart could still thump at the thought of discovering the ice and fire of the Mountains of the Moon, or squatting in a mud-hut village and listening once again to the throb of African drums.

Having written down the fantasy, she paused for some minutes, thinking that when the teachers read her dream perhaps they would dismiss it as impractical, even if they understood her yearning.

She wrote down a second career choice. It was to be a nurse. In her mind she did not see herself donning a white uniform and carrying a tray of medications around a hospital ward. Her image was much more romantic, influenced by a library-book picture of Florence Nightingale tending the wounded and the dying in a candlelit basement. Elisabeth visualized herself cradling bandaged heads and writing down last whispered messages for loved ones far away.

She blotted the page, leaned back in the desk chair, closed her eyes and then gravely evaluated her assets. She decided her major attribute was her ability to work very hard—harder, she felt, than her sisters. She recognized that she had a good mind. She understood most lessons faster than her sisters, and she took half the time they did to complete her homework.

Once over the dining table she had spoken about her hope of becoming a physician. Her father dismissed the idea and the subject out of hand. Had Elisabeth any idea, Mr. Kübler said, what a medical career would cost him? He certainly would not be able to afford to send all the girls to college. The cost of keeping Ernst at commercial college was already stretching the family budget. Thus snubbed, Elisabeth had not raised the subject a second time.

However, since her father was unlikely to read her school composition, and since the teachers had urged the class to be "absolutely honest" about their deepest aspirations, Elisabeth leaned over the desk and dipped her pen in the inkwell once more. In the last paragraph of her composition she wrote, "Above everything else in the world I would like to be a physician. Of course I know that attending medical school is an impossible dream, but this is what I most want to do."

In the adjacent seat Eva, already beginning to develop a handsome figure, trailed blond braids across the desktop as she wrote her reasons for wanting to become a ski instructor. Farther back in the room Erika, the "quiet one," would get the best class marks for literary style. Erika had written that she wanted to be a writer.

Shortly after they wrote these career compositions, and toward the end of the spring semester, the whole school prepared for the annual classroom hiking expeditions. The distances of the hikes were governed by the ages of the students. The triplets were almost thirteen and for the first time they were scheduled to hike for three days under the leadership of the redoubtable Mr. Wegmann. There would be rest stops at night, of course, but the distances between camps were designed to test stamina.

Equipment for the hike included heavy hiking boots, a knapsack containing enough food for the trip and changes of clothing. Some of the children carried small musical instruments to be played while walking.

Elisabeth and Eva were eagerly looking forward to their longest school hike. Erika alone in the class was not excited by the prospect of three days on the high trails. She had never had Elisabeth's love of the outdoors, but on this occasion she was obviously fearful, even tormented by the approaching date. She pleaded with her parents to allow her to stay at home. Mr. Kübler firmly shook his head. To refuse a physical challenge was unacceptable behavior for any member of the Kübler family.

The children set out for the hills, but the hikers had not gone far before Erika became ill and had to be sent home. The illness was treated as a psychosomatic ailment by her disappointed and disapproving parents, who did not call in the family physician until four days later. By this time Erika was scarcely able to walk. She was suffering from a fever and from a pain in her hip.

After ten days, with the ailment still undiagnosed and with the condition clearly not improving, Erika was sent to the Children's Hospital in Zurich. There she underwent a series of elaborate tests which revealed no physical cause for the pain or fever, although some suspicion of poliomyelitis was voiced. Because of the possibility of polio or of some other contagious ailment, neither Elisabeth nor Eva was permitted to visit her sister. But whenever there was an opportunity, Elisabeth visited the courtyard of the hospital. Erika peeked through the window of her room and the two girls waved to each other, communicating nonverbally with that special empathy peculiar to identical twins. Erika spent some weeks in a second hospital, where she was given therapy that proved of no benefit, and at midsummer she was sent home. Mr. and Mrs. Kübler were still persuaded that Erika's illness was psychosomatic. They were not discouraged in this belief by some of the physicians who had failed to diagnose any cause for the inflamed hip. Hope was expressed that the family environment would aid the patient's recovery.

But Erika's condition worsened. Through hot summer days she lay in an upstairs bedroom, tolerating the constant pain only if no one moved her. When she was moved for the necessary making of her bed or for ablutions, her screams could be heard by neighbors. If a door slammed, the child was shattered by pain. The Kübler home became a place of whispers and tiptoe walking. The mailman was ordered to drop the mail at the garden fence to avoid making some noise that would exacerbate the pain of the patient upstairs.

In late August Erika had another spell in the hospital, this time in Zurich's Orthopedic Institute, where therapists tried to compel her to walk with the aid of a walker. But her suffering only increased. With this suffering came a sense of resignation. She started to read adult books and to write poetry and short stories.

While Erika was in the hospital, she and Elisabeth exchanged many letters. In one letter, Erika wrote that she would really love to be a doctor. She had selected writing as the career of her choice because as a writer she would not have to use her frail legs.

Elisabeth wrote back that she would be her identical twin's alter ego. She, Elisabeth, would be the physician. She promised Erika that she would come home every night and tell Erika all about the patients so that she could vicariously experience the profession she was to be denied.

Although these promises given and received were childlike, they were made with utmost gravity. The twins had always complemented each other, without competition. The world saw them as physically identical, but they themselves had always known that their personalities, their spirits, were quite different.

While Erika lay ill, Elisabeth grew stronger in wind and limb. She ran and bounded with the energy of a gazelle, ran so swiftly that no other girl of her age could catch her. Although she weighed only a scrawny seventy-five pounds when she was thirteen years old, she was constantly in scraps with other children, more often with boys, whom she was delighted to taunt, probably, she believes, because she wished to be one of them. In her reveries she invariably pictured herself as a male. She was always an Indian brave, for instance, and never a squaw; always Robin Hood and never Maid Marian.

Many times when her mother inquired why Elisabeth was late returning from school, she was advised (as likely as not by the butcher's boy, who seemed to know more about what was going on in the village than anyone else) that her missing daughter was fighting another boy down the hill. When Elisabeth eventually turned up with a torn dress and a bruised eye, she would be sent to the cellar to cool off. This was hardly punishment. The animal hospital was in the cellar! The schoolyard fights continued.

Looking back upon her early childhood, Elisabeth speaks of its "feather-touch sorrows and joys." The dominant recollection, though, is of loneliness. Not, of course, physical loneliness, for aside from those snatched moments on the secret Sundance Rock and rarer moments of being on her own in the mountains, she was, in fact, hardly ever by herself. Hers was the loneliness of "feeling different," of being so often misunderstood, of coveting the parental affection given to Eva and Erika. She remembers struggling unaided to comprehend life's meaning. Hers was a loneliness of the head and the heart. It was linked somehow to a sense of special destiny and an intuitive awareness that she would have to struggle on her own to discover paramount truths. At times, even in her tender years, she was conscious of having set her face toward a mountain that would fully, sometimes cruelly and grimly, test her faith, courage and endurance.

4

The Vow and the Rebel

FRIDAY, SEPTEMBER 1, 1939, dawned without omen in the village of Meilen. Distant mountain peaks carried an unseasonable first mantle of snow, and in the vineyards the leather-skinned grape pickers shouldered baskets to gather the harvest. Within the Kübler home the dawn developed into a commonplace morning, with Mr. Kübler striding to the station to catch the train for Zurich, and Mrs. Kübler chasing Elisabeth and Eva—Erika was still an invalid—from the breakfast table and off to school.

It was at lunchtime that the day developed into a date of great consequence for Elisabeth—not only for Elisabeth, of course, but, infamously, for millions across the earth.

Arriving home shortly before one o'clock, Elisabeth and Eva saw their father staggering into the Big House under the weight of a bulky parcel. Some moments later they watched him heave out of a cardboard carton a walnut-encased radio. The excited children exclaimed with delight, for it was the first radio bought by their thrifty father. In their excitement they did not at first observe his tightened jaw as he placed the radio on a side table in the living room, plugged it into an electric outlet and switched it on.

After the few seconds that the radio took to warm up, a newscaster came through loud and clear. "At dawn this morning, German military forces moved across the Polish frontier . . ."

So it had happened: For weeks past everyone had been talking about the possibility of war. Fear in the eyes of grown-ups, especially in the eyes of a family of Jewish refugees who had settled in Meilen, meant more to Elisabeth than all the talk of treaties and storm troopers.

Her father was on one knee adjusting the volume of the radio. The newscaster went on: "German panzer divisions are reported to have penetrated forty miles into Poland. . . . Hitler is believed to be with his advance troops . . . Britain and France have issued ultimatums to Germany. The people of Warsaw, including old people, women and children, are digging tank traps around the city . . ."

In Elisabeth's mind, magazine pictures of war suddenly became animated. They may have been pictures of the Spanish Civil War or of Italy's invasion of Abyssinia, but they were pictures of burning towns, of terrified refugees huddling together, of dive bombers bullet-spraying innocent people. In one magazine there had been pictures of bodies lying in the streets, of children with bandaged heads.

The illustrations were alive now. People cried. Huge tanks, their guns blazing, thundered through villages resembling Meilen. Elisabeth imagined children like herself, younger perhaps, digging trenches and fortifications to halt the invaders.

The voice on the radio continued: "Poland's Prime Minister has appealed to the world for help. The people of Poland, he said, would fight to the last ditch. . . ."

Elisabeth looked over her shoulder at her aproned mother leaning against the door. Mrs. Kübler was listening to the radio too, while the lunch she had prepared was cooling on the dining-room table.

Elisabeth remembers feeling a dread sinking sensation. She knew it was a critical moment. Yet, except for the newscaster's voice, everything was so quiet, so normal. At breakfast that morning the family had been planning to go to Furlegi for the weekend. Elisabeth and Eva would play with their friends in Amden. At sunset the old farmer

45

who lived next door would come up to the mountain cabin. He would sit on the wooden bench, smoke his pipe and talk about the rock climbs of his youth.

But out there, far beyond the mountains, it wouldn't be the same. People were being killed and wounded. People were watching their homes burn to the ground. There had to be something she could do.

But she was just a young girl far away from the fighting. It was pointless to think she could do anything practical for the victims of war. She could try to understand their pain, of course. But if only she were older, if only she were a man . . .

"Although overwhelmed by superior forces and superior armament, the Polish Army is reported to be fighting stubbornly . . ."

At the doorway Mrs. Kübler moved and beckoned. The lunch was getting cold. Elisabeth and Eva would be late for afternoon class.

Suddenly she knew what she could do. She could make a promise. She could promise to help the gallant Polish people just as soon as the Swiss frontiers were opened again. It was no time to rationalize, to think about growing up or how she would travel to Warsaw. She simply accepted a feeling deep inside her that one day she would go to people who needed help.

Her father's eyes were still fixed on the radio. From the dining room she heard the sound of crockery. No one was watching her as she moved her lips to form the words of her promise. To herself and to the people of Poland she said, "I promise that as soon as I can do so I will come to you and help you."

Yet it still didn't seem quite right. It wasn't enough. Promises could be broken or forgotten. Unless she fulfilled her promise, she would be making no gift at all. It had to be more than a promise. It had to be a vow, an irrevocable committal of heart and flesh, an absolutely unconditional gift of her mind, body and spirit.

She closed her eyes and tried to imagine more vividly the horror of war. The images changed. She remembered newspaper pictures of Jewish refugees. She remembered the stories they had told of persecution, of friends disappearing in the night, of concentration camps, of torture and death. In her mind's eye the faces of the refugees were the faces of the people now trying to hold back the ruthless invader.

Her lips moved again. She whispered, "I vow that unless I die, and no matter what else happens, I will come to your help as soon as I can."

Now her gift seemed real to her, not merely the pledge of a young girl. Later she was able to articulate her feelings at that moment. It was as if, she has said, her vow had been mystically sealed.

As she joined her mother and Eva at the dining table, Elisabeth was strangely comforted by the belief that her unconditional promise had already been received as a gift by the people of Poland.

In Meilen life was, in fact, little changed by war, at least in the early years of conflict. The most significant first consequence for Elisabeth was the disappearance of her new class teacher, beloved Mr. Wegmann, who was called up for service in the Swiss Army Reserve. When giving his valedictory address to the class—an occasion for which he impressively wore a captain's uniform—Mr. Wegmann urged his students to reach out for the best of which they were capable. The talk was simple, but Elisabeth can recall no speech that stirred her more. She took it as a personal challenge when Mr. Wegmann, obviously much moved himself, looked at each member of the class individually and then said he would take with him to the frontier his own pride in all of them.

In the months and years that followed, Mr. Wegmann's words of farewell inspired his class to gain the community's top awards for conservation, for wartime drives to salvage metal for industrial recycling, for harvesting crops and for destroying crop pests. The children's wartime salvaging drives and their labor on the farms were undertaken not consciously as a patriotic gesture (although they were not in fact paid) but as a response to their teacher's appeal and trust.

Mr. Wegmann's replacement as class teacher was Miss Anna Peter, who was immediately obliged to overcome two handicaps. First, she was uncommonly plain. Her very fine scarce black hair was drawn to a tiny knot over a thin neck that supported an unusually pale and angular face. Her unevenly hemmed dresses covered an almost shapeless body. A graver handicap was that she was a substitute for the school's most popular teacher.

Miss Peter was given a rough reception. On her first day the boys booby-trapped the classroom. They stretched cords at ankle height across the floor and placed powdered blackboard chalk behind pictures and maps that had been deliberately set askew.

Bruised from her tripping and blotched from the chalk, Miss Peter survived the initiation. Her forbearance and tolerant smile gained her respect. The quality of her teaching and her genuine concern for the welfare of every student quickly won her near adoration. Miss Peter soon became the school's most beloved teacher, and on rainy days the children fought for the privilege of holding her umbrella when escorting her to the train station.

Although still crippled, Erika eventually returned to school. She was not able initially to walk the distance, so Elisabeth and Eva took turns pulling her in a handcart, a simple four-wheeled contraption with a shaft, the type commonly used by the Swiss for shopping or collecting fruit and vegetables from farms.

Erika's illness was eventually diagnosed by the veteran obstetrician who had delivered her. The doctor, who always spoke of "my triplets," postponed her retirement solely to unravel the mystery of Erika's ailment. When she had collected all the data on the course of the disease, she proved with X rays that Erika had in fact suffered simultaneously from both poliomyelitis and osteomyelitis. A now slowly healing cavity was found in the hip bone. The girl's suffering was finally comprehended by the rest of the family, who now watched her courageous struggle to regain strength, although she remained a semi-invalid through all her teenage years.

Elisabeth was overjoyed to have her identical twin back in the classroom and was fiercely protective of her. One morning shortly after Erika's return to school (she was crippled enough to have to be carried from the cart to her desk) the class bully walked down the aisle and splattered ink over Erika's workbook. The teacher (not the empathetic Miss Peter) asked the reason for the sloppy pages. In character, Erika did not protest her innocence even when her hands were rapped with a ruler.

The bully had counted on Erika's not accusing him, but he had not counted on Elisabeth's loyalty and fury. At the end of the class, Elisabeth ran outside and waited for him. Choosing her moment, she jumped onto the boy's back and pummeled his face with her fist. The bully, head and shoulders taller than Elisabeth, mopped his bleeding nose as he slouched off followed by a shrill threat that the beating he had just received would prove merely a taste of what would happen were he ever to offend Erika again.

With her wiry frame, and in the intensity of her emotions, Elisabeth was beginning to cast the shadow of her adult physique and personality. She seemed to possess more energy than she needed and she was always likely to overreact to any slight or injustice, real or imagined. Elisabeth saw the sky bluer than her fellows. The grass was always greener. There were no pastel colors on her palette. By conventional standards she was not a pretty girl. Her hair was too thin, and any artificial curls that were given to it vanished with the first puff of wind. There were no soft puppy-fat lines on her tanned face. In rare repose, her mouth was too small. Her dark brown darting eyes were her most attractive physical feature. Her body was slow to develop. At the age of fourteen it would still be like a boy's—flat-chested, lithe of limb. Now only strangers would confuse her with Erika, for her identical twin had put on weight as a result of obligatory inactivity, and she walked with a pronounced limp.

Aside from her school lessons, which generally continued to bore her, Elisabeth tackled everything she undertook with passionate intensity. Patience was not one of her virtues. Life was "out there" somewhere and waiting to be attacked with a rapier.

But life in the village meandered, and no amount of wishful thinking could speed the years. The first Christmas of the war approached, and had it not been for newspaper headlines and radio bulletins, Meilen might have been unaware of the great conflict beyond the frontiers. Not the sound of cannon but the tinkle of sleigh bells was heard in the streets. Elisabeth's desire to "do something" for people in need had not cooled. Of course, it was a waste of time to consider doing anything immediately for the victims of war, but she found alternative outlets. Typically she decided to help an impoverished, fatherless peasant family who subsisted in a shack on a hillside above the village. She was especially troubled by the thought that the family would be overlooked by the most welcome of Christmas visitors. Conspiring with her closest friend, Klara, she elected to be a Santa Claus surrogate.

49

She half filled a burlap bag with oranges and tangerines (already in short supply) "borrowed" from the family larder. Emptying her piggy bank, she bought candy, and then with Klara's help repaired discarded toys. The burlap bag was topped by a bundle of outgrown children's clothes.

On the evening of December 6, the traditional day for Santa's visits, the two girls pasted cotton waste to their eyebrows and chins and pulled the sack up the hill on a sled. Through a window of the shack they saw six children, who rushed to the door as soon as Elisabeth rang the hand-held "angel" bell. Elisabeth and Klara dumped the gifts and fled. The widowed mother overtook them and offered money. In her gruffest voice, Elisabeth told the woman that Santa Claus never charged for gifts. The mother sobbed her gratitude, and the two girls cried with joy as they ran down the hill.

No one in Meilen responded with more fervor than did Elisabeth to the government's appeal to grow more food. She doubled the size of the backyard vegetable garden at the Big House. Her hands became calloused from digging and hoeing. She helped her mother to can and bottle fruit and vegetables. Soon shelves in the basement groaned under the weight of garden produce.

With its native population of four million, Switzerland, the one island of peace in Europe, gave wartime sanctuary to 300,000 refugees. The first refugees, mostly Jews from Germany and Austria, arrived before the outbreak of hostilities. Sometimes the stream of refugees was thin; sometimes, and especially after D Day, they came in a flood tide, mostly from France.

Ernst, who was of military age, was now in the army, and Mr. Kübler also served, in a special army of volunteers. Both were stationed for weeks and months on the Swiss border with Germany, sometimes in the same town. Returning home after spells of duty, they spoke of refugees and prisoners of war swimming the Rhine River to find Swiss sanctuary. Many times they witnessed escapes and attempted escapes. When the Germans were alerted, they opened up with machine guns. Mr. Kübler and Ernst saw men die within a few yards of safety. But many times father and son waded into the river to rescue exhausted men, women and children who miraculously survived the hail of bullets and ice-cold water. Elisabeth could never hear too many stories of such escapes and rescues. She could conceive of no task more glorious than that of helping escapees. Still, if her wartime tasks were less militant and exciting, they were hardly less vital to the common cause.

Because many young farmhands were called up to man the frontiers, there was an urgent need for auxiliary help to bring in the harvests. On most weekends and in the summer and during school vacations she and other children went out to farms to pluck the fruit, stack the hay and kill the bugs. She learned to scythe, to glean and the art of milking. She could not imagine being happier than when working on a farm from sunrise to sunset. She was proud of her industry, proud of discovering new strength in her berry-brown arms and legs. Her fatigue at the end of a day in the fields was always linked in her mind to a continent's struggle for freedom.

Other reminders of the war included shortages of food, clothing and gasoline. Elisabeth devoured the news in the newspapers and on the radio. She wept over the fall of France and remembers listening spellbound to newscasts from London reporting the rescue by the "little boats" of 300,000 Allied troops from the bloodied beaches of Dunkirk. Her heart wanted to explode when she listened to a translated speech by Winston Churchill declaring that "we shall fight on the beaches . . . fight in the fields and in the streets . . . fight in the hills . . . we shall never surrender."

She recalls thumping a sofa pillow and shouting, "No, no, no! We'll never surrender!" It was her war too, her struggle, and the next weekend she would climb the apple trees and pick more bugs off the potato plants than anyone else.

The excitement of the Battle of Britain, the horror of the U-boats— these were her victories, her disasters. And there was one enemy just down the street. With the German victories, the first-grade teacher, Mr. K, brazenly proclaimed his admiration of Hitler and his conviction of ultimate Allied defeat. Her father too growled his fury over Mr. K's preening and boasting.

Yet another winter, another spring, another June; and the sixteenth birthday of Elisabeth, Eva and Erika was on the calendar. In the midyear of 1942 the girls were about to complete their compulsory education. Each of them had now to come to a firm decision about her life career.

Six years earlier Ernst's career had been decided. He was now writing his final examinations at Zurich's business school. Because he was so much older than his sisters, Ernst had rarely seemed to Elisabeth to have been within the inner circle of the family. He had always had his own interests, his own friends. He had become a young man while they had still been children. Ernst would shortly leave for India to join the staff of a well-established export-import company.

Erika was still hobbling down the long road to recovery from her illness. Her frailty had virtually decided her future. She was not strong enough to become an apprentice. In the inactive period of convalescence, Erika had further demonstrated her flair for writing and had won parental approval for her expressed hope of becoming a journalist. It was understood that Erika would take higher education. She would leave the school at Meilen for the gymnasium (the equivalent of junior college) in Zurich. Then she would go to university.

Several times when the subject of careers had been raised, Mr. Kübler had stated flatly that he could afford to send only one of the girls to university. Both parents had also indicated that since healthy Elisabeth and Eva could be expected to earn their keep until they found husbands, it would be a waste of money to send either of them on to a higher education.

The three girls had some idea of what was on their father's mind when, one spring evening after supper had been eaten and the dishes washed and stacked, he summoned them and Mrs. Kübler to a conference at the dining table. The head of the household was about to dictate career decisions.

Elisabeth's dream of becoming an explorer and researcher in Africa had not faded. However, it was three years since she had written her composition on what she would like to be. Her thinking was now tempered by practicality, but her hopes of becoming a physician were still in the back of her mind. If a chasm lay between where she now stood and this citadel, and there was obviously no way of spanning it, still, one day . . .

So she was thinking as Mr. Kübler took his seat at the table and cleared his throat. He looked first at Eva. A long moment passed before he spoke. Eva sat back confidently in her chair, her hands resting on her lap, her burnished hair spread over her athletic shoulders. Excitement had colored Eva's cheeks, and for a second or two Elisabeth was stabbed by envy of her sister's beauty. No one in the family doubted that Eva would be the first of the triplets to marry or that she would eventually become the efficient mistress of a gracious home. She was, as the clairvoyant physician had prophesied fifteen years earlier, her mother's daughter.

Eva, announced Mr. Kübler, would go to a finishing school, an establishment where she could polish the natural attributes of a Swiss-German lady of the upper middle class. Eva smiled. So did Mrs. Kübler.

Erika was the next focus of Mr. Kübler's gaze. It was a brief sympathetic glance. That Erika had always been closer to him than the other two girls was puzzling, for she had never much enjoyed climbing, skiing and hiking, the pastimes that her father loved, and lately had been unable to participate in them at all. Perhaps she stirred in him a masculine protectiveness. With her he revealed an otherwise veiled gentleness. From very young childhood it was usually to Erika that he had offered a lap. He said gently that Erika would now go to the gymnasium.

In the silence that followed this pronouncement a sudden tension mounted. Mr. Kübler may have discussed his plans for Elisabeth's future with his wife, but the girls had been given no clue to his intentions. Mr. Kübler's eyes veered left to the eldest of the triplets. He started by speaking quietly, deliberately so.

For the past year he had been evaluating Elisabeth's qualities and shortcomings. She was a bright but rebellious child. She tended to be an impractical idealist. She would continue to need firm direction and correction. He had observed with gratification that when she set her hand to a task that interested her she was both conscientious and methodical. In rock climbing and when hiking she had proved that for her size she was physically strong. She would not, he was fully persuaded, buckle under hard work and long hours. But she still had something to learn about punctuality, tidiness of dress and the need to conform. There had been incidents, still fresh in memory, of her temper. She possessed a somewhat aggressive nature, which if properly channeled could be positively used. Indeed, under control her assertiveness could be a spur to ambition. Academically she appeared to have shown a leaning toward mathematics.

Mr. Kübler paused and tapped his fingers on the tabletop. He savored a significant moment of paternal authority. Elisabeth's eyes never left his face.

Then the verdict. Elisabeth would join his business. She would be apprenticed to him as a secretary and bookkeeper.

Mr. Kübler's voice was matter-of-fact. Elisabeth was appalled. She had never had even a passing thought about becoming a businesswoman. Mr. Kübler mistook her stunned silence for acquiescence. He became expansive. He was offering Elisabeth a first-class opportunity. He hoped she would appreciate this. In spite of the wartime difficulties of supply, his business remained prosperous and progressive. He himself would undertake to give Elisabeth instruction out of his wide experience. In due course, if she was diligent, she could look forward to a nice income. She would continue to live at home, of course, and commute to Zurich every day with her father.

The paralysis of limb and tongue caused by the shock of her father's decision was ended by a spurt of adrenaline. Elisabeth's heart pounded. Her small fists thumped the table as she shouted that she would never go into business. She hated everything to do with business and with the making of money. She would die if she had to work in an office. She would be a disaster as a secretary and bookkeeper.

Mr. Kübler's eyes widened in disbelief. No one in the family had ever dared to question his decision, let alone to defy him. Elisabeth glanced at her mother to seek some support. But Mrs. Kübler's eyes were downcast, her face pale. Eva and Erika sat rigid in their chairs.

Mr. Kübler bellowed for silence. When he had achieved it, he icily reminded Elisabeth that he was offering her the opportunity of a lifetime. He was not going to stand for any immature objections. He was not prepared to listen to any more of this nonsense.

But Elisabeth was not yet finished. She stood up. Her breath came in short stabs, not out of fear of her father but because of her fury over the way he believed he could manipulate her. She shouted that it was her life that he was talking about. Nobody was going to tell her how to live her life. Nobody!

"I'd rather be a domestic servant than join your business!" she concluded.

Mr. Kübler also rose to his feet. His big shoulders were squared, and to Elisabeth he seemed like a giant on the other side of the table. His voice was now quietly menacing. All right, then, Elisabeth could make her own choice. She could either join his business or she would be sent away from home, and so far as he was concerned she could become a domestic servant.

Father and daughter held each other's angry eyes for another long moment. Mutual pride and stubbornness eliminated all chance of compromise. Then Mr. Kübler pushed back his chair, turned about and strode from the room. Years later Mr. Kübler told Elisabeth that he had guessed, even as he left the dining room, what her choice would be.

It was a practice of many Swiss-German girls on leaving high school to go to the French-speaking part of Switzerland to work as housekeepers while they learned their country's second language.

The Kübler household could survive the blow to family dignity by informing relatives and friends that one of their daughters had chosen to be a "housekeeper" in order to learn colloquial French.

On the day following the fierce clash of wills across the dining-room table, Mrs. Kübler found a newspaper advertisement inserted by a widow in the French-speaking village of Romilly on the Lake of Geneva. Mr. Kübler applied for the position on Elisabeth's behalf. A week later a letter was received from Madame André Perret, offering to engage Elisabeth for one year's employment as a "housekeeper." She could start work immediately.

An old leather suitcase was brought down from the attic, and Elisabeth packed her clothes. A continuing mood of defiance now helped offset the first weight of anticipatory homesickness. She still had absolutely no intention of retracting, just as she knew her father would never reconsider his decision about her future. She smothered painful thoughts of leaving her mother, Erika and Eva, and leaving behind beloved and familiar places. As the day of departure drew near, she was determined not to show her feelings. She was convinced that were she to cry, her father would hear about it. She would not give him that satisfaction.

Her eyes were the only dry ones when she said goodbye to her sisters. She quickly agreed with Erika and Eva when they said they could not face up to going to the station. It was better this way, she told them. She would keep in touch with them. She would write every week.

Mrs. Kübler had bought Elisabeth her first adult large-brimmed hat and what she called a "very practical" brown woolen dress. Barely reaching five feet (she was to grow no taller) and weighing almost exactly a hundred pounds, the sixteen-year-old looked like a little old lady as she boarded the train for Lausanne.

Mrs. Kübler dabbed her eyes and talked banalities. Elisabeth tightened her jaw and brushed away the offer of a handkerchief. As the train whistled its departure, Elisabeth stretched her lips into a tight smile. She was on her own.

5

Cutting the Cord

As SHE WATCHED the Swiss countryside slide past her window, Elisabeth's emotions swung from nostalgia to excitement. The rhythmic beat of train wheels on the track were moment-by-moment reminders of her widening separation from the security of home, from well-patterned ways and from the people she held most dear.

The train rattled over a bridge spanning a white-water river, and the sudden staccato sound broke her reverie. Elisabeth remembers this moment because it seemed to her symbolic. She was crossing a bridge between her childhood and adulthood. The challenges would be tougher now, the gradient steeper.

Her exultation over being really on her own for the first time in her life (discounting her spell in the hospital) did not completely shield her from darts of doubt. Even changing trains at Lausanne for the connection to Romilly prompted some anxiety. Was this the right train? Suppose she were to miss the station sign at Romilly? Would Madame be there to meet her? How would she recognize her?

The journey was, in fact, completed without a hitch, for Swiss trains run with clockwork precision. Romilly's stationmaster shouted the arrival. Elisabeth heaved her suitcase to the platform. She was conscious of being critically examined by an overweight woman. Three young children, all girls, were clinging to her black dress. Elisabeth advanced, smiled shyly and put out her hand. There was no responsive warmth in Madame's sensuous and heavily made-up face or in the limp beringed hand she proffered. The children eyed Elisabeth suspiciously.

Elisabeth voiced a greeting in Swiss-German. Madame pursed her rouged lips and snapped, "*Nous parlons francais tout le temps, maintenant.*"

The rebuke, and warning that she would be prohibited from speaking her own tongue, caught Elisabeth off guard. She was among strangers now—seemingly unfriendly ones.

Madame's corsets squeaked as she waddled to the station's yard and to a vintage car, and there were large sweat stains under her arms. Elisabeth later guessed that Madame Perret was in her late thirties. She was still ostentatiously in mourning for her husband, who had been a prominent official in the city of Lausanne, and had been twice her age when he had died six months earlier.

It was a short drive up the hill to Romilly and to a three-story red brick mansion set in the middle of a large unkempt garden. On arriving at the house, the eldest girl, Louise, a sophisticated twelve-year-old, immediately ran off to join some friends. Elisabeth was to see little of the rebellious child, who treated the "housekeeper" with studied disdain.

The second girl, plump seven-year-old Renée, was obviously going to grow up to be as large as her mother. She too had been encouraged by her mother to look down on servants, but Elisabeth was soon to capture her confidence and friendship. She whined her needs, but she and the youngest child, Marie, were to find in Elisabeth the affection they craved.

On arriving in the kitchen, Madame Perret again looked Elisabeth up and down as if she were re-examining a questionable purchase and surely doubting the young girl's stamina and ability to cope with an outrageously crowded schedule of domestic duties.

The tasks of the housekeeper were pinned to the kitchen door.

Instructions were written out in French. Elisabeth would rise at 6:00 A.M., wax and polish floors, help to dress the children, polish the silver, feed the chickens and rabbits in the yard, water plants and vegetables—all before breakfast. After breakfast she would wash the children's clothes and household linen, read to and otherwise entertain the younger children and then prepare lunch. She would prepare and serve afternoon tea, then cook and serve dinner, wash all the dishes and put the children to bed. At midnight she would lock up the house (except for the back door) and take two cups of tea on a tray to her employer's bedroom. Additional duties would be assigned from time to time.

Nodding her understanding of what was expected of her, Elisabeth turned to face her employer, who was holding out a small maid's cap and dainty white apron. These garments were to be worn when serving at table, instructed Madame.

The salary for Elisabeth's eighteen-hour working day would be the equivalent of three dollars a month—one dime a day better than slavery. She would have half a day off each week. She would be careful not to talk to strangers or get into any sort of mischief. There was a nice walk to the lake, Madame advised her. Naturally when there were guests the housekeeper would take her meals in the kitchen. She would on no account cook anything extra for herself, as there would be sufficient leftovers from the family table.

Then Madame Perret panted ahead of Elisabeth up two flights of stairs to a cubbyhole of a bedroom in the attic. The furnishings were an iron bedstead with a horsehair mattress and a small musty closet. A washbasin and water pitcher rested on a marble slab. A curtainless window looked onto the yard.

Wheezing from her exertion, Madame informed Elisabeth that she could start work immediately, and that she would be expected to cook and serve dinner that night.

So the new housekeeper unpacked her clothes and few belongings and smothered persistent thoughts of flight. It wasn't alarm over the schedule of duties that disturbed her. Indeed, she looked forward to being physically tested, for there had hardly been a day in her life, except when she had been ill or when working on a farm, when she had felt really exhausted. The duties would be a challenge. No, it was the studied curled-lip contempt of her employer that chilled her. In Meilen she had encountered negative personality traits—irrational anger, cynicism, injustice, hatred—but this frigid indifference was something new. Elisabeth now understands that Madame Perret projected upon the young girl her own self-loathing.

Work proved a partial relief from loneliness. By the end of the working day Elisabeth discovered a new level of fatigue, caused in part by undernourishment, for the leftovers from the family table were invariably slim. She often ate these morsels alone at the kitchen table. In the weeks and months that followed, she spent most of her pittance on loaves of fresh bread and irresistible pastries. She saved only some pennies to buy stamps to write home.

Her letters were long and mendaciously cheerful. Pride forbade her to speak of her exploitation and her loneliness.

In an early letter to Erika, she wrote:

> I am learning a lot of French, and the two younger children are my best teachers. Renée and Marie laugh at me, of course, but my vocabulary and accent are improving every day. When the children go to bed I read to them in French, and they can never have too many stories.
>
> The chickens and bunnies are getting to know me. They are already feeding out of my hand. I guess you'd call the children spoiled brats. Little Marie really misses her father, who must have been a very nice man because everybody speaks well of him. The house is full of beautiful *objets d'art*. You've never seen such fine tableware which is brought out whenever Madame entertains people to dinner—which is quite often.
>
> I've found a friend in the village, Dorothea. She is a year older than we are and she's a housekeeper at a home nearer the lake. Dorothea comes from Winterthur and it is nice to speak Swiss-German again. I wish I could see her more often.

Madame Perret proved a chronic faultfinder. Elisabeth grew to loathe the voice that whined about a dull patch on the waxed floor or a soggy potato or crystal that didn't have a diamond shine or linen not perfectly ironed.

She began to understand that her employer was playing the role of an aristocrat to camouflage her humble background. Elisabeth was part of the game playing. She overheard Madame tell one visitor that she employed several servants—presumably one who opened the front door with a curtsy (Elisabeth had been told very precisely how to receive guests), one who cooked the meals, one who served them at table, and a nursemaid who looked after the children!

It was a couple of months before Elisabeth understood why Madame's men friends called so late at night and why they entered the house through the back door. Because she was so naive she had not initially understood why she had been instructed to take always two cups of tea to the boudoir door at midnight. The realization that the voluptuous widow kept open house for men friends was a shock to the young girl. In Meilen the word sex, if mentioned, had been whispered behind a hand. Sex was what made babies. She knew that. Sex was vaguely associated with menstruation and, intimately, with marriage. There was, her mother had told her, no need to think about sex until you were fully grown up.

Elisabeth tried not to think about the male voices and the seductive laughter behind the door of Madame's boudoir. Unless bidden to enter, she left the tea tray on a table in the corridor and tapped gently on the door to indicate to Madame that the final duty of the day had been completed.

Anyway, there was very little time to think seriously about anything beyond the task at hand and about trying to catch up with the clock. Just when she felt she had ten minutes to herself, perhaps to write a letter home, one of the children would arrive with a broken toy to be mended or Madame Perret would shout from the hall that she had found some dust on a bookcase.

The tolerable part of a day came when she was outside with the children. When inside the house, the children were brats, but their attitudes changed when they were in the garden or yard. They respected her love of nature, and she grew fond of the two younger children and they of her. But they knew that they gained their mother's approval when, indoors, they treated Elisabeth as a servant.

The only person to whom she could really open up was her friend Dorothea. Their meetings were rare but thoroughly enjoyed. The two girls tried to synchronize their shopping and their time off duty. Dorothea was hardly happier than Elisabeth and just as homesick. The girls promised to support and help each other if they were ever in need.

With little variation in the routine, summer blended into the fall,

fall into winter. The tiny bedroom at the top of the house became so cold that Elisabeth slept in underwear under her nightgown. Sleep itself was no problem, but getting up at six on a frosty morning after only six hours' rest demanded all her willpower.

In early December Madame Perret gave her biggest dinner party. It was for her late husband's colleagues and friends. The widow was particularly offensive and demanding as Elisabeth prepared the elaborate meal. By the time she had changed into her parlor maid's white cap and apron to serve at table she was faint from fatigue. She noticed that one of the guests, a white-haired man with a kindly face, frequently looked at her with sympathy.

After she had cleared the dishes from the table and washed them up, she sat down at the kitchen table to eat the remnants of the meal. These were slim pickings—a few scraps of meat in congealed gravy and lukewarm asparagus. Suddenly the elderly man walked into the kitchen. He introduced himself as Professor Fouché.

To her surprise, the professor pulled a second chair to the table. Speaking Swiss-German, he asked bluntly why an educated young girl from what was surely a good family was doing such menial work.

It was the gentle way he looked at her that prompted Elisabeth to pour out her story. She told him how she had virtually run away from home because she could not face the prospect of working in her father's business. Her lips trembled as she spoke about Meilen.

The professor asked her what she really wanted to do with her life, and Elisabeth replied shyly that her dream was to be a physician. She naturally recognized that this hope was impracticable, at least in the immediate future, because first she would have to take the formidable Mature examination and she had not had any higher education. (The Mature is a prerequisite to entering a Swiss university.)

The old man nodded thoughtfully. So what would she like to do in the immediate future? She had by now given some thought to this and she answered without hesitation that she would like to find an apprenticeship in a laboratory. Laboratory work was related to medicine. It would be a sort of first step. Then, as a qualified laboratory technician, she could study to pass the Mature and then finance her medical training.

The professor got up and walked around the kitchen in silence. Then he came to her chair and patted her shoulder encouragingly. He urged her to hold on to her dream. He took a business card from his wallet and told her that on her next day off duty she should call at his home in Lausanne. He had some connections in the field of biochemistry. He promised he would find her a job in a laboratory.

Elisabeth was still euphoric when five days later Madame Perret waddled into the kitchen to announce that she was off to a funeral. She casually added that it was the funeral of Professor Fouché, who had been a dinner guest the previous Saturday. He had died of a heart attack on the Monday morning.

Elisabeth reeled. It couldn't be Professor Fouché—not the kind man who had spoken to her! Madame confirmed it. In her room Elisabeth wept for Professor Fouché, and then on Saturday, still only half believing that the kindly old man had died, she took a train for Lausanne and found his home. The curtains were drawn. His widow opened the door. Elisabeth haltingly explained why she had come. The widow nodded her head. On the morning he had died her husband had phoned a friend of his. She had overheard the conversation. It was something about a laboratory job for a young girl. But the widow could remember no more than that. Her husband had so many friends, his conversation could have been with any one of them. She was sorry she couldn't be of more help.

Numbed by her misfortune, Elisabeth returned to Romilly and to her employer.

A week before Christmas a number of Madame Perret's relatives arrived to stay. They doubled Elisabeth's work load. Only one of the visitors, her employer's eldest sister, Madame de Villiers, gave her any assistance in making the beds and cooking the meals. Madame de Villiers took a real interest in the young housekeeper and expressed concern over Elisabeth's physical condition. Elisabeth heard Madame de Villiers rebuke her employer for "half starving" the housekeeper, and she made sure that Elisabeth's meals were adequate.

Two days before Christmas Elisabeth found Madame de Villiers standing in the hall with her bags packed. Her eyes were blazing. Although she didn't say so, it was obvious that the sisters had quarreled. Madame de Villiers was leaving. She gave Elisabeth a tip and scribbled her Geneva address. If ever Elisabeth was in Geneva, said Madame de Villiers, she must be sure to look her up.

On Christmas Eve a big pine tree was hauled into the house. Elisabeth joined the children in the drawing room to help them decorate it. When Madame Perret entered the room, she immediately ordered Elisabeth back to the kitchen. This was a family festival, and Elisabeth had plenty of work to get on with in the kitchen.

It was this act—this exclusion from Christmas festivities—that carried Elisabeth into a depression like none she had known before. She climbed the stairs to the cold attic room and sobbed into her pillow. She recalled the Christmas Eves of her early childhood and how her father would take the triplets for a short walk in the snow; and then on returning to the house, they would see the Christmas tree aglow with lighted candles. Her mother would always greet them with a contrived expression of disappointment and declare how the children had just missed the Christmas Child who had lighted the candles on the tree.

As she shivered and sobbed on her bed, her grieving turned to anger. Why was she in this horrible house when she could be home at Meilen? She beat her fists into the pillow. She hated Madame Perret more than she hated anyone else in the world. She would rather be anywhere than spend another night in this house. The sudden thought of escape halted a slide into hysteria. She would be gone in the morning. She would leave when the household was asleep. With trembling hands she counted the few francs in her purse.

The hour was badly chosen. The night was bitterly cold and the landscape covered by a foot of snow. But Elisabeth's mind was made up.

At midnight she took the two cups of tea to Madame's boudoir and returned to her room to pack her bag. Her first problem was that her mother had sent extra winter clothing and she could not manage to cram everything into her one suitcase. She would have to borrow an extra bag from her friend Dorothea.

Taking one of the children's sleds, she worked her way down through the snow to the place where her friend was employed. The house was already in darkness, but Elisabeth attracted Dorothea's attention by throwing snowballs at a window. Whispering, she told her what she planned to do. Dorothea lowered a wicker suitcase on a rope.

When she returned to her bedroom, Elisabeth struggled with second thoughts. It was now one o'clock on Christmas morning. Her money was not enough to buy a train ticket home. She thought of the children and was saddened that she would be leaving them without saying goodbye. Marie would miss her, perhaps Renée too. She thought of her father. Surely her father would understand.

What moved her to a firm and final decision was a fresh image of the sour, disdainful face of Madame Perret. She resolved that she would never again look at that face, never again have to tolerate that grating nagging voice.

She wrote a brief note saying goodbye to the children and added that she had been obliged to borrow their sled. She would leave it at the station in Romilly. She pinned the note to her pillow.

By the time she reached the station, it was six o'clock in the morning. She tied the sled to a pillar. Her hands were swollen from cold as she carried her suitcases to the ticket office. With one franc to spare, she paid the price of a ticket to Geneva; the sleepy official told her the Geneva-bound train would be arriving in ten minutes. It was only then that she remembered that she had the address of Madame de Villiers.

The cold and her fatigue and hunger made her light-headed. In a strange way she felt she was being guided—as if there were someone beside her, as if she herself were not in charge of events.

She seemed to be the only passenger on the train. It was Christmas morning! That was what was so hard to believe. She slept for a little while, but it was still dark when the train pulled into Geneva. Using her last franc, she telephoned Madame de Villiers. Dawn was breaking when Madame de Villiers picked her up in a taxi and took her to her apartment.

With little explanation, Madame de Villiers seemed to understand Elisabeth's situation. It was many hours later, and only after Elisabeth had bathed, eaten and slept, that she asked about the abuse she had suffered at the hands of Madame Perret. Elisabeth recalls very little of the remainder of that Christmas Day. But that night she telephoned her home and spoke to Erika. She learned with surprise that her parents and Eva were in the mountains on a skiing holiday. Erika, who was alone, was overjoyed to hear that her identical twin would be home very soon.

Two days later Madame de Villiers loaned Elisabeth enough money to buy a train ticket to Meilen. Erika was at the Meilen station to meet her. The girls hugged each other and laughed and cried together. The suitcases were put into a handcart, and they pulled the cart up the hill to the Big House.

On January 2, when Mr. and Mrs. Kübler and Eva returned, they were amazed to see Elisabeth, who was obliged to repeat her stories of Romilly. Her mother was appalled. Her father reflected that an experience like this was bad only if one did not learn from it. The following day Erika left to start the new semester at the Zurich gymnasium, and Eva left for her domestic science college.

The night after her sisters had returned to their studies, Mr. Kübler again raised the question of Elisabeth's future. He expressed the hope that the hard lesson Elisabeth had learned over the past nine months would stand her in good stead for the rest of her life. He likened her experience to that of a mountaineer caught in a blizzard, obliged to make do as best he could. However, Elisabeth was now back in the protective warmth of the cabin, as it were. It was time to lace up her boots again and face the next challenge.

Mr. Kübler refilled his wine glass and sipped meditatively. Elisabeth correctly anticipated the direction of his thoughts. She would not be taken off guard again. Mr. Kübler said that he was just as ready as he had been earlier to take Elisabeth into his business. Bygones were bygones. In fact Elisabeth could start work immediately and take the train with him to Zurich on the following morning.

She shook her head, but kept her voice low. She was, she said, grateful for the offer. She understood now that her father wanted what he believed was best for her. But it would be as hard for her to go into business as it would be to return to Romilly.

Mr. Kübler shrugged. Elisabeth was still being stubborn and foolish. That was her right. However, she could not stay at home doing nothing. He would give her exactly two weeks to find alternative employment. Murmuring something about his stamp collection, Mr. Kübler rose from the table and went to his office desk. He always withdrew in this manner when he wanted to avoid confrontation.

Over the next few days Elisabeth and her mother scanned all the job-vacancy advertisements in the Zurich newspapers. Mrs. Kübler remembered that a new biochemical research laboratory had just been opened in Feldmeiler, a few miles from their home. Perhaps the staff quota had not yet been filled.

The owner-manager of the small laboratory, Dr. Hans Brun, was a young man who was not prepared for the breathlessly eager applicant for an apprenticeship. Nor was Elisabeth initially sure what the work entailed. But by the time she returned home that evening she had been signed on. (Entering an apprenticeship is a legal procedure in Switzerland, and there were legal papers which she and her employer had to sign.)

The laboratory was divided into two departments. Cosmetic creams and body lotions were manufactured in one department. The other, consisting of large greenhouses, was for cancer research. Plants forced in the greenhouses were exposed to a variety of known and suspected carcinogens. Dr. Brun had a theory that carcinogens could be botanically identified in procedures that would be far less costly and much quicker than testing them on animals.

Dr. Brun's enthusiasm matched Elisabeth's as he demonstrated his techniques of feeding nutritious agents to some plants and suspected carcinogens to others. The agents had to be added at precise intervals and with extreme care, and the growth of the plants carefully measured. The greenhouses were kept at 90 degrees Fahrenheit.

Within a few days Elisabeth believed she could not be happier. As the staff was very small, she took her turn making cosmetic creams and lotions, but the precision of the work in the greenhouses and the possibility of achieving a breakthrough in cancer research made the job purposeful.

There was, however, a problem—and a big one. Dr. Brun was a manic-depressive whose mood swings became increasingly severe. One day he would be an extrovert, blazing with zeal for his pioneering work. The next day—and perhaps for the next week—he would be languid, slovenly and deeply depressed. Sometimes he would not turn up for work at all. Telephone calls to his home were unanswered. When he was not at work, Elisabeth and two junior staff members took complete charge of the laboratory.

Then, in one of his hypermanic moods, Dr. Brun ordered thousands of dollars' worth of mostly unneeded equipment. The huge order gravely depleted the resources of the small company. After six months of prodigal spending, bankruptcy was imminent.

The news was alarming to Elisabeth not only because a progressive and potentially profitable company was threatened with closure but because, under Swiss apprenticeship laws, she was expected to spend a minimum of three years in one laboratory if she was to graduate as a technician. Unless she obtained a special dispensation, she would have to start her three-year apprenticeship over again from scratch.

It had all seemed so promising. She was living at home. She was traveling to Zurich two afternoons a week to take apprenticeship courses in chemistry, physics, mathematics and allied subjects. She was one of only two girls in her class, and was consistently at the top.

Her job allowed time too for some social activities. The other students in her classes, all apprentices, were cheerful company. She occasionally joined them at a cinema or to go dancing. Then on the weekends there was the opportunity to go to the mountains for skiing or climbing.

But early one autumn morning she arrived for work at the laboratory and found the police barring the entrance. The company, they told her, had been closed because of non-payment of debts.

Labor Department officials advised her that unless she found another laboratory position immediately she would lose her nine months' credit toward qualifying as a technician.

To Mr. Kübler it was quite obvious that his daughter had made the wrong career choice. She would now be obliged to shed her pride and take up his offer of office work.

Elisabeth's response was to write to every listed laboratory in Zurich. Within the short period her father allowed her to remain unemployed, and because it was the middle of the academic year, she received only one positive answer. It was from the dermatology department of the Canton Hospital. They had just one apprenticeship vacancy.

She arrived an hour early for the interview, and she wandered about the hospital corridors inhaling the smell of ether and carbolic as if these were exotic essences of Araby! She relished the hustle and bustle of physicians and nurses. Nothing, she resolved, would prevent her from making this environment her world. She would plead or claw or crawl her way into their exhilarating company.

The seventeen-year-old initiate was on the outer fringes of the healing profession's temple. But the time would come—and of this she was now convinced—when she would enter the inner chambers. She resolved that one day she would walk through these corridors as someone fully qualified to perform all the Hippocratic practices and rituals.

The laboratory of the dermatology department was in the hospital's windowless basement. The office of Dr. Karl Zehnder, the director, was not much larger than an average-sized bathroom. From behind a desk piled with files and textbooks he looked up inquisitively. He was a rather inconspicuous-looking man with bushy fair hair and pale blue eyes ringed by fatigue—the eyes of someone who spends long hours reading small print. With an expression of kindness and interest, Dr. Zehnder studied the girl at the door. He waved her to a chair and then glanced at her scholastic records and testimonials.

Besides being a research scientist (he was later to become eminent in the fields of water pollution and purification) Dr. Zehnder was a shrewd student of human nature. Several years later he told Elisabeth that within the first minute of meeting her he decided to sign her on for the coveted laboratory apprenticeship.

═══ 6 ═══

The Dream and Reality

AS A JUNIOR APPRENTICE in a drafty old-fashioned basement laboratory of a large urban hospital, Elisabeth was a long, long way from her citadel. There was still time to dream, and her fantasies featured heroes and heroines like Madame Curie and Albert Schweitzer, and indeed all those scientists, philosophers and explorers who have helped to ease man's suffering or probed the frontiers of man's understanding of himself.

Reality was not at all glamorous. Elisabeth spent most of her first months at the hospital preparing microscope slides of the syphilis spirochete!

Dr. Zehnder supervised the lab work and the training of the apprentices. His job allowed him time enough to study his scientific journals. He occasionally emerged from his cluttered office to peer at the lab benches or advise in a mild-mannered voice on a different method for preparing a solution or on some other lab procedure.

The qualified technicians tended to keep aloof, but Elisabeth found an instant friend in an eighteen-year-old lab technician with the rather un-Swiss name of Baldwin. Cheerful, irresponsible and gangling, Baldwin provided needed humor with his practical jokes. His duties ranged from message running to cleaning the benches at the end of the day. Elisabeth was amused by Baldwin, but placed a margin on their relationship, as she did with all the young men in her technical college class who suggested closer ties.

A romance was simply out of the question. Elisabeth had set her sights on a distant target, and there could be no diversions. Her first goal was to graduate as a technician. That would take another two years. Then, if ever she was to get to a medical school, she would have to study for the Mature exam. After that? . . . But the time to consider the crossing of bridges would be as she approached them.

The job at hand was what mattered. She would be the best technician the hospital had ever engaged. The director would always be delighted with her research and, she was determined, her work would always be a challenge to her searching mind. Also she would remain in the top position in her class at the technical college. Such was the gravity of her resolve.

Of course there was time for some social and outdoor activities. She enjoyed dancing occasionally, but always with a group from her class. One of her more frequent dance partners was Roberto Niederer, with whom she had grown up in Meilen. He had a regular girl friend, so the relationship between him and Elisabeth was comfortably platonic. Roberto was new in her class at the college and already showing skill in glassblowing, for which he was to become internationally famous. There were class picnics too and occasional visits to theaters.

Each night Elisabeth took the lakeside train home to Meilen, and the family met over the dinner table to share their experiences.

Eva was growing into a young woman of unusual beauty. She had a long list of attentive boy friends, and indeed was never without a date. Erika's social life was still handicapped by her lame leg. She was never happier than when reading a book. Her children grown, Mrs. Kübler now sought her satisfaction in her kitchen.

For Mr. Kübler the mountains still beckoned, and it was to Elisabeth that he turned for company. In spite of the clashes in the home, there was never a harsh or angry word exchanged between Elisabeth and her father when they were on the high trails. When they hiked, it was usually an easy silence. Each was conscious of the other's love of nature, of climbing and skiing. Elisabeth remembers walking for eight or ten hours at a stretch with her father, with barely a dozen words passing between them. Smiles exchanged at the end of a day in the mountains would convey their mutual respect and contentment.

The fighting war remained as close but no closer than the Swiss frontier. However, food, clothes and gasoline were in increasingly short supply. Although Switzerland had not heard the sounds of guns, bombs and jackboots, the country remained on wartime alert. Patriotism in a country of three races and four languages had never been more fervent.

Waste was the ugliest word in the dictionary, and no family was more conscious of conservation than the Küblers. Elisabeth had taken upon herself responsibility for the vegetable garden. Flowerbeds and lawn were sacrificed to potato patches and for the growing of cabbages, beans, peas, brussels sprouts, carrots, radishes, tomatoes and cucumbers—indeed almost every vegetable that could be grown between March and November. Vegetables and fruits that could not be immediately consumed were bottled and stored in the basement. Beans and peas were dehydrated by threading the pods together and hanging them in the sun to dry. Cabbage, cauliflower, beets and carrots were stored in garden pits. The Kübler family was more than self-sustaining in fruit and vegetables and was able to provision neighbors, friends and the needy.

Elisabeth's workdays were not always rhythmically patterned. When, for instance, one of the senior laboratory technicians went on vacation, Dr. Zehnder called upon the zealous teenager to take additional responsibility. She was introduced to hematology and histology (the studies of blood and of tissues), branches of science that would be of value to her in the years ahead.

Her first contact with patients came about through the need to take blood samples. She was initially apprehensive and shy because most of the patients were suffering from venereal disease. The sheltered life at Meilen had given her no preparation for unexpected confrontations with prostitutes. She discovered that they were not the scarlet women of fiction and popular prejudice but generally disillusioned women who told stories of abandonment, cruelty and poverty.

72

This early contact with patients whose problems were not merely physical stirred within her feelings which she couldn't fully articulate—not then. But there was something terribly wrong, she thought, when the dispassionate technology of medicine could not be linked to the cries of the heart and an understanding of the mind. What these prostitutes needed—and their clients too—was old-fashioned humanity. The patients desperately needed somebody to sit at their bedsides, somebody with time to listen, somebody who was non-judgmental and who could empathize with shame and loneliness, pain and fear.

While Elisabeth was too young and inexperienced to counsel prostitutes, she could seek out sick children, and she began to visit the children's wards. Wearing her white lab coat and white shoes, she would walk up two flights of stairs from the basement and, without seeking authority, simply sit down at an ailing child's bedside. She usually picked out the child who was most heavily bandaged or one who was crying.

She made these visits in her lunch hour. Sandwiches and a glass of milk could be quickly consumed, and she still had forty-five minutes in which to talk to a sick child or to read a story or simply to hold a hand.

Then suddenly there was no time for anything except the very basic care of people in dire need. On June 6, 1944, the radio broadcast the anticipated D-day landing in Normandy. Within a few days of the Allied invasion of France, refugees from the battle zones began pouring across the Swiss frontier.

Elisabeth arrived at the Zurich train station one morning to find a column of two or three hundred refugees stumbling up the hill to the hospital. Aside from a handful of old men, the refugees were women and children in about equal numbers. Some were in rags, some incongruously in fur coats, but whatever garments they wore, their expressions were the same. Faces bore the shadows and lines of fatigue, suffering and hunger.

Bounding up the hill ahead of the ragged column, Elisabeth learned that the refugees were being directed to her own department in the basement. They were coming to be deloused. Breathlessly she told Baldwin to tell Dr. Zehnder that she wouldn't be reporting to her lab bench. She was needed for the emergency.

The delousing department in the dermatology wing was run by an elderly woman who was in a state of panic. The woman immediately accepted Elisabeth's offer of assistance.

Within a few minutes Elisabeth was stripping the refugees of their clothing and leading them to the baths. Their bodies were covered with scabies, the highly contagious skin disease caused by itch mites. For Elisabeth it was on-the-job training. The adults were able to wash themselves, so Elisabeth took charge of the children and the babies. She gently washed their skin, covered the bodies with antiscabetic lotion and later brushed off the scabs. She collected the lice-ridden clothing for steam disinfection. Then she covered open sores with ointment.

It was eleven o'clock at night by the time the last of the refugees had been cleansed. She had just enough time to catch the last train to Meilen. Her lab coat was filthy and her white shoes ruined by dirt and water. It was, she decided as she walked up the hill to the Big House, the happiest day of her life.

But her parents weren't happy. Indeed, they had been frantic with worry and had waited up for her. How, they asked, could she be so thoughtless as to arrive home half an hour after midnight without warning them? From the state of her clothing she looked as if she had been ravished. Nothing like this was ever to happen again. As she sank into her featherbed, Elisabeth realized she had had nothing to eat since breakfast.

Next day she found another column of refugees outside the delousing department. Some had walked from Paris and beyond. Elisabeth put in another thirteen hours' work at the basement baths.

That first tide of refugees lasted several weeks. The older woman in charge of the operation collapsed under the strain and meekly handed over responsibility for the department to the seemingly tireless and very happy teenager. Mr. and Mrs. Kübler realized that their protests were useless. Mrs. Kübler continued to express concern over the effect on her daughter's health of the long hours at the hospital, but Mr. Kübler spoke with grudging admiration of the "family's Pestalozzi."

Elisabeth discovered a new talent—an ability to organize. She streamlined the delousing operation until it ran with the efficiency of

74

a mass-production factory. By the time the refugees had been bathed, dried and anointed, their clothes had been steam-disinfected and were ready to be worn again.

But "the best delouser in the world," as she laughingly described herself to Erika, involved herself in more than logistics and efficiency. She realized that what the refugees needed at least as much as their cleansing was encouragement and empathy. The colloquial French she had learned in the home of Madame Perret now came in useful. She had a comforting word for everyone and made time to listen to stories of peril and privation, to cries of grief and fear.

After three weeks of almost continuous work in the delousing department, Elisabeth's skin became pallid. Because of missed meals she lost weight. Mrs. Kübler, fearing that another of her triplets might become an invalid, extracted a promise from Elisabeth that at least she would rest up on Sundays. She intended to keep this promise and to soak up the sun, but on the third Sunday when she was planning to rest she received a message that another large contingent of refugees had arrived at the hospital.

Telling her mother that she was off to see some friends, Elisabeth went to the hospital. That night she just managed to catch the last train to Meilen. When she arrived home, she found the house in darkness and the doors locked. She attempted to squeeze her way in through a kitchen trapdoor designed for milk bottles. The door was a fraction too small, and she got stuck! She could move neither backward nor forward, and the groans and grunts from her straining aroused the household. Her father rescued her, and she accepted parental reproof for her deceit, but she added that the refugees were indeed her friends. After this incident even her mother gave up protesting about her daughter's late hours.

Elisabeth was more anxious about her absence from the laboratory workbench than she was about parental castigations. Dr. Zehnder had just accepted another hospital appointment, and a new physician, Dr. Abraham Weitz, a Polish-born Jew, headed the dermatology department. Elisabeth feared he might not be wholly sympathetic to the excuses of a young apprentice who had not lighted a Bunsen burner for three weeks but who was still drawing a modest salary for the work for which she was ostensibly employed. Her most disquieting thought was that she could be fired. If she were, all hope of qualifying as a technician would be crushed.

She was debating whether to tell the new head of the laboratory about her dilemma when she was forced to a confrontation. Baldwin arrived in the delousing area, his expression unusually serious. Dr. Weitz wanted to see her before she went home.

It was a Friday, and Elisabeth hoped that if she could spend the weekend preparing her defense she could muster an argument to convince Dr. Weitz that she had been doing very necessary work and that she didn't deserve to be fired. She spent a long time bathing the last of the children, hoping that Dr. Weitz would become impatient and leave. But he didn't. In fact, he came to the delousing bathrooms himself. In a neutral voice, he asked Elisabeth to come at once to his office.

Her heart pounded, but she saw a glimmer of hope when she was invited to sit down. When about to reprove a junior, a department head traditionally kept the miscreant standing.

After a silence in which Elisabeth could hear her watch ticking, Dr. Weitz said that he had been observing her for the past week and that he had not seen anyone work with more dedication. He paused and gave her a faint smile, and then added that he had not seen anyone more contented.

A compliment was certainly not what she had expected. Overwhelmed by a feeling of relief that after all she wasn't going to lose her apprenticeship, she felt the tears well up.

The doctor handed her his handkerchief. Then he spoke quietly about the war, and about his home country, Poland, about his intention of returning to Warsaw as soon as hostilities ceased. The people would urgently need medical help. Poland would need strong young people who could work with the dedication that Elisabeth had shown in the delousing department.

Elisabeth sat on the edge of the chair and nodded her head. She was very conscious of the dirt stains on her lab coat and that her face and hands were begrimed.

The tears she had tried to stem now rolled down her cheeks as she heard Dr. Weitz tell her that, so long as she didn't publicize the fact,

76

her prolonged absences from her laboratory bench would not be recorded in the employment register.

When the hospital ran short of supplies for the refugees, Elisabeth became a community mendicant. Usually alone, but occasionally accompanied by the irrepressibly enthusiastic Baldwin, she begged neighborhood housewives for spare clothes, farmers for milk and pharmacists for baby bottles. She felt no qualms about telling a wealthy Swiss woman that she hardly needed five coats when there were women in the hospital basement who didn't possess one.

Diapers were more difficult. She and her sister Erika raided the linen chests in the attic of the Big House and cut old sheets into appropriate squares. If Mrs. Kübler missed her mothballed sheets, she never mentioned the loss.

Baldwin was a born trouble attracter. One day he and Elisabeth got into serious trouble. It was a day when two hundred refugees arrived without any warning. Already undernourished—much of Europe was hungry, some areas starving—they had had nothing to eat on the last part of the journey from the Swiss frontier to Zurich.

Baldwin went to the hospital kitchen and when the eyes of the cook were averted "borrowed" a cart loaded with seventy meals destined for the convalescent wards. The hypertensive director of the hospital, a caricature of an administrator, was incensed by what he described as "this blatant theft." He summoned Elisabeth and Baldwin and apoplectically demanded a quantity of food similar to that which had been "stolen" or the equivalent in food coupons (food ration cards had been issued to a population swelled by refugees). Indeed, unless the food or coupons were forthcoming within twenty-four hours, Elisabeth and Baldwin would be out on the street.

It was impossible to find such a quantity of food in so short a time. Even the black market had dried up. But the prospect of imminent dismissal was a goad to action. Elisabeth approached Dr. Weitz and told him of the threat. He listened in characteristic silence before he told her to report to him on the following morning.

Next morning he presented Elisabeth with enough food coupons to allow for the replenishment of the hospital's larders. The previous night, Elisabeth learned later, the doctor had visited his Jewish friends in Zurich—friends who clearly understood the needs of the

77

homeless and persecuted—and readily obtained all the food coupons needed.

A couple of weeks after this incident Baldwin came to Elisabeth's rescue in a more personal way. She was back at her laboratory bench boiling an alcoholic solution over a Bunsen burner when the flask exploded into a fireball. As the flames leapt upward she was able to protect her eyes, but at the cost of seriously burned hands. Parts of her mouth, neck and ears also received third-degree burns.

Quite unaware of the extent of her injuries, Elisabeth coolly doused the fire on the bench and then walked up a flight of stairs to the emergency room. Some of the waiting patients screamed at the sight of the almost hairless apparition. Doctors came running.

Sledgehammer blows of pain now struck her—pain that could not be fully controlled by morphia.

Elisabeth spent the next six weeks in a hospital bed. In the first ten days her head was completely bandaged, except for a small opening in the area of the mouth to permit her to be fed by a tube. Her arms were immobilized and her bandaged hands throbbed excruciatingly, for the spill of blazing alcohol had burned the flesh to the bone. Her earlobes were charred.

Once a day the suppurating skin and flesh were treated with silver nitrate, an agonizing procedure. In fact, in the first week the pain was so acute, in spite of heavy doses of analgesics, she twice kicked out and broke hot water bottles that had been placed at the foot of the bed.

Her parents and sisters were informed, of course, and came to visit her. Dr. Weitz also came at least once a day and with paternal affection assured her that a new batch of refugees was being properly cared for; and the senior medical staff took the keenest interest in her progress. But her most constant visitor was Baldwin. He tried to cheer her up with his jokes, and he read to her too, haltingly but gamely.

It was Baldwin who, after she had spent weeks in bed, wheeled her to the medical school at the request of the professor of plastic surgery. The professor said that because of the extent of the injuries the patient would never again have fully effective use of her hands.

Elisabeth was appalled by this prognosis. Baldwin, however, as he wheeled her back to her bed insisted with characteristic optimism that if they worked on the therapy together they could prove the professor wrong.

He set to work at once. Borrowing apparatus from the laboratory in the basement, he designed and rigged up a system of pulleys and weights. Every evening that followed, and until she fell asleep, Elisabeth worked on stretching the tissue of her hands. Every evening Baldwin provided additional weights, and every morning he smuggled the borrowed apparatus back into the lab.

The new skin on the back of her hands began to stretch, the joints to loosen. Three weeks later, and just before Elisabeth was to be discharged from the ward, the professor of plastic surgery once again asked Elisabeth to attend his class for the practical instruction of the medical students. He invited the students to look at Elisabeth's hands and he extolled the effectiveness of the silver nitrate treatment. The wounds, he noted, had healed well, but, he added, the patient's fingers would be permanently inflexible. Thereupon, in spite of the stab of pain caused by stretching the pearly white and glistening new skin, Elisabeth fully opened and closed her fingers. The professor's jaw sagged. Elisabeth and Baldwin relished their moment of triumph.

At the request of the professor, Elisabeth explained to the students how she and Baldwin had worked with the improvised apparatus. The professor regained some dignity by expounding at some length on how recovery from serious injury could be expedited by patient motivation.

After taking some sick leave at home, Elisabeth returned to duty at the hospital, where she was distressed to find that Baldwin had been fired as a result of his playing some harmless practical joke on the administrator. She made attempts to trace him but failed to do so, and she never saw him again. However, she still carries on her hands the scars of her debt to a young man of irrepressible humor and optimism and of extraordinary deftness and ingenuity.

7

To France with Love

On the Friday of the first week in January 1945 Elisabeth returned to the Big House without knowing that she was close to a landmark encounter. Over the dinner table that evening Mr. Kübler asked her if she would help him prepare the Furlegi Mountain cabin for twenty members of the International Voluntary Service for Peace. The name of the organization was new to her.

She had some time on her hands, because the flow of refugees had temporarily stopped. The thought of a weekend in the mountains made a strong appeal. It would be a chance to recharge the batteries, and there would surely be an opportunity for some skiing. She nodded to her father. Yes, she would be glad to help him tidy up the cabin.

Elisabeth and her father had hardly arrived at the cabin on the following midmorning when the visitors turned up. Most of them, men and women, were in their twenties or early thirties, but one grizzled veteran boasted of his eightieth year.

The party was obviously not the usual group of rowdy holiday-makers. No sooner had they off-loaded their backpacks than they set about domestic chores—cooks to the stove, others using brooms, still others splitting wood and collecting water for the copper tank. All the members of the group seemed to be much more interested in each other's welfare than in skiing and in the other recreations of the mountains. The Volunteers were not only self-disciplined but obviously possessed a collective sense of purpose. That evening Elisabeth and her father joined the group for an evening meal and a sing-along.

Then for the benefit of Elisabeth and Mr. Kübler, the Volunteers spoke about the work of their organization, which had been started after World War I. The Volunteers came from diverse cultural, religious and economic backgrounds, but they shared a commitment to peace and to helping the needy anywhere in the world. No one was paid for work. Some members worked for a few weeks, others for a year or more. Though not government-supported, in its structure and service the organization was to serve as one of the models for the American Peace Corps.

Another round of songs, and then some of the Volunteers related their personal experiences. One told of helping to rebuild a Greek village that had been devastated by an earthquake. The oldest member spoke of helping to distribute food to starving villagers in India. The stories were told with humor and humility.

Then one of the Volunteers spoke of the enormity of the need in war-torn Europe. The reason for the meeting on Furlegi was to discuss how the Volunteers could ready themselves for the day when the Swiss frontiers would be open again.

With her feet tucked under her, Elisabeth listened spellbound as two of the older members reported on the outrage inflicted upon the small French village of Ecurcey, not far from the eastern Swiss frontier. The village had been almost totally destroyed in a punitive raid by the Nazis, who had wrought vengeance following a successful exploit in the area of the village by the French Maquis (the anti-Nazi resistance forces).

In the light of the flickering oil lamp Elisabeth studied the faces of the men and women around her. They were ordinary faces, the faces of the Swiss town and the farm, but there was something special about the company, some quality not easily defined. It was kindness, she decided, true unselfishness. A deep contentment too. She looked at a huge ruddy-faced, tousle-haired man who was now speaking about the plight of children in a coal-mining village in Belgium. He was a lumberjack, he said, and she could imagine him wielding an ax with his coarse, calloused hands. Yet his voice held avuncular tenderness as he spoke about children dying from diseases caused by coal dust.

At his shoulder sat a dark elfin girl who said she was a seamstress and that she was ready at the drop of a pin to move into any area of need.

Elisabeth studied them each by turn—the young bearded professor of music who had led the community singing; a farmer from the Italian area of Switzerland; a heavy-set bank manager, one of the few senior men and probably a contemporary of her father; and a dozen or so students. They were her sort of people, all of them.

She looked across at her father too. He was in the shadows, a little apart. She couldn't read his expression.

From the time of the arrival of the Volunteers at the mountain cabin, Mr. Kübler had played the role of the courteous host. None could play it better. She understood his pride in being honorary custodian of the Furlegi cabin. Perhaps that was why, thought Elisabeth, he remained a fraction separated from the company.

Could her father, she wondered, be feeling the sense of excitement, indeed the intoxication, that she now felt? It was an excitement that tightened her stomach muscles, made her pulse quicken. These were the kind of people who would understand her vow to help the people of Poland!

Impulsively she turned to the student sitting next to her—a clean-cut young man who could have posed for a shaving cream advertisement. How, she asked him, could she join the Volunteers?

The student replied that there was a branch office of the International Voluntary Service for Peace in Zurich. The office could always use some help. When the war was over, there would be the chance to help rebuild places like Ecurcey.

Elisabeth found little sleep that night. She tossed on her bunk as she thought about Poland, thought about Ecurcey.

On Monday during her lunch hour Elisabeth rushed to the Zurich branch office of the IVSP. She filled out and signed a form listing her modest qualifications. The organization had its newest and most ardent recruit ready in any spare time that she had to roll bandages, collect old clothes, sew blankets and make whatever other preparations were requested or necessary for the day the frontiers opened.

One practical preparation was to forgo her annual vacations. She would need the accumulated vacation days when the war ended.

The news that the war in Europe was over reached Zurich on May 7, 1945. Elisabeth was on duty at her laboratory workbench when someone dashed into the lab and shouted the news. Everyone cheered and hugged one another. As Elisabeth ran upstairs to the wards, the bells of Zurich's cathedral began to peal.

Spontaneously, the medical staff assisted or carried the patients to the flat roof of the hospital. Almost every patient, even those who were very sick and those who were dying, wanted to get up into the sunlight where he could hear better the clamor in the streets and the sound of a thousand bells.

Elisabeth carried half a dozen children up to the roof. Even a very sick three-year-old seemed to understand the significance of the hour. Beds were carried up for some dying patients. One ninety-year-old woman murmured that she held on to life only to see this day of peace. (In fact she died the next day.) Few people said anything. Many cried.

Elisabeth's elation was heightened by the thought that after five years she would now be able to fulfill her vow. She would go at once to the wastelands of war.

The bells were still ringing when she descended to the basement again and knocked on the door of the office of Dr. Weitz. She was going to blurt out her request for an immediate leave of absence, but the words died on her tongue as she noticed the distant and sad expression in the doctor's eyes. She wondered whether Dr. Weitz had heard the news, or perhaps not understood the meaning of the bells, muffled in this office.

Dr. Weitz at once explained. He was thinking, he said, of his own people. Those who had survived to see this day would be mourning those who had not.

The doctor picked up a letter opener from the desk and turned it slowly in his hand. He seemed to be speaking as much to himself as to Elisabeth. As a Jew, he did not know if he had a single relative left in

Poland. The Nazis were known to have taken away even the youngest children.

Elisabeth remembers precisely one phrase he uttered. "We who have survived the war may find that we have not tears enough for our homecoming."

She had no ready words of comfort. It was hard to shift her own feelings from the jubilation she had experienced on the hospital roof to the grief in this cramped and cluttered office.

Eventually she asked him if he would be going back to Poland. He nodded. There would surely be some victims to save, some to whom he could give succor and hope.

It was then that she told Dr. Weitz of what had happened on the first day of the war when as a thirteen-year-old she had listened to the newscast of Germany's invasion of Poland. The doctor listened without interruption. Then he said how good it would be if he and Elisabeth were to find themselves in Poland working as colleagues once again. She smiled acknowledgment of the tribute and was about to leave the office when Dr. Weitz waved her back to the chair.

He looked at Elisabeth so frankly that she folded her arms across her chest self-consciously. She was aware that with her small height and wiry boyish figure she appeared to be a very young girl.

The doctor lifted his eyes to her face and asked what it was that motivated her. Why was it that she was not like other girls of her own age? Wasn't she interested in young men, in finding the right man to marry, in settling down and raising a family?

The questions caught her off guard and the color rose to her cheeks. She didn't, she replied, feel different from other girls of her age. It was just that there were so many things she wanted to do that she never gave any thought to having a steady boy friend or to marriage. Of course, she hoped that one day she would have a husband and babies. All she was thinking about now was working with the Volunteers.

She told the doctor about the destruction of the village of Ecurcey. The Volunteers were ready to move there immediately. Then, when the opportunity presented itself, she would go to Poland. It was, in fact, about Ecurcey that she had come to see him. Could she have immediate leave of absence? She had, she reminded the doctor, accumulated nine weeks' vacation leave!

Dr. Weitz smiled. Even if he were to turn down her application, he said, Elisabeth would still be on her way to the frontier. He reached for her personal file and noted that she was only one year from completing her apprenticeship. Her marks at the technical college had been straight A's. He presumed she would return in the late summer to complete her final year of apprenticeship. Elisabeth promised she would be back in Zurich in the last week in August.

At home at the Big House that night the family's excitement over the ending of the war was dampened by what Mr. Kübler called Elisabeth's "madcap" plan of going immediately into a war zone. The dining room was again a place of confrontation and anger. Didn't Elisabeth understand that although the fighting had officially stopped there could well be pockets of resistance from desperate men?

Mr. Kübler drowned Elisabeth's protests with his thunderous voice. She was a young girl who knew nothing about war. Did she realize that much of the territory just over the border would doubtless still be mined? What was more, there was an acute food shortage in Europe. If she wasn't blown up by a land mine she'd probably starve.

Certainly he respected the ideals of the Volunteers and the caliber of the men and women he had met at the Furlegi cabin. But the idea of a starry-eyed child going into the war zone was absolute madness.

While her father drew breath, Elisabeth reminded him that she was within a month of her nineteenth birthday. Some of her contemporaries were already married and had babies. Some of the men and women who had fought in the war were no older than she was.

Mr. Kübler tried a different tack. What about her apprenticeship? Was she going to throw away the chance of becoming a full-fledged technician?

She told him of her conversation with Dr. Weitz and her promise to return in August to write her final exams and complete her apprenticeship.

All at once Elisabeth realized that her father was looking old. Six weeks earlier he had broken his hip in a fall at a spa. He now walked with a cane, even in the house. His days of mountain climbing were over. His shouting could no longer perturb her. She suddenly felt deep affection for him. She would have liked now to go around the table to him and hug him and tell him that if they could change identities he would do exactly what she proposed to do. But a gulf of pride and stubbornness still lay between them.

It was an old man who suddenly flung up his hands in resignation and hobbled to his desk in the other room.

Elisabeth still had to overcome her mother's opposition. Mrs. Kübler had been her ally in the past in her confrontations with her father. But not now. If anything, she was even more opposed than Mr. Kübler to Elisabeth's plans.

She now used delicate euphemisms to warn Elisabeth what happened to young girls caught by licentious soldiery. Elisabeth smiled to herself, recognizing that her mother felt insecure if she was fifty miles from home. After this warning Mrs. Kübler must have felt she had done all she could. She retired to the security of her kitchen.

Erika and Eva took a neutral stance in the dispute. Eva's mind was on her date with a new boy friend. All the young people were gathering at the lakeside to celebrate the peace. She too left the room, and a couple of moments later Elisabeth watched her through the window as she mounted her bicycle.

Now only Erika was left in the dining room—Erika the dreamer, Erika the quiet one, who was now working part-time as a secretary. Hers was a predictable future. Elisabeth was aware that her identical twin lived vicariously through her own, Elisabeth's, adventures. Her semi-invalid sister did not have the strength to join the Volunteers in active service but she would be close to Elisabeth in spirit.

Next morning Elisabeth reported to the Zurich branch office of the International Voluntary Service for Peace and was issued preliminary identification papers, essentially a document declaring that she was a member of the peace organization. Passports were not yet being issued.

Two days later by prearrangement she joined ten Swiss male volunteers and one young woman who were awaiting her arrival at the French border. The other woman had come only to wish the party well, so Elisabeth soon found herself the only female in it. With the exception of a couple of middle-aged men, the Volunteers were in their mid-twenties or early thirties. She had met some of them before at the Furlegi cabin.

One of the men had already made a reconnaissance at Ecurcey and

86

had returned with a usable bicycle he had discovered among the ruins.

With exaggerated gestures of chivalry, and with the observation that since she was to be the cook and thus "the most important member of the party," the young man who had retrieved the bicycle handed it over to Elisabeth. The men walked the few miles to devastated Ecurcey, but Elisabeth rode into the village against a stiff breeze that sent her corduroy skirt flaring.

Shielding her eyes against grit swept up from the dusty country road, Elisabeth surveyed the first foreign land she had ever seen. She remembers having a surge of feeling that her life would be spent "out there"—beyond the rampart security of Switzerland's mountains.

She had, of course, still no focus on the nature of her lifework. There was simply an inexplicable certainty that she would, as she had once dreamed she would, explore new lands, new people and new philosophies.

Ecurcey proved a shock beyond her imagining. The only visible inhabitants were women with backs bent under loads of firewood, children with the saddest eyes and several men, some very old and others who had lost one or more limbs.

Before the Nazis had attempted to crush its soul, Ecurcey had been a pretty village of thatch- and tile-roofed brick cottages. Nine of the homes had been leveled and thirty-eight of them had been badly damaged, but not wholly beyond repair. The task force of the IVSP, soon to be joined by another nine men, immediately set to their task of reconstruction and restoration.

The Volunteers had brought some food with them, but when this was consumed they intended to live off the land. Immediately after her first inspection of the village Elisabeth set up an outdoor kitchen, the center of which was a huge iron cooking pot slung over a wood fire. The chief culinary skill she was soon to develop was how to vary the menu by altering the flavor of vegetable stock stews.

She slept on a mattress and under a rough blanket in a small room of a crumbling house. The men slept in a partly reconstructed house nearby.

At first light on the day after their arrival at the village, the Volunteers set about collecting reusable bricks and lumber from the ruins. Those who were not students had professions or trades, but none was a professional builder and they had no tools. They were healthy and strong and fired with enthusiasm. One of the first jobs was to make ladders. Then sixteen men, and Elisabeth when she could spare time from her pots, salvaged bolts, screws and nails from blackened buildings. Elisabeth spent hours sitting on her haunches straightening nails.

Once the Volunteers had settled into an efficient work routine, Elisabeth took shifts at the building sites. She was sometimes part of the human chain passing bricks to the builders, and sometimes she scaled a roof to lay tiles or thatch.

Her back ached, her fingers were soon blistered, and when she sometimes hit her thumb instead of a nail, she took it matter-of-factly. The Volunteers always sang as they worked, and the singing eased fatigue.

For three years the village people had suffered occupation by a ruthless enemy. When the villagers came to stare at the reconstruction work, it was initially with a sense of wonder and curiosity rather than admiration. Even the children could not understand why people had come from a foreign country simply to help them, expecting nothing in return.

The cooking of meals always remained Elisabeth's main task, but finding food developed into a major problem. Every day two of the men were detailed to scour the countryside for food, to barter nails, screws and other salvaged material for potatoes, cabbages, carrots, perhaps a chicken or duck. To transport the food, they constructed a handcart out of timber and bicycle wheels. Elisabeth took her turn at scavenging. She gained top honors when she returned from one foray with a ten-pound fish which nobody was able to identify, or even guess where it had been caught. She was also rated the best mushroom hunter, essentially because she got up before first light to glean the meadows.

On some days, fortunately few, there was simply nothing to eat. The Volunteers refused to beg for food from the village people, because the local populace was finding it no easier to survive in a countryside that had been ravaged by retreating Germans.

Elisabeth's most embarrassing moment occurred on the day when she was given what she assumed to be a jarful of herbs by one of the grateful women of the village. She spent the afternoon preparing a vegetable stew. When the men returned from work, they sniffed the appetizing odor and urged the cook to speed the meal. She emptied the full jar into the pot. It was only when the stew was served and the first recipient exploded in a paroxysm of coughing that she learned that the jar had contained red pepper! The stew was uneatable. Jokes about the cook eased Elisabeth's embarrassment, but that night everyone in the camp went to bed hungry.

Another group of people in the village was hated as much as the Volunteers were admired. Germans rounded up at the end of hostilities were being held in the basement of the village school. Each morning the prisoners were marched into the adjacent fields. Elisabeth noticed that on some evenings when the German soldiers returned to the makeshift prison there were two or three fewer than there had been when the squad marched out in the morning. At first she assumed that some German prisoners must have escaped during the day. Then she inquired about the discrepancy. It was the village mayor who explained. The prisoners were being used to clear the fields of land mines.

The German Army, said the mayor, had planted some wooden mines among the metal ones. These wooden mines could not be readily detected by the usual devices. With gendarmes' rifles at their backs, the German prisoners were compelled to cross the mine fields. On some days two or three of the human mine detectors were blown up. This savage practice raised no feelings of guilt among the villagers. They were filled with hatred against the Nazis.

But Elisabeth was horrified. She recounted to the other Volunteers what was going on and at what cost.

Next morning she and the Volunteers downed their building tools and marched ahead of the German prisoners. They took positions in front of the squad when they were deployed to cross a mine-trapped meadow. Embarrassed gendarmes summoned the mayor. The Volunteers told the mayor that unless he stopped employing human mine detectors and requisitioned appropriate devices they would march ahead of the German prisoners into the fields.

The carnage stopped.

But Elisabeth was still deeply distressed by the way the Germans were herded into the dank cellar of the schoolhouse. The place was so crowded that the prisoners could barely squat. From dusk to dawn they were in almost total darkness and without proper sanitation.

Elisabeth found it easy enough to understand the animosity of the people of Ecurcey against the Germans—the feelings of widows, of fatherless children and of the homeless. She herself reacted with a bitterness she had never previously felt when she found small human bones and baby clothes in the ruins of one cottage. But her revulsion over what the Nazis had wrought upon innocent village people was offset by her empathy for the abject misery of men who were treated worse than cattle.

By mid-August Elisabeth was counting the days to when she would have to go back to her hospital apprenticeship. She knew the faces of the prisoners, mostly young faces prematurely lined and drawn by suffering. Each morning when they were marched through the village on their way to labor—repairing a road perhaps or digging a ditch— she smiled shyly at them. Sometimes she sang familiar German songs. The prisoners could smell the meal she was cooking in the big iron pot in her makeshift kitchen. She always had to overcome a temptation to share a loaf of bread or mushrooms with them. The prisoners appeared to be terribly undernourished.

The prisoners knew her too. They had learned the name of the girl who had stopped the suicidal practice of forced marches across mined fields. Some of the men waved to her, aware of her femininity, of course, which perhaps stirred memories of their homes, their sisters, mothers and girl friends. Just the brief glimpses each morning and evening of a girl with a friendly smile may have reminded them that they had once lived in a place where they had been loved.

The sunshine of high summer beat down on Ecurcey. Elisabeth watched the calendar, conscious that she must fulfill her promise to return to Zurich. A dozen houses had been made habitable again and there were cheerful celebrations when families were able to move back into their homes once more.

But Elisabeth was nagged by unfinished business. She had to do something for the prisoners, and the thought suddenly struck her of something she could give them. It could not be food, for there was barely enough for the Volunteers themselves. She spent half a day collecting writing paper and pencils, mostly donated by the one village store, and a few candles. When darkness fell, she crept out of the camp and, seeking out the shadows, made her way to the schoolhouse. Through a grilled window at ground level she attracted the attention of the men herded below.

She was obliged to whisper, because a sleepy gendarme was on duty a few paces away. She tossed paper, pencils and candles through the bars on the window. She spoke in German.

She would be going back to Switzerland in three days, she whispered. If the prisoners would like to write letters to their families she would mail them when she was across the frontier.

Below her in the cellar she heard exclamations of surprise and noises like the sounds of restless cattle in a stall. Then lights flickered as the candles were lighted. Elisabeth lay down by the grilled window and waited, praying that the gendarme would not notice the unusual activity. After about twenty minutes one of the prisoners came to the window and handed up a fistful of letters. His voice was choked. What the prisoners had wanted more than anything—even more than good food—was the chance to let their families in Germany know that they were still alive.

Elisabeth was about to leave when another face appeared at the window. He was the one she had called the "Old Man." He had looked like an arthritic grandfather as he shuffled past her kitchen. The Old Man handed up a single sheet of paper. He told her that she was to read this letter herself.

On her return to the camp Elisabeth read the note addressed to the "Little Cook." It said, "You have rendered the greatest humanitarian service. I write to you because I have no family of my own. Want to tell you that whether we live or whether we die here, we shall never forget you. Please accept a deep, heartfelt thank you and love from one human being to another."

On the night before she left for home, Elisabeth managed to smuggle a few basic requisites to the prisoners. She found a few cakes of soap, some more candles and toilet paper, which she dropped through the grilled window. The prisoners whispered her name and their gratitude. This time she didn't say anything. She knew that she would not be able to control her voice.

Next morning, when she was about to take the road back to the Swiss frontier, the news that the Little Cook was leaving was spread around the village. The people came running; so did the mayor, wearing his badge of office.

The mayor waved his hands for silence and made a flowery speech about the "eternal debt owed to the visiting angel." After kissing Elisabeth on both cheeks, he handed over a freshly penned scroll of commendation. Everybody cheered. The Volunteers hoisted her to their shoulders and carried her triumphantly to the edge of the village, where they sang "Auld Lang Syne."

Elisabeth, lean and suntanned, strode down the dusty road toward the Swiss frontier. A mile or two out of the village another group waved to her from a distance. The German prisoners were repairing a footbridge. A flower-scented breeze bore the sound of their farewell. Her last view of the prisoners and the village of Ecurcey misted over as her eyes brimmed with tears.

8

The Swallow Must Fly Again

ELISABETH HITCHHIKED from the frontier to Meilen and arrived at the Big House to find it half stripped of furniture. Mr. Kübler had bought an apartment in Zurich, because with his hip injury he could no longer tolerate the workday journey to his Zurich office. The family was in the midst of moving.

The sale of the Big House was not a surprise to Elisabeth. Mr. Kübler had spoken of his intention before she left for Ecurcey. But it was a shock all the same to find most of the furniture already gone and to hear her footsteps echo in uncurtained empty rooms.

Her sisters were not at home—they were spending a year in England—and her mother was confined to bed with pleurisy. Elisabeth was obliged to take on responsibility for the move to Zurich after what her mother called her "nice vacation in France." However, there was a letdown after the drama of Ecurcey, and she was glad for the hard work of packing up.

Next day she organized a yard sale of unwanted furniture, garden tools and the like, and she watched numbly as pieces of furniture, most of them linked to some special memory, were sold for a few francs.

Although she was learning to shield herself against the hurt of nostalgia, the disbursement of so many familiar things was far from easy. The innocent joys of her childhood seemed to be tolled by the auctioneer's hammer. The tangible reminders of halcyon days—toys from the attic and animal cages from the basement—vanished in the hands of strangers.

Before the day was spent, Elisabeth revisited the Sundance Rock, where, Indian-fashion, she once more stretched her arms to the setting sun. She thanked the Spirit of Heaven for her happy childhood. The ritual brought some peace of heart, some restoration of a sense of purpose.

After the move was completed, Elisabeth boarded in the new duplex family apartment, a large and well-appointed home with wide verandas spilling red geraniums. The apartment house on Klosbachstrasse, a little up the hill from the lake, was only a few yards from the trolleybus routes. The site had been chosen essentially for Mr. Kübler's convenience; he was now only a few minutes from his office.

Mr. Kübler was in need of pampering, for not only did his physical condition deny him outdoor activity but he had been demoted at his office. The proprietor of the business, one of her father's closest friends, had suddenly died. The new owner made staff changes and appointed his son, a young man, to the top executive position—an action that deeply wounded Mr. Kübler's pride.

Mrs. Kübler too needed care. Her pleurisy did not readily respond to treatment, and for the first month in the new apartment she was confined to bed. Elisabeth delayed her return to the hospital in order to nurse her mother and, indeed, to run the household.

However, when at last in October Elisabeth went back to the hospital laboratory, she slipped easily into her old routine. Dr. Weitz had left, presumably for Poland, but her colleagues gave her a big welcome. She paid a brief visit to the delousing department. It was almost eerily quiet. It was hard to believe that a comparatively short time ago the area had been filled with refugees.

She spent most of Christmas Day that year at the hospital, in the children's ward. For some blind children and children whose eyes were bandaged after surgery she devised a special Christmas tree. She made delicate glass bells and other decorations at the technical college, and when candles underneath the bells were lighted the decorations tinkled. The sightless children were enthralled.

In the new year her energy was given to studying for the final apprenticeship exam, which she took in June. Of the thirty-two students who survived the course, Elisabeth gained first place. She was now a qualified laboratory technician.

She was strongly tempted to rejoin the Volunteers and go to war-torn Europe again, but she had successfully applied for a job as an assistant to an internationally known hematologist, Professor Karl Köller. She would, she was told, have to sacrifice the job unless she reported for work in July.

There was, however, time for a brief holiday in the mountains. Elisabeth remembers it because there she met a woman psychiatrist, Dr. Lisa Müller, who was an authority on Szondi tests. (Lipot Szondi, the Hungarian psychiatrist, had devised a test designed to bring forth the hidden dynamic processes in the human personality.) Dr. Müller was intrigued when Elisabeth proposed adapting Szondi tests to a study of herself and her sisters. The fact that the three girls had lived together since birth might throw new light on the effects of environment in contrast to hereditary factors in personality development.

Some weeks later the psychiatrist actually administered the Szondi tests and other psychological tests to the three sisters. The tests proved what Elisabeth had already assumed—that she and Erika were indeed mirror images of each other, that together the two of them completely complemented each other, and that Eva was a totally different entity.

Although there was no immediate follow-up to these tests, Elisabeth later showed the results to Professor Manfred Bleuler, the internationally renowned Zurich psychiatrist. The meeting between Elisabeth and the professor was the beginning of a lifelong friendship.

In July Elisabeth reported for work at Professor Köller's laboratory and found to her disappointment that although she was working with a team that was on a frontier of science she was now completely

95

out of touch with patients. It wasn't that the work lacked interest and challenge. Indeed, she recognized that the research was pioneering and always held the potential for major medical breakthroughs. But spending her days separating blood cells from plasma, peering through microscopes and preparing and cataloging a thousand slides were labors that fell far short of giving satisfaction.

She respected Professor Köller, admired his drive and total dedication to his work. She enjoyed the chemistry involved in the research and enjoyed working on new techniques. Somebody, she admitted, had to undertake the wholly demanding business of classifying blood factors. But surely it wasn't meant to be Elisabeth! Her discontent fed resentment against those postgraduate medical students who used the results of her painstaking laboratory work for what they claimed were original dissertations. This kind of plagiarism was, she learned, quite common in the research laboratories, and she decried it for the exploitation that it was.

In the spring of 1946 she arranged through a friend to be introduced to the head of the department of ophthalmology at the University of Zurich. He was Professor Marc Amsler, a scholarly elderly physician from the French part of Switzerland. He too was a disciplined scientist, but he was also a clinician committed to working directly with patients. He was a man of unusual charm, warmth and sensitivity.

She had to wait in an outer room for her appointment with the professor, whose office was in an old building known as the "eye clinic." When the door of the office opened, Professor Amsler appeared with a patient. She recognized the patient. He was the Emperor Haile Selassie of Ethiopia. The next patient entered the office. Elisabeth recognized her too. She was one of the cleaning women at the hospital. What profoundly impressed Elisabeth was that the professor treated the cleaning woman with exactly the same old-fashioned courtesy he had accorded the emperor.

During her interview with Professor Amsler he asked her about her work with the International Voluntary Service for Peace. Elisabeth was soon pouring out stories of the reconstruction of Ecurcey. Only after the interview did Elisabeth recall that the professor had not asked a single academic question. It was, she learned from him later, essentially her vitality and intensity that gained her the coveted job as a member of his eye clinic's laboratory staff.

Elisabeth's only disappointment was that she was expected to start work at the clinic as soon as she had completed her year with Professor Köller. She had hoped that there would be a summer opportunity to go to the devastated parts of Europe. Once again she was obliged to postpone her journey to Poland.

However, in this year there were compensations. Her work at the clinic brought her into the closest contact with patients. Her small office was located in the basement of the crumbling building. With its slit lamps and other optical instruments, the Amsler laboratory resembled an alchemist's cave.

Professor Amsler had developed an intricate technique for the treatment of eye injuries which, in many instances, prevented total blindness. A common complication of traumatic injury to one eye is that the other eye may become diseased too—a phenomenon medically known as "sympathetic ophthalmia." Unless treatment is rapid and effective, the patient is likely to lose the sight in both eyes. In 1946 the only prophylactic treatment for preventing total blindness in cases where sympathetic opthalmia was considered a serious risk was the immediate surgical removal of the injured eye.

The professor instructed Elisabeth in his technique, which amounted to injecting a fluorescent dye into a patient's bloodstream and then, with a slit lamp and other apparatus for gauging light intensity, evaluating the strength of the fluorescence in the interior of the eye. In a healthy eye the degree of fluorescence would be within a specific and measurable range of intensity. In an unhealthy eye the degree of fluorescence increased beyond the normal range.

The technique permitted the physician or one of his aides to monitor the healthy eye. Only when some deterioration was observed in the healthy eye was the injured eye surgically removed. Thus the sight of the good eye could usually be preserved without risk, and the precise timing for the removal, if necessary, of the injured eye was known.

The monitoring of the uninjured eye and measuring the fluorescence were extremely delicate procedures, and work to be entrusted only to someone of total reliability. Professor Amsler soon found that his new lab technician was meticulously careful and accurate.

After working some months in the laboratory, Elisabeth observed that the monitoring of an eye also revealed the presence of other pathological conditions, especially systemic diseases, such as lupus. She drew the professor's attention to her diagnostic findings, and he enthusiastically encouraged her to pursue this avenue for research.

For Elisabeth, the special benediction of her new work in the basement laboratory was that it gave her the chance to spend many hours with patients in one-to-one relationships.

The patients who came to Elisabeth's small black-walled windowless room, known as the "darkroom lab," were frightened. Some were threatened with total blindness. Others feared losing their jobs. A few were fearful for their lives. These patients found themselves being ushered into a darkened room by a young woman who, they often sensed at once, completely understood their fears. Within a few minutes of starting the delicate tests most of the patients were ready to share their innermost thoughts. Many admitted before long that they had never before talked like this to anyone.

Elisabeth's laboratory thus became in effect a confessional box. Hurts and heartbreaks, long-suppressed anger and guilt, were poured out in the darkness.

Because she empathized, because she listened, because she did not appear too wise or offer cliché answers, Elisabeth serendipitously became a psychological therapist. Naturally, she did not think of herself as a therapist. She simply knew that the people who came to see her requiring physical care were often in deep emotional, mental and spiritual need, and that sometimes she could help.

The long hours these patients spent in total darkness were probably a major factor in encouraging their outpourings, for no one could have been further removed than Elisabeth from the popular conception of a father confessor. On first meeting her, an occasional older patient protested that he had been put in the care of a child. The white laboratory coat lent her professional dignity, but the first impression of her was still not reassuring, for Elisabeth continued to look like a teenager. Almost without exception, though, even the most sophisticated of the patients acknowledged that she knew her business. Some reported their confidence in Elisabeth to Professor Amsler.

He was delighted. Each month he allocated more and more responsibility to his young assistant. One of the responsibilities was to be the bearer of bad news.

Bearing bad news is an undefined art. But it is an art, as Elisabeth now stresses. After making initial mistakes when with the best intentions she tried to soften a negative diagnosis with evasions and euphemisms, she realized the paramount importance of speaking with absolute honesty and frankness.

"Playing games with patients," as she now calls it, invariably compounds tragedy. When it was necessary, for instance, to tell a mother that her child's eye had to be removed if the vision of the healthy eye was to be saved or—in an extreme case—that the prognosis was total blindness, Elisabeth soon learned to explain the unpalatable truth in a simple, straightforward manner.

Of course there were tears. Of course there was grieving for the loss. But alongside the patient or the patient's relative was someone who clearly understood the pain and the grief.

Spending up to ten hours at a stretch in a darkened basement laboratory would not be everyone's concept of pleasant working conditions. But Elisabeth soon so loved her work, with its opportunity for intimate association with patients, that she blurted out to an amused Professor Amsler that she would be prepared to work in his laboratory at half her modest salary. The relationship between the tall, stooped grandfatherly physician and the zealous twenty-year-old lab technician blossomed into affection.

Six months after she had started working with him, the professor accorded Elisabeth the unprecedented honor for a lab technician of assisting him in surgery. Few among even the most senior medical students at the university were handpicked to assist Professor Amsler in the operating theater.

At her first operation, the removal of a tumor behind an eye, the professor insisted that Elisabeth stand at his shoulder. He explained to her in detail the surgical procedure. After several operations—and they were almost always of the most delicate nature—Elisabeth was actually using retractors and other instruments, and the professor often treated her as his first assistant. Soon she knew his ways so well, both in the operating theater and in the laboratory, that she was able to anticipate his requests before they were uttered.

She had spoken to him once about her hope of one day becoming a doctor. The professor had nodded thoughtfully, but without making any comment. However, from the day she had shared this aspiration she gained the impression that he was training her for the time when he would be ready to hand over his scalpel.

But before she could consider even the formidable preliminary steps of getting into a medical school, Elisabeth was determined to fulfill her vow to go to the aid of the people of Poland.

On one of the first mornings of spring, when Elisabeth was scrubbing up to assist Dr. Amsler in surgery, she suddenly felt that this was the right time to tell him what had been on her mind for so long—that it was time for her to leave, time for her to return to the still devastated war zones of Europe.

She would not, she explained quickly, leave him and her work at the eye clinic for any other reason. The words suddenly gushed out. How much she loved her work! How grateful she was to him for giving her so much responsibility! If when she returned in the fall there was still a position for her in the clinic, she would like so much to come back and work for him. But if he didn't want her back, if someone else had her job, she would quite understand.

A nurse tied a surgical mask across the professor's nose and mouth. She could only see his eyes a foot above her own and she tried unsuccessfully to read in them his answer.

Then, rather gruffly, he said, "So the winter is over, and the swallow must fly again!"

9

To Save the Children

THE ADMINISTRATOR of the Zurich office of the International Voluntary Service for Peace consulted his files. Yes, he told Elisabeth, in a village near Mons, in Belgium, there was a group of Volunteers who urgently needed a cook. The present cook for the fifty Volunteers at this work camp was an eighty-three-year-old woman who was finding the task beyond her strength.

The administrator looked up from his desk and caught the flicker of disappointment in Elisabeth's eyes. So that was not what she had hoped for? he inquired sympathetically. Elisabeth admitted it wasn't. She had, of course, no objection to cooking, she quickly added, and in fact she enjoyed cooking for large groups. But she had hoped so very much that she could be sent to a work camp in Poland.

The administrator closed his file. The strength and effectiveness of the Volunteers, he reminded her, was that each member was prepared to go where the immediate need was greatest. There was no request in his books for immediate help in Poland.

Elisabeth assured him that she understood this. Of course she

101

would be ready to go to Belgium, not only to cook but to dig latrines if necessary. Her knapsack was already packed and she could leave at once.

The administrator reopened his file and entered Elisabeth's name, the name of her next of kin and other details. He offered to buy her a rail ticket to Mons, but he warned that beyond the frontier the trains were not running on schedule and were always very crowded. It might take more than a week to get her a firm train reservation.

That was too long, she agreed. She was quite confident she could hitchhike to Belgium.

At home that evening parental opposition was surprisingly low key. Mr. Kübler made some reference to rolling stones gathering no moss, but he was mollified by the fact that Elisabeth would be working in Belgium. It was, he reminded her, his favorite country. He expanded on a visit he had made to Belgium before the war. He had met no friendlier people.

Next morning Elisabeth hoisted to her shoulders a large hiking rucksack containing a change of clothing, a spare pair of boots and a first aid box that included bandages, bottles of iodine and aspirin, some antiseptic ointment, a syringe and hypodermic needles. She found space for a box of emergency rations and a cheap Kodak box camera. She had her first passport. Resting on top of the knapsack and against her shoulder blades was a rolled army blanket. In her purse she had the equivalent of twenty-five dollars.

On the advice of a friend, she avoided Germany. In a journey via Basel, Nancy and Rheims, where she rested for a night at a youth hostel, it took her a couple of days to reach Mons. Her ultimate destination was a brooding, grimy coal-mining village a few miles beyond the city.

The Volunteers composed a cosmopolitan group of Swedes, Danes, Italians, a few Austrians, a large group from Britain, one Spaniard, half a dozen American Quakers and about eighteen Swiss nationals.

The work, it turned out, was unrelated to the war. In fact it was a project that had been scheduled before the war by the IVSP; the group was fulfilling a commitment made in the 1930s.

The octogenarian cook, who had been awaiting Elisabeth's arrival, explained that the village people died at an average age of thirty-four from silicosis and black lung disease, because from infancy they breathed coal dust. The Volunteers were engaged in building a playground on top of one of the mine dumps in the cleaner air above the ever-present pall of dust. The goal was to give the village children a chance for a reasonable life expectancy.

The day after her arrival Elisabeth toured the village and the project site. Coal dust was everywhere, graying lace curtains behind the almost opaque windows of small brick miners' houses. Elisabeth took shelter from a rainstorm under the porch of a house and watched a stream of black water swishing down the gutters. Coal dust gritted her teeth, reddened her eyes, darkened her hair.

When the sky cleared, she looked up to see the pyramid-shaped tailing dumps—huge ugly monuments to man's grimmest labor—towering alongside the latticed head-gear of mining shafts. The self-appointed task of the Volunteers was to level the top of one of the black pyramids so that a playground could be built there, perhaps three hundred feet above the grimy streets.

Leveling the top of the man-made mountain was proving a herculean task. No bulldozers were available, so the work had to be undertaken with picks, shovels and wheelbarrows. Incredulous mining families watched the labor of those who asked nothing in return for their sweat, blisters, thirst and fatigue.

Within a generation the village had twice experienced military invasion. Three generations were familiar with the sounds of shells and tanks, and they had seen much bloodshed on their cobbled streets. These new invaders brought with them not guns but grass seed; not hostility but good humor, songs, love and selfless service.

The village had its natural leader, a young pastor who had opened his large manse to the Volunteers. It was in the manse that Elisabeth set up her kitchen.

One of her first duties was to organize the local hospitality without offending the generous village housewives. She called a meeting of the women and persuaded them to take turns baking pies and washing the Volunteers' clothes. No one in the village was to be denied the privilege of making some gift or rendering some service to the Volunteers who, in the villagers' phrase, were "finding sunlight for our children."

Elisabeth also took her turn with pick and shovel. At the end of a shift she resembled, as one village woman said, a "pickaninny." Everyone knew the young Swiss woman who looked no older than some of the schoolchildren but who put in a full day's work alongside the men. She was held in special affection after a bucolic incident in a meadow near the manse.

She was washing her clothes when she looked out of the window and saw a cow walking backward in small circles. The beast was bellowing and clearly in distress, but it was some moments before she realized that it was calving. Her shouts that the cow was "going to have a baby" alerted the community. She ran to the animal and attempted to heave the calf loose from its mother. Since the cow was still walking backward, Elisabeth was obliged to hop on one foot while pressing her other foot to the cow's flank in full view of a laughing group of miners' wives and children. Thereafter, until she left the village, she was greeted good-humoredly by children who cried out to her that "the cow's going to have a baby!" and re-enacted her one-footed midwifery.

The best part of every day was the Volunteers' evening meal and the community singing to which the village folk were invited. Each national group sang and taught the others their favorite songs. Ballads from Denmark and Austria were followed by songs from Spain and Italy, Swiss yodeling, traditional songs from Britain and lively contemporary tunes from America.

At a sing-along one evening Elisabeth found herself sitting beside one of the American Quakers. He had a friendly, open face, and Elisabeth guessed he was in his late thirties. He introduced himself as David Ritchie. Appreciating that Elisabeth's understanding of English was still limited, the American spoke to her slowly.

Elisabeth was sleepy. She had spent the hottest hours of the day with the work party leveling the top of the mine dump and the rest of the afternoon preparing the supper for the fifty Volunteers. She was looking forward to getting to bed.

However, she listened politely to David as he spoke of his recent work in a Philadelphia ghetto. Her head was nodding and she was about to excuse herself and sneak off to the women's dormitory in the manse when David mentioned Poland.

She was instantly alert. She asked him to repeat what he had just said. David then told her that he was waiting to go to Poland, would be leaving for that country as soon as his papers were in order.

Elisabeth seized his arm. With a passion that astonished the soft-spoken Quaker she begged him to help her get to Poland. She would crawl all the way on her stomach if only she could get to Poland. In stilted English she told him of the commitment she had made when she had heard the newscast announcing the outbreak of war.

She was wide awake now, and in the light from the campfire she eagerly studied David's face for some positive reaction. Eventually he said that when he got to Poland he would try to send for her. She made him repeat this statement. David laughed and said that she had been given a Quaker's promise, and that that was surely good enough. He would keep in touch with her through the Zurich office of the Volunteers.

Impulsively, Elisabeth hugged him.

But it wasn't to Poland that she was summoned next. Three days later, on the first day of June, she received a letter from the Zurich office saying that she was needed immediately in Sweden. In Stockholm a camp had just been established for the training in Volunteer work of a group of young Germans who wanted to make some restitution by helping to alleviate the suffering the Third Reich had caused. The IVSP was apparently having difficulty in obtaining German-speaking teachers and interpreters because there was still a great deal of animosity toward Germans and widespread distrust of their motives.

Elisabeth did not have to go to Sweden. Since she was a volunteer, no one could force her to do anything. The thought of going to a country that had suffered no war privation was no more appealing than the idea of returning to Switzerland. She had very negative feelings too about working with people, no matter how remorseful, who had been responsible for the kind of brutality she had witnessed in Ecurcey.

Such was her first reaction on receiving the letter from Zurich. But she had second thoughts. She took time to be alone. She went for a walk through the meadows beyond the manse. She saw the events in her life as "links in a chain"—each experience having some purpose. Even the horrific nine months at Romilly had its own positive meaning, surely honing her, toughening her for whatever challenges lay ahead. She had a sudden comforting feeling that "nothing happens by chance." It was, as she remembers it, a "sort of mystical insight" that in the years ahead she should follow the "inner promptings." The request that she should go to Stockholm seemed suddenly to have a special significance. She had no idea what it was, but going to Sweden "just felt right."

On the evening of her last day in Belgium Elisabeth had an accident in the kitchen. She was helping to prepare a valedictory meal on the stove at the manse when the handle of a saucepan she was carrying snapped in her hand. Scalding oil spilled over her leg, and the skin immediately blistered.

One of the Volunteers salved and bandaged her leg, but the pain kept her awake into the small hours. Even so, at five in the morning and after perhaps a couple hours' sleep, she dressed for her journey and heaved the heavy rucksack to her back. She was about to creep out of the dormitory alone when suddenly out of the shadows there appeared a ring of people. All the Volunteers, including the newest arrivals at the camp, had awakened an hour early to bid her goodbye with the traditional singing of "Auld Lang Syne."

After hugs all around, the exchanging of addresses and promises to write, Elisabeth hobbled off to the train station. She had been given a train ticket to Hamburg and Copenhagen.

Through the window of the crowded coach she gained her first glimpse of Germany, but the pain in her leg so dulled her impressions that Elisabeth has little memory of the journey. At the Hamburg station she went to a grubby restroom and unwound the bandage. What she saw alarmed her. The skin over her shin bone was scarlet and suppurating. She had a fever. Her purse contained the equivalent of five dollars in Belgian money, and she had not eaten in eight hours. Germany was the last country she wanted to remain in, if only because it was the hungriest country in Europe.

Her plight raised nagging doubts as to whether she had made the right decision in leaving Belgium. She didn't know a soul in Germany, and people were so busy simply trying to survive that no one was likely to be concerned about a sick itinerant girl. But something had to be done because she so rarely felt sick and the pain was excruciating.

Elisabeth limped out of the station, and as soon as she came to a residential street she started to knock on doors. If someone answered she asked for a doctor. At the first dozen doors she received cold blank stares. At the thirteenth door a middle-aged woman nodded. Yes, she was a doctor, but she was a psychiatrist. Elisabeth explained her condition. The doctor took Elisabeth inside her house and examined the suppurating wound, but she shook her head and said that she had no drugs, no dressings and no food. But the doctor went to a desk and wrote out a prescription for 55 cc of alcohol (the maximum she could prescribe under existing regulations), and then walked with Elisabeth to a pharmacy at the end of the block.

A potentially dangerous infection was obvious; but perhaps, said the doctor, bathing the wound with alcohol would clean it up and prevent the pus from seeping into the shin bone.

A pharmacist measured out the alcohol as if it were gold dust.

Set on getting out of Germany as quickly as possible, Elisabeth boarded a train for Copenhagen, where she made her way to the ferry for Malmö, at the tip of Sweden. In Malmö she hitchhiked to the nearest hospital.

Suddenly luxury! The hospital outpatient rooms were whistle clean, and blond nurses in starched uniforms were at her beck and call. Medication was prescribed and administered. With the help of strong analgesics, the throbbing pain she had endured for the longest hours began to ease.

She felt marvelously relaxed as medical and administrative staff fussed over her, but the VIP treatment puzzled her. She was taken to a lounge, where her leg was propped up and cushioned. Nurses came in bearing trays of food, the quality of which she had not seen for a long time. She was not to worry at all, she was told. All arrangements for her journey to Stockholm were being made. She would be met at the Stockholm station and be driven out to the camp. A messenger had already been sent to the Malmö station to change her train ticket to one for a first-class sleeping compartment.

When she arrived next morning in Stockholm, she was driven out to a large youth camp where hundreds of people were milling about among wooden barracks-type buildings. Most of them were taking instruction on various kinds of peace work. A senior Swedish official at the camp told her that in gratitude for being unscarred by the war

Sweden was anxious to make a contribution to its crippled neighbors.

During the next weeks Elisabeth could have believed she was on a different planet. Cafeteria tables at the camp groaned with food, yet just a few hours away in Hamburg Elisabeth had seen a couple of old women picking over garbage.

There was something obscene, she felt, not only in the amount and quality of food consumed but in the amount of food thrown away. On her first Friday evening in Sweden she was invited to join a party driving into Stockholm. Almost everyone on the streets of the city seemed to be blind drunk. She was told that she was witnessing a Swedish tradition. Liquor coupons were issued on Fridays and that was the night of the week when Swedes went on a collective binge. Elisabeth leaned against the parapet of a bridge and watched with amazement and disgust a group of lurching young teenagers drinking hard liquor straight out of bottles. She thought about the precious 55 cc of alcohol so carefully measured out for her when she had been in Germany.

She thought too about her thrifty home, where it had been a family fetish to conserve everything that was edible—to bottle or pickle or re-hash the leftovers. She remembered those hungry nights in Ecurcey.

Swedish hospitality overwhelmed her. Neighbors of the camp played host to the foreigners, and Elisabeth found herself at tables where she was served seven-course dinners. She usually couldn't manage more than a couple of courses. Her stomach, long used to the smallest helpings of the plainest food, simply could not cope with big meals. She was often overcome by nausea as the meals dragged on. She did, however, manage to regain the weight she had lost previously.

Moreover, there was too little to do. Soon after her arrival at the camp she was expected to "acclimatize" herself and learn the language. Then she was to start teaching a group of Germans every aspect of work camp leadership. She spent most of her free time studying Swedish (not difficult for a German-speaking person with knowledge of English), and she was soon proficient enough in the language to translate a lecture from Swedish into German.

Many of the Germans at the camp kept to themselves. Elisabeth was convinced that some of them—certainly the most arrogant ones—

had signed on for the peace work simply to escape the privation in their own country. There was not one German she spoke to about the war who didn't deny supporting Hitler. Anyway, the past should be forgotten, they insisted. It was the future that mattered.

She had a long conversation with a young German intellectual, and she spoke to him about Ecurcey and of the child's bones she had found in the rubble. The German merely shrugged. He had been a child himself when Hitler had come to power, so how could he feel responsibility for Ecurcey?

Elisabeth's eyes blazed. Was no one responsible for Ecurcey? she asked him. Was no one responsible for all the horrors of war? The German got up and walked away. Elisabeth chided herself for being so judgmental. Her anger cooled when she took out the letter written to her by the old German prisoner of war, the one who had spoken of the love of one human being toward another. There was so much, she admitted, that she still had to understand about her own attitudes and feelings.

For the first time since she had left Switzerland, Elisabeth was homesick—homesick for the openness and honesty of her family. She thought with affection about her father. Her father was strong-willed and sometimes he was wrong, but at this moment she would have given a lot to be with him, to sing with him at the piano, to hear his rich familiar laugh, to tramp with him along a mountain track. It was a new feeling—this sudden and pressing yearning for the company of a strong man to whom she wouldn't have to explain her feelings but who would understand. She remembers it as a wistful longing for a male shoulder to lean upon, not a sexual stirring but an awareness of her loneliness and limitations.

She had just celebrated her twenty-first birthday. She had let the day pass without telling anyone about it. No message had reached her from her family. Erika and Eva would have had a party at home. Friends would have called. Gifts would have been exchanged. Perhaps the family had gone to the mountains and celebrated the birthday with a feast of wild strawberries and cream.

She walked limply to a lecture room where she had been asked to translate for a Swedish physician giving a talk on first aid. She sat down on a chair on the dais. A babble of tongues filled the room. Suddenly she was aware of being watched. She turned her head and saw the nut-brown weatherbeaten face of an old man. The eyes that were fixed on her were deep-set and dark, eyes full of sagacity and humor. The man's back was poker-straight. He was wearing a high-collared shirt, buttoned at the neck, and a braided red coat. He looked, she first thought, as if he might have come from the Himalayas bearing with him the wisdom of an ancient monastery.

Affinity was instant. The idea flickered across her agnostic mind that the old man was an answer to her yearning, a guardian sent to her, a related soul, someone who had known her in some other time, some other place.

After the lecture Elisabeth approached the old man, who could have been in his eighties. He greeted her in French. He was, she learned from him, a Russian émigré. He did not tell her why he was at the camp, and she did not ask, yet in the days that followed he remained as close to her as her shadow. He was simply there—in the lecture halls, in the cafeteria. When she went for a walk in a nearby forest, she saw him standing quietly in a glade, offering comfort and protection without words.

It was "a sort of love affair," Elisabeth recalls, a love silent, mutual, without claims, without demands. The old man's effect on her was to free her from negative attitudes. She now found herself seeing potential for good in even the more arrogant of the young Germans. As suddenly too she was conscious of the stunning beauty of the Swedish countryside, of the sweep of dark forests, of the cold and crystal fjords and the charm of the tidy timbered farmsteads.

A few days before she left Sweden—and the old Russian seemed to know instinctively of her going—he approached her when she was writing in her journal. He asked if he might write something too. In a shaky hand, but in flawless French, the Russian wrote, "Your shining eyes remind me of sunshine. My hope is that we'll meet again and that we'll have the opportunity to greet the sun together. Au revoir."

The old man's leathery face creased into a smile, and then he walked away. Elisabeth watched him until he had vanished from her view. Then she reread his message and she realized that he had not signed his name. He had never offered his name and she had never asked for it.

She was not to see the old man again, although she made a number of inquiries about him in the camp. No one knew who she was talking about. She began to wonder if she alone had seen him, whether he had been sent simply to care for her, a guardian angel. For the next day or two she had the strangest sense that he was still close by, that she would see him across a table in the cafeteria, or that he would suddenly come around the corner of one of the barracks.

Then the long and anxiously awaited telegram arrived from David Ritchie, the American Quaker. The telegram, redirected from the Zurich office of the Volunteers, read tersely, "Come to Poland as soon as possible. Greatly needed. Letter follows."

She counted her small change. It was barely enough for a bus tour of Stockholm. Then she remembered a local farmer she had met at a smorgasbord at a hospitality house. The farmer had complained bitterly that because of a local shortage of labor he was unable to gather in his fruit harvest. Next day she visited and he told her that if the young Swiss girl was really prepared, as she claimed, to work sixteen hours a day in his orchards and at scything hay, he would certainly pay her the going rates, and a bonus too.

When she had completed her lecture assignments she packed her knapsack once again. For the next twelve days she worked at the farm from five in the morning until late in the evening. It was mid-July, and the summer days in the north are long. But Elisabeth loved the job. The money the grateful farmer paid her was more than enough for a boat ticket from Stockholm to the Polish port of Gdansk.

Then, as promised, David followed up his telegram with a letter which bore the address of the Warsaw office of the Quakers. He gave her travel instructions. She was to get a visa at the Polish Consulate in Stockholm, which had already been advised that she would be asking for one. A steamer would be leaving Stockholm for Gdansk on July 20. When she reached Gdansk, she must ask the stationmaster for a prepaid ticket to Warsaw. From Gdansk she should send a telegram to the Warsaw Quakers to advise them of what train she would be taking.

Elisabeth was elated. It was all working out so smoothly. At last she was all but on her way to fulfilling her vow.

═══ 10 ═══

A Vow Fulfilled

ELISABETH NOTIFIED the Swedish camp authorities that she was leaving and gave them the Quaker address in Warsaw for forwarding mail. Then she went to the farmer to say goodbye and to collect fresh fruit for the journey. He had been more than generous, and her purse was bulging with hard Swedish currency.

She had never felt healthier. After days in the orchards, her face, arms and legs were walnut brown, her hair bleached several shades lighter than its natural color. She closed the farm gate and, with her thumb upraised, stood on the side of the Stockholm road. Her intention was to pick up her visa at the Polish Consulate and board the Gdansk-bound steamer on the following day.

Almost immediately a car crunched to a halt on the shoulder of the road and a door was flung open. As she ran toward it, dragging her knapsack, she made a mental note of the registration number—a precaution she had learned in France from a veteran hitchhiker who had had some trouble on the road.

Her first glimpse of the driver was not reassuring. He was an unshaven man of middle age, and there was something sinister about his pig eyes and his almost salivating invitation to sit beside him in the front. Elisabeth hesitated, but smothering an intuitive warning against taking the ride, she climbed into the back seat.

When the driver swung the car off the main highway to a dirt road flanked by dense forests, Elisabeth's concern heightened to alarm. On pages torn from a notebook she scribbled the registration number of the car and the word "Help!" in German and Swedish. She wound down the window a fraction and at intervals tossed the pages into the road. She figured that in the event that she was really being abducted someone might pick up the clues.

After a drive of perhaps twenty minutes, the driver pulled up at a large two-story house fronted by high railings and a grilled gate. He invited Elisabeth to sample "real Swedish hospitality." There would, he assured her, be plenty of time to drive to Stockholm.

She had little option but to leave the car, and when he led her to a comfortably furnished room and brought in a tray of pastries, she was still unsure whether to cry murder or express gratitude. When the man attempted to kiss her, however, she ran through open French windows into a walled garden. She noticed the movement of curtains in an upper window. Three young women were observing her.

Recalling the incident, Elisabeth is not sure how much she imagined, but at the time she was convinced she had been taken to a brothel and that, unless she acted quickly and resourcefully, she might be inducted into the "second oldest profession."

Returning to the house, she told the driver that she had left clues to her whereabouts on the road. He seemed to be nervously impressed. Protesting his innocence and her ingratitude, he drove her to Stockholm, but insisted on calling at his bakery near the docks, where she could help herself to all the pastries she could carry. To Elisabeth's surprise there was indeed a bakery. She had just filled a paper sack when the man started to close the door of the building. Elisabeth ran and didn't stop running until she had reached a police station. The police seemed to be quite impressed by her story and murmured something about the disappearance in recent months of several young girls. She recalls too some reference to white slave traffic.

Before the police drove her back to the farm, they asked her to help them try to find the dockside bakery. By this time she was quite disorientated and was unable to recognize the place. She never did learn whether the women in the upper window of the house in the country were about to be shipped to an oil sheik's harem or whether she had merely denied a kiss to a lecherous baker who had three daughters. The only bonus of the episode was that she still possessed a bagful of pastries.

After a last night on the farm, she reported next morning at the Polish Consulate, and thence to the ticket office where the consulate officials helped her buy a one-way ticket on a Polish packet boat due to sail that evening for Gdansk.

She had expected a sleek white steamer like the ones that cruised Lake Geneva, and hazarded that the small rusting hulk she boarded had not been sunk in the war because it had not been worth sinking! The packet boat had a few berths below deck, but Elisabeth, conserving hard-earned money, elected to travel on the open top deck. At ten o'clock that night, with a milky sun low on the western horizon, the engines wheezed into life. Winches rumbled, ropes were cast off and the ancient craft nosed through the oily waters of Stockholm harbor.

Elisabeth was apparently the only woman aboard. She wrapped herself in a blanket and curled up on a dew-wet bench. Four rather gaunt-looking men, one of them seeming to be seven feet tall and as thin as a lamp post, stood at the rail and talked animatedly in a language she didn't understand.

The timbers of the ghost ship (as she thought of it) groaned as it heaved to the Baltic swell. Soon she was asleep.

She was awakened in what seemed to be the middle of the night by someone gently stroking her hair and adjusting her blanket. It was one of the hungry-looking men she had seen earlier. She was ready to scream, but feigned sleep. Peeking through her lashes at the man's face, now softly illuminated by the midnight sun, she saw that his expression was not rapacious but protective, even tender. The man moved away to rejoin his friends at the rail. In spite of the experience of the previous day, Elisabeth felt secure.

She slept through the long dawn of the northern summer, and stirred only when those passengers able to afford bunks had clambered up the companionways to stretch and to breathe the fresh sea air. As she folded her blanket, she saw she was being watched by the men who were again standing at the rail. The very tall man greeted her in what she presumed to be Polish. She responded with a cautious

114

good morning in Swedish. She stood at a little distance and studied the men keenly. All four seemed much of an age, perhaps in their mid-thirties. They were dressed in rumpled, ill-fitting suits. One of them wore a patched and frayed coat. Were it not for their faces, which were sensitive and intelligent, they could have been laborers.

She opened the sack of pastries given to her by the lecherous baker, more food than she could eat. Shyly approaching the man who had tucked in her blanket, she asked, in German this time, if he and his friends would like a pastry. The man's face clouded, and she realized the need to explain, as she had had to do when she passed through Denmark, that she was not in fact German but Swiss. The other three men overheard her explanation. They fastened on the word Swiss and repeated it. They beamed at her and accepted her offer of pastries.

German was obviously not their language, so she murmured something in French. Two of the men spoke French, although not very well. As they ate the pastries, they introduced themselves. They were all physicians and all of different nationalities. The very tall man was a Rumanian. The man who had stroked her hair was an aristocratic-looking Hungarian. The third was a bearded Polish national and the fourth, a red-haired man with a square jaw, a Czech. Speaking in French, the Pole explained that they had just attended a medical convention in Stockholm sponsored by a Swedish philanthropist. Like Elisabeth, they too had been stunned by Swedish opulence. They were happy to be returning to homes where the need for medical care was acute, and fascinated by her tales of working as a Volunteer and her intention of joining a working camp in Poland.

Elisabeth warmed to them immediately, and they to her. The Polish doctor translated some of the dialogue into Hungarian, and soon they and Elisabeth were communicating in a sort of lingua franca. They all roared with laughter over the struggle to understand one another, and they resolved to stick together for the journey to Warsaw.

It was a memorable moment for Elisabeth when she walked down the gangway at Gdansk and first stepped onto Polish soil. The sun symbolically burst through the overcast. She walked a few paces alone along the dock. A brisk on-shore breeze whipped the scudding white waves and flattened her faded brown corduroy skirt and thin green cotton shirt against her lean body. She wanted very much to remember the moment, to recall its smell, its sounds and, most of all, its feel.

Looking back over her shoulder, she saw the physicians beckoning her to hurry. Her mood changed. She felt elated, buoyant, even pretty, despite her dowdy clothes and heavy boots. She had four gallant escorts, and this should be an interlude of enjoyment, adventure and laughter.

With the help of one of the physicians, Elisabeth collected her train ticket from the stationmaster, who cautioned that they would find the Warsaw-bound train crowded. This was an understatement. The compartments were packed not only with people but with livestock. Geese, chickens, even goats added to the cacophony. There was only one way to get to Warsaw on that train, decided the Polish physician, and that was to ride the roof.

By standing on the shoulders of the giant Rumanian, the Pole managed to scramble to the roof of one of the cars, and he hoisted the others aloft. All five were now in high humor. Elisabeth could have believed she was playing some childish game—a perilous game for sure. Their safety, indeed their lives, depended upon the strength of their arms and upon the convenient placing of a ventilation chimney that protruded two feet above the roof. The group of five encircled the chimney and gripped each other's shoulders.

The train began to move and gathered speed. From the platform a railway official observed the roof passengers for the first time. He waved his arms and shouted angrily. But it was too late now! They were on their way!

The big knapsack on Elisabeth's back tended to pull her backwards. White-knuckled, she clung to the coat sleeves on each side of her. Suddenly the tall Rumanian's eyes saucered. He nodded in the direction of the locomotive. The train was heading for a tunnel. Elisabeth's fantasy was horrendous—a vivid picture in her mind of five headless people, their arms still intertwined, arriving at Warsaw!

The last seconds before the train thundered into darkness seemed to last little short of eternity. But two minutes later, coughing from smoke and blackened by soot, the five roof travelers emerged once again into daylight.

Elisabeth knew well enough that she could not possibly last out the journey to Warsaw up there on the roof. Each lurch of the train almost pulled her arms from their sockets. Fortunately the train half emptied at a station about an hour out of Gdansk. Her companions climbed down ahead of her onto the platform, and Elisabeth jumped into their arms, bruised and exhausted. The party of five scrambled into a completely empty compartment, its hard wooden benches a good deal more comfortable than the roof. The physicians bought some fruit, bread and sausage from a platform vendor. After they had eaten, Elisabeth fell asleep. When she awakened it was quite dark. For a moment she wondered where she was, for it seemed as if she were lying on a couch. It wasn't quite that, but while she had been asleep her companions had laid her across their knees. They were holding her with tenderness, as if she were a young child.

As the train clattered and swayed through the short summer night, the five traveling companions passed the time by singing the ballads of their countries. At the time the train pulled into Warsaw early next morning, an incongruous sound of yodeling filled the compartment!

Warsaw's train station seemed to be reasonably intact or rebuilt and gave few clues to the devastation of large areas of the city. David Ritchie, wearing the broadest grin, and a middle-aged married couple, also American Quakers, were on the platform to greet Elisabeth.

It was time for yet another goodbye. Elisabeth had known the four physicians for little more than forty-eight hours. She was in love with all four of them. To indulge in extended grief for parting friends was a luxury she could no longer afford. Farewells to people whose company she loved were "little deaths," as she now describes them.

She hugged each of her four cavaliers. Then the physicians lined up and lustily sang a song of the Swiss mountain men—the one she had taught them. Passengers and officials stopped and stared in amazement as the yodeling echoed off the station's walls.

After David and the Quaker couple had driven Elisabeth to a tiny apartment, which also served as an office, they took her on a tour of Warsaw in a jeep. They traveled through miles of almost total devastation of what had once been among the proudest and most noble cities in the world. Warsaw, which had once had a population of two million, now had less than 300,000. In the previous twelve months, more than two years after the end of hostilities, the remains of 150,000 citizens, the vast majority of them civilians, had been dug out of the ruins. The exhumations were continuing. The only way of knowing that people actually lived in some of the ruins was from the smoke of countless little chimneys.

Elisabeth had never been more moved than she was by the sight of thousands of people, many children among them, sorting out the rubble, still attempting to recover whatever was usable for the rebuilding of the city.

She was especially touched by the sight of crosses and bunches of fresh flowers placed against the crumbling walls of homes and ruined churches. Each cross, David explained, and each bouquet marked the loss of someone killed in the war. The flowers were changed two or three times a week. They were brought in from the countryside, and the grieving people often sacrificed money badly needed for food to purchase wreaths to pay tribute to a loved one.

The Quakers had arranged for her to join a Volunteers' camp at Lucima, near Lublin, not far from the Russian border, in an area that had been savagely raked by war. After a second day in Warsaw, a quiet day spent washing clothes and writing letters (which for some reason never reached her family and friends in Zurich), David drove her in the jeep south through flat steppe country, following the Wisla River, stopping occasionally in a village for a drink of water or milk.

After a bumpy, dusty journey that took five hours, David pointed ahead to a cluster of cottages. "Lucima!" he shouted above the rattle of the jeep. As they approached the village, Elisabeth saw that many of the cottages were in ruins; the village had been half flattened by tanks and shells. However, there was evidence of reconstruction and industry. Outside one cottage a tailor was busy pedaling an old-fashioned sewing machine; outside another some older women were weaving blankets. On the perimeter of the village, near the river, stood two large tents, accommodations for forty-five Volunteers.

David sounded the horn as he drove through the village. Children waved and chickens scattered. Volunteers, engaged in construction of a new school building, downed their tools and greeted the new recruit.

At once Elisabeth was introduced to her new kitchen. It was almost as primitive as the one in Ecurcey, but at least there was an old-fashioned brick stove, and coal to fire it. Convinced that she could not possibly be happier, she rolled up the sleeves of her shirt.

Eight years after making her vow, she was at last honoring her solemn contract with the Polish people.

11

A Handful of Blessed Soil

FOUR TIMES in the final throes of World War II the flame and steel of battle swept back and forth across Poland. Many of those who survived had done so by burrowing into the ground like animals. Thousands of people near the Russian frontier had starved to death. Untold numbers of others, Elisabeth learned, had been frozen to death in savage winters. Those who managed to hold on to life were the ones for whom the Volunteers had traveled from distant countries.

What astonished Elisabeth was the stoicism of the Polish people. She was amazed to encounter no self-pity, no bitterness. Privation, physical suffering and death were simply accepted as part of the gamble of life. None of the peasants seemed to have money. If one family slaughtered a pig or a goose, neighbors were invariably and naturally invited to share the meat, or perhaps a portion was bartered for a pair of pants from the village tailor.

Fifteen nations were represented in the Lucima camp. About half of the Volunteers were from the British Red Cross or were American

Quakers. The next largest group was made up of Polish nationals. For a while Elisabeth was the only Swiss. She is not sure who first gave her the name "Peterli" (Little Peter), but that was what everyone called her. It was a name that stuck through the rest of her work-camp experiences in Europe.

Not so much because she was only five feet tall, but rather, she assumed, because of her eagerness to tackle any job, from mixing concrete to lugging timber, and because of an enthusiasm she simply couldn't repress, she was often taken for a teenager, at least by those Volunteers who were sophisticated and widely traveled. She didn't mind, and anyway she soon proved she was no camp mascot.

As she had in Ecurcey, so now she enjoyed the challenge of trying to vary the menu of basic food purchased or bartered from local farmers. A family for whom a house was being constructed or repaired would return to the village from a foraging expedition into the countryside, and then bring to the kitchen bags of apples, cucumbers, tomatoes, eggs and goat's milk. Once in a while a truck drove in from Warsaw with canned food, dried fruit and vegetables, sugar, coffee and tea. The imported food had been shipped into Poland by American Quakers or the British Red Cross.

The Volunteers concentrated most of their energy on building the school, because the children in the area had had no chance of education. Teachers had been among the first to be liquidated by the Nazis. The Volunteers believed that through education of the new generation they would best be able to restore culture and commerce, and thus prosperity, to the wasteland that was Poland.

The idea was to hand over a usable school to Polish-speaking teachers before the end of the summer. Lucima had been selected for the site because it was at the hub of an agricultural area, and Poland's first priority was to get the land back into full production.

Elisabeth had plenty of local help in the kitchen and took time off for construction work. Her first alternative job was mortar mixing. She and a muscular Danish girl, Karen, took turns mixing cement, sand and water to the proper consistency. By the time she had mixed mortar for a couple of hours under the midsummer sun her shirt would be wringing wet and every muscle in her body would protest. Her colleagues would take pity on her then, and for the next hour or two she would be a bricklayer or a thatcher.

Within a few days Elisabeth knew most of the forty-five people at the camp and many of the villagers too. She was drawn especially to a painfully thin Polish girl, Rita, not much older than herself. Rita was dying of leukemia and had philosophically accepted her failing strength. She could not mix mortar or heave bricks, so she assigned to herself the chore of washing the clothes of the Volunteers.

Elisabeth joined Rita before sunrise every day. The young women collected bundles of clothes from outside the tents and carried them down to the River Wisla. Usually without soap (always one of the rarer commodities) Elisabeth and Rita washed the clothes on old-fashioned scrub boards. As she scrubbed and rinsed, Rita sang lilting Polish folk songs in a soft melodic voice.

Elisabeth vividly remembers those predawn hours on the banks of the Wisla River, and especially the moments when the sun rose over the steppes—the clarity of Rita's voice, the sudden fire of the sunrise, the cool river water slapping at her feet. With Rita she spent many hours talking about life and death, about human vulnerability and about God and the meaning of existence. It was Rita who taught her Polish, and soon Peterli amazed veterans at the camps by being able to translate basic Polish into German, English and French, and vice versa.

As in her previous Volunteers camps, so the workday at Lucima ended with a sing-along, with each national group contributing songs. In short order, Elisabeth taught her colleagues the songs of the Swiss mountain men.

After a while, however, there was a change in her routine. Most Polish physicians, nurses and even midwives had been displaced or liquidated by the Nazis. A few hospitals were beginning to reopen in the bigger towns, and one of them was in Lublin, more than twenty miles from Lucima. But this hospital was known to be overcrowded and refusing outpatients. So the village people had handed over one of their cottages to be used as a clinic. (In fact, the clinic was only half a cottage, the second room being used for the storage of food.) With its mud floor and thatched roof, furnished with a wooden table, a couple of chairs and a few shelves, the clinic could hardly have been more primitive; but as soon as news of its existence spread abroad it was handling up to fifty patients a day.

When it was known that Elisabeth had worked in a hospital and that she possessed medical syringes and hypodermic needles she was asked to join the clinic, which was run by two young Polish women known to everyone as Hanka and Danka. These two women had both had front-line surgical experience with the Polish resistance forces. Their pharmaceutical resources were limited to a dozen basic drugs, including aspirin and herbal emetics, but they were remarkably skilled general surgeons.

Although Elisabeth's surgical experience had been confined to assisting Dr. Amsler, she was a fast learner. Patients lined up outside on the dusty Lucima street at sunrise. Some came in horse-drawn carts, others came up the River Wisla in small boats, but most walked, some for several days and nights.

The procedures of Hanka and Danka would not be found in modern medical textbooks. For instance, a patient suffering from a chronic infection was likely to be given an injection of his own blood. Elisabeth's syringes and needles came in handy for these auto-transfusions, in which the blood was drawn from one arm of a patient and injected into the other. Though the procedure had the appearance of witchcraft, it seemed remarkably effective. Elisabeth believes that the factor which played the most significant part in recovery was the total childlike trust of the patients in the skill of their "doctors."

So unconditional was the patients' trust that there were times when Elisabeth believed all she had to do to effect recovery was to lay her hands on a patient's head! Sometimes that was about all she could do, because there were few drugs, and the patients arriving at the clinic suffered from almost the whole gamut of human ailments.

A not uncommon problem was wounds caused by shrapnel. For several years patients suffering from shrapnel wounds had carried small bits of metal from bombs, shells and grenades in their bodies. The shrapnel not immediately excised tended to work its way through the body to the surface, and cause a septic wound.

Since the clinic had no anesthetics, the shrapnel patients were obliged to endure the pain of perhaps a dozen incisions while fully conscious. Elisabeth can recall no adult patient uttering any sound except words of gratitude.

She was soon wielding a scalpel alongside Hanka and Danka, and with as much dexterity. She simply undertook what had to be done, or

122

at least what could be done under such primitive conditions, and then smiled encouragement and expressed admiration for courage.

Her competence as a surgeon was fully tested one day when the two Polish doctors left hurriedly for the countryside to see if they could track down the source of a sudden outbreak of typhoid. Elisabeth was about to close the clinic after a busy day when a peasant woman, obviously in the last weeks of pregnancy, came to the door.

The woman explained that the advent of her baby was not her problem, and she then exposed in her groin a swelling the size of a melon. She went on to say that she had walked twenty miles to see the "lady doctors" at Lucima because she believed (correctly) that the swelling was a threat to the life of her unborn child.

One of the village women was within hailing distance. Elisabeth called her to the clinic and asked her to hold the pregnant woman down on the wooden table during the operation. She made an incision and pressed from the wound a quantity of pus and fluid. She then urged the patient to remain at the Lucima camp for a couple of days, but the mother-to-be shook her head. No, she had to hurry home for the birth of her child. Awed by the stoicism of her patient, who had not uttered a sound throughout the procedure, Elisabeth watched the woman walk down the dusty street toward the sunset.

A few days later another patient from the same area arrived at the clinic and reported that the woman had given birth to a healthy baby boy.

Elisabeth had moved out of the women's tent so that she could sleep on the ground under the stars. After the heat and pressure of full days, she relished, in the few minutes before falling asleep, the quiet, the space and the isolation of what she lightly referred to as a "Quaker silence"—a chance to sort out her thoughts, to express to "the Spirit of Heaven" her gratitude for health, strength, friendship and work that were so enormously satisfying. She would then glance with wonder for a few moments at the star-studded sky before succumbing to sleep.

One midnight she was awakened by the sound of a child crying. Her first thought was that she had heard the cry in a dream, but then in the light of the moon she saw a woman sitting at the foot of her mattress. The woman was rocking a small fretful child.

The woman apologized for awakening Elisabeth. The child

wrapped in the shawl was Janek, her three-year-old son. Janek was ill. He needed help from the "doctor." Elisabeth reached out and touched Janek's forehead. It was hot with fever. Between his plaintive cries, the child's breathing was rasping, shallow. The symptoms were all too familiar at Lucima. Janek had typhoid.

Elisabeth walked the mother and child to the clinic, where she lighted a lamp and made two cups of herbal tea. She listened to the woman relate unemotionally how she had walked three days and two nights carrying her son. The woman had been told in her own village that the "lady doctors" at Lucima would help her child to get well again.

Across the rim of her teacup Elisabeth gently told the woman that there was no medication at the clinic for the sick child, and that the long walk had been in vain.

The woman listened impassively, her coal-black eyes locked to Elisabeth's. After a long silence, with the woman slightly tilting her head as if she were listening for some inner voice, she said evenly, "Doctor, you will save the life of my son because he is the last of my thirteen children. Janek is the only one to survive the gas chambers of Maidanek."

The mother's absolute faith felt like a knife in Elisabeth's heart. How would she explain to this woman that the chances of emaciated Janek's survival would be very small even if he were now to receive intensive medical care?

The mother simply sipped her tea and waited for Elisabeth to make some move. The flickering lamp in the center of the table threw grotesque shadows across whitewashed walls and almost empty shelves. Only Janek's harsh breathing broke the silence. Still the woman did not move, save occasionally to rock the glassy-eyed child.

Her mind desperately scanning for options, Elisabeth fastened on one small hope. Surely the overcrowded hospital at Lublin could not turn away so sick a child. But Lublin was more than twenty miles away, and at the moment there was no transportation at the camp.

Elisabeth rose from the table and blew out the lamp. Then, taking turns carrying Janek, she and the mother walked down the rough Lublin road through the remainder of the night. As they walked, the mother told Elisabeth how the whole of her family had first been moved to a slave labor camp and then, at the end of 1943, to Maidanek concentration camp, where Janek had been born. It was nearly noon by the time they reached the gray stone walls of the Lublin Hospital.

They entered a wrought-iron gate, but found the hospital door closed and locked. A physician—so they assumed from his white coat and stethoscope—came around a corner of the building and confronted them. With not even a greeting exchanged, the doctor gave the child a glance and felt the pulse in his neck. Then he shook his head vigorously. Even if the hospital had a single spare bed, he said, it would be purposeless to take in this dying child.

The doctor turned on his heel and strode away. Elisabeth ran after him and seized his arm. Her anger flared. Mixing her Polish with German expletives, she shouted at the physician that he had no heart at all. She, a Swiss, would tell the world of the callousness of the Poles. She would report how a Polish doctor at Lublin had refused to give medical help to a young child who had miraculously survived a Nazi concentration camp. Some Poles were no better than the Nazis! That's what the world would believe after she had told her story.

Where pleading had failed, Elisabeth's anger and threats proved effective. The doctor would, he grunted, take the child into the hospital on one condition only—that neither Elisabeth nor the child's mother would visit Janek for the next three weeks. In three weeks Janek would either have been buried or would be fit enough to take home.

The doctor spoke so rapidly that Elisabeth did not completely understand him. But the mother did. She stepped forward and simply handed the child over to the doctor.

During the long walk back to Lucima, through the blazing afternoon and the cooler evening, the mother shed no tears at all, and indeed she made no mention of her son. Back at the camp Elisabeth put the woman to work cleaning out the clinic, fetching water from the river, boiling syringes and rolling bandages. At night the woman shared Elisabeth's blanket.

Then, exactly three weeks later, Elisabeth awakened to find the woman gone.

A week later she found a knotted handkerchief alongside her bed. The handkerchief was filled with soil. She assumed it and its contents played some part in one of the superstitions that were common among the peasantry. She took the small bundle to the clinic, where she placed it on a shelf. Later in the morning when treating a patient from the village, she made some reference to the mystery of the handkerchief. The patient urged Elisabeth to untie the knots. Lying under the knots and the soil was a penciled note. Written in Polish, it read, "From Mrs. W., whose last child of 13 you have saved, a gift of blessed Polish soil."

The mother, it seemed, had carefully kept track of her days at Lucima, and had at the appointed time returned to the Lublin Hospital to pick up her son. The child had recovered, as she had known he would. After taking Janek back to her home and leaving him in the care of neighbors, the mother had gone to her church and had asked a priest to bless a handful of soil. Then the woman had walked two more nights and two more days to bring this special gift to the "lady doctor." There had been no need for words of gratitude, no need for farewells. The priceless gift of blessed Polish soil said it all. Her gratitude thus expressed, the woman had left as quietly as she had arrived and walked home to a living child.

The following morning while washing clothes at the riverside, Elisabeth shared with Rita the story of the mother's gesture of gratitude. Rita sang a special song of the faith and endurance of the Polish people, and of the new seed being sown in the Polish earth, seed which would surely mature to harvest.

It was September now, the days shortening and the nights much cooler. Elisabeth had been away from her native land for many eventful months. In the past month she had been exposed to a variety of diseases and she had lived on a simple and often inadequate diet. Yet she had never felt healthier. It was strange then that as she walked back from the river with Rita to help prepare the camp breakfast she had a strong conviction that it was time to leave, not because of the advent of autumn but because of a vague sense of danger.

After the morning clinic she sought out David Ritchie and told him of her premonition. David reminded her that the new school building, a simple one-classroom structure, was now completed and that many of the Volunteers would be leaving Lucima within the next week. In fact, on the following day there was to be a fiesta to mark the official

126

opening of the new school. David, who was to be master of ceremonies, invited Elisabeth to make a short speech in Polish. The fiesta would be a suitable moment for Elisabeth to say goodbye to her friends.

One other thing she asked of David. Before leaving Poland she wanted to visit a concentration camp. She needed a deeper understanding of the suffering of the victims of the holocaust and of man's capacity for hatred and cruelty. David understood and agreed at once. A jeep had just come in from Warsaw. After the celebration he would arrange for Elisabeth to be driven to Maidanek. Then later the Quakers' office in Warsaw would try to help her to get home.

Elisabeth was shy and nervous about making the first speech of her life in a language in which she was barely proficient. Although Rita promised to come to her aid and interpolate a few appropriate idiomatic phrases, Elisabeth's knees knocked as she ascended the makeshift rostrum outside the new school. The village people, especially the women, were dressed in colorful finery, their heads covered in silk scarves, their long skirts starched and buoyant with petticoats. The village tailor had worked overtime making new pants and shirts for the men. Many of the women wore necklaces and jangling bracelets, treasured family heirlooms that had been successfully hidden from marauding soldiers. A priest came from Lublin to bless the school, and the children formed themselves into a choir. The first Polish teacher had arrived, and the school was ready for classes.

Elisabeth does not recall much of what she said in her maiden speech. She was not sure whether the ovation she received was for audacity or oratory! However, it was the happiest of days, followed by a late night of singing and dancing to an accordion band.

The villagers and the Volunteers were still dancing and singing as Elisabeth left for the women's tent to pack her knapsack for an early departure next morning.

At the bottom of her knapsack she carefully placed a handful of Polish soil tied up in a white handkerchief.

══════12══════

Barbed Wire and Butterflies

THE GATES OF MAIDANEK were sprawled open as if they had been rammed by a tank (as well they might have been). Elisabeth walked slowly through them. From both sides of the gate drooping rusting barbed-wire fences skirted the camp's perimeter. At intervals the watchtowers from which guards had kept round-the-clock vigil still stood, squat and purposeful. At closer range now, the tall chimney of the crematorium, which had seemed a mere smokestack from a mile away across green fields, rose sinister and ominous against the azure sky.

A few paces inside the gates she paused and closed her eyes. She heard the sound of the marching feet of thousands of Jews, peasants, intellectuals and Gypsies—a host of innocents who had entered here never to return. In her mind's eye she saw a shuffling ragged column of the condemned snaking down a desolate cindered road. She heard the coarse shouts and commands of SS guards and Capos, the thud of rifle butts striking flesh.

She was thankful to be alone. At the gate she had bid goodbye to Karen, the Danish girl who had driven her to Maidanek. Karen had offered to serve as Elisabeth's guide, but she had turned down the offer. She did not need a guide; she knew this place, from pictures she had seen and the simple words of Janek's mother.

She continued walking, across two rusted railroad tracks partially concealed by encroaching weeds. She paused again and then turned down the track toward two railroad cars. At the first one she hesitated, then slowly she climbed the ladder and looked inside. The car was half-filled with shoes—large shoes and children's shoes fused by fungus into an amorphous mass.

She peered into the second car. It took her a moment to realize that the tangled material on the floor was human hair.

Sickened, she walked slowly to the nearest of the barracks. A few other people, some in small groups, moved silently along the paths. She guessed they were relatives or friends of those who had perished here.

After her eyes had adjusted to the shadows of the interior of the barracks she saw the tiers of wooden bunks where inmates had been crowded five abreast. And the graffiti on the walls. Hundreds of initials were carved into the wood, and pathetic messages, among them drawings of butterflies. Scratchings of butterflies were everywhere.

Within days, perhaps within hours of their dying in the gas chambers, the doomed men, women and children had left their last messages—not of despair but of hope, not of grief but of conviction of freedom!

She stood in silent awe, only her eyes moving from butterfly to butterfly. She heard no sound, but suddenly she became conscious of being observed. She turned away from the wall. A slim young woman was gazing intently at her. The woman's dark hair was swept back from a pale heart-shaped face, and her eyes were full of sorrow. She might have posed for an artist's Madonna. The woman smiled and murmured a greeting in Polish. Together they walked out of the barracks into sunshine.

The woman introduced herself. Her name was Golda. She was German-born and Jewish. While the two young women sat on a patch of grass and shared sandwiches, Golda, speaking German, related how her father, a Bavarian merchant, had been taken away one night by the Gestapo. She had been twelve years old at the time, and she had not seen her father again. When the war began, she, her mother, and an older brother and sister had first been deported to Warsaw and then in 1944 sent to Maidanek. The whole family had been herded to the gas chamber, but because she had been pushed by a Capo to the end of the line, a steel door had been closed in her face and she had been left outside. Save for this slim chance, she would have died with the others.

Golda pointed to the crematorium chimney. "The ashes of my mother, brother and sister floated up there," she said quietly.

Elisabeth had calculated that her companion was exactly her age. She asked Golda what she was now doing. The young woman hesitated as if she were unsure that Elisabeth would understand. She was working at a children's hospital in Germany, she said at last. To purge her bitterness she had deliberately chosen to help German children. Most of the children were war victims, many of them paraplegics.

In the long silence that followed, Elisabeth tried to fathom how within the human mind and heart there lay the potential for such cruelty and hatred as could create a Maidanek, and such forgiveness and love as was epitomized by Golda. Elisabeth was to carry in her heart and down the years the images of Golda and of the butterflies scratched on the stark walls of the prison barracks.

Golda had come to Maidanek with a small party of foreign visitors, a couple of American cousins among them. The party had rented a truck, and their immediate plan was to travel north to visit a community where one member believed he might find relatives. They offered to give Elisabeth a lift to Warsaw, but she had other plans.

For some time she had carried a hope of visiting Russia. This desire was not merely a tourist's whim but a feeling that in visiting Russia she would gain some understanding of the patriotism and motivations of the people of that vast land. She had read much about the heroic defense of Stalingrad and of the enormous sacrifices the Russians had made to throw back the invaders. She knew there would be no immediate opportunity to visit the cities or even to get to know anyone; but simply to cross the border might, she felt, help her to understand. She did not attempt to explain all this to Golda's party when she accepted a ride only to the outskirts of Bialystok, about twenty-five miles from the Russian border.

Golda was the only member of the party who did not try to warn her of the obvious dangers of traveling alone. She seemed to comprehend Elisabeth's motives and also, it appeared, why their paths had crossed at Maidanek.

On her own again, Elisabeth struck out on the road into Bialystok. In her knapsack there was little of material value. One of the Quakers had given her some money in Polish currency, but besides this and her well-worn and faded clothing she had nothing worth stealing. She did not even possess a spare pair of boots. She had her blanket, of course, and in the bottom of the knapsack the handful of Polish soil.

Her immediate concern was where to spend the night. With luck, she thought, she would find a farmer who might allow her to sleep in a haystack. As she approached the outskirts of Bialystok, she moved off the road and made her way to the top of a grass-covered knoll. As there were no promising farms in sight, she was about to settle for sleeping behind a hedge when a woman suddenly appeared, as if from nowhere. She seemed to be of middle age and wore a brightly colored scarf over her head and a long dress, full-skirted with many flounces. As Elisabeth studied the handsome walnut-colored face, the woman greeted her in a language she had not heard before.

When she grasped Elisabeth's hand and studied her palm, Elisabeth guessed she was a Gypsy. With smiles and gestures, Elisabeth expressed admiration for the woman's attire and bangles, and she indicated that she had no spare money. In any case, Elisabeth said in Polish, she was not interested in prognostications of her distant future, but keenly interested in where she might safely sleep. The Gypsy seemed to understand, smiled agreeably, sat down and spread some cards on her skirt. From the cards, apparently, the Gypsy understood that she should take Elisabeth under her care. She stood up and beckoned her to follow.

It was quite dark by the time they reached a caravan of several decorated wagons. A man sitting on the steps of one of them was playing romantic music on a fiddle. Other women prepared food, and children of all ages busied themselves with chores or played rough-and-tumble near a campfire.

Elisabeth remembers her first night in the Gypsy caravan as "the animation of a children's story." Under a night sky so clear that the stars seemed to be within reach she listened to the melodies played by the wizened fiddler. The children brought her food and smiled and danced for her, and the woman she had first met insisted that she sleep in one of the wagons.

A couple of the men spoke adequate Polish and a little German. The group seemed suspicious only when she asked where the caravan had come from and where they were going. They shook their heads at these questions and talked among themselves. She gained an impression, however, that they came from deep inside Russia, and presumed that that was why they had been able to evade Hitler's extermination of Gypsies in Eastern Europe.

She remained with the caravan for four days as the wagons rumbled along country roads, usually heading eastward. The Polish-Russian frontier was unmarked, but Elisabeth believes she moved across the border two or three times in what seemed to be an aimless journey. Whenever the caravan reached a community, the adults immediately set about selling their wares—mostly brooms, costume jewelry and hand-woven baskets—or bargaining for food. Tolerant of Elisabeth's visibility when they were on the move, they insisted that she conceal herself when they stopped at a village.

In sharing the Gypsies' companionship and hospitality, in sharing their music, which seemed to her to echo the sounds of centuries past, Elisabeth experienced a deep contentment. She would happily have stayed longer with them had she not once more felt the nagging concern that she must not delay her return home.

She had been completely out of touch with her family for many weeks. She worried that they had no idea where she was. She had written home from Lucima, but had received no letters. Were she now simply to disappear on this distant frontier (Hanka had warned her that friends on the Russian frontier had disappeared), no one—not even the Volunteers—would know what had happened to her.

When she told the Gypsies that she needed to leave, they used extreme caution in putting her on the road to Warsaw. She knew the direction she must take, but had no idea of how to get to her destination.

She walked for an hour before coming across a stalled vintage car and two cassocked priests changing a tire. The older priest spoke German and Elisabeth explained her situation. Yes, the priest told her, they were driving to Wysokie, and on the following day to Warsaw.

They drove that night to a war-damaged convent where she was given a bed, and by the next afternoon she was back in Warsaw.

The couple in charge of the Quakers' office told her that the political situation in Europe had deteriorated while she had been at Lucima. With the Russians trying to stop the human flood tide now surging from Eastern Europe to the West, it might prove difficult, even dangerous for Elisabeth to attempt to return by train to Switzerland. Instead, the Quakers would arrange for her to travel on a military plane which would be leaving Warsaw for Berlin in a couple of days. From there she would have to try to make her way across Germany to Switzerland.

She was out of funds, but undaunted. She had never asked anyone for a penny and she wasn't about to do so of the Quakers, who themselves were living sacrificially. She would manage somehow. Then, on the evening before she was due to leave for the Warsaw military airport, a Polish businessman well known to the Quakers for his generosity but believed to have made a fortune on the black market arrived at the office with a package of butter. Learning that Elisabeth was about to depart next day, and guessing from her worn clothes and shoes that she was impoverished, the Pole gave her four pounds of butter, then almost worth its weight in gold. As an afterthought he also gave her the equivalent of ten dollars in Polish currency.

At the airport at dawn next day she discovered that the converted bomber she was to travel on had flown in from China with half a dozen American officers. It had stopped in Warsaw for refueling. She learned too that the crew and passengers had been alerted to pick up "a distinguished Swiss national who had rendered outstanding service in Eastern Europe"! No one could have looked less like a VIP than the brown-legged young woman wearing heavy boots and a patched skirt, whose back was bent under the weight of a knapsack and who clutched a package of butter.

In the cabin she found the six American officers already seated on benches facing each other. Their eyebrows arched and their jaws sagged as Elisabeth took her seat and innocently asked in heavily accented English how to fasten her safety belt. Ignoring the stir she had created, she pushed her battered knapsack under the bench and smiled happily at her fellow passengers. This was her first international plane trip and she was determined to enjoy it.

The flight to Berlin took about two hours. Elisabeth exchanged few words with the other travelers, because she was fascinated by the topography seen through portholes the size of dinner plates.

When the aircraft reached Berlin, her most pressing need was to find a restroom. The Americans were quickly whisked away in a limousine; and since the crew seemed to be busy, she left her precious package of butter, which she intended to sell in Berlin, under the wing of the aircraft. When she returned from the women's restroom the butter had vanished. Now all she possessed was the ten dollars in Polish currency, and it was still a long, long way to Zurich.

The American, British and French sectors of Berlin were under siege. The Russians had made it virtually impossible for unauthorized civilians to travel by land through the Soviet-occupied corridor to West Germany. Every vehicle running the Russian gauntlet had to be registered, and every driver and passenger was obliged to carry a fistful of documents signed at high level.

Elisabeth shouldered her knapsack and made her way on foot through the British-occupied sector to the heavily guarded barrier. For a while she simply stood at the checkpoint watching Russian soldiers interrogating every driver that came or went. It was obvious that she couldn't simply stand at the gate and raise her thumb.

Then a light military truck pulled up to the curbside near where she was standing. An officer, whom she correctly presumed to be British, got out of the driver's seat and lit a cigarette. He looked authoritative and trustworthy. Elisabeth approached him and explained her problem in English. Would it be possible for him to take her through the Berlin corridor to West Germany? The story tumbled out. She was a Swiss who had been doing relief work in Poland. She needed to get home. The officer studied Elisabeth, his British sense of chivalry struggling with his awareness of personal risk were he to attempt to smuggle an illegal passenger through the Berlin corridor.

Then suddenly he made up his mind. Yes, he told her, he would be prepared to take the risk if she would agree to being nailed into a crate. Yes—she nodded—if it was the only way.

The officer backed his truck to a spot out of sight of the guards at the checkpoint. There he whipped aside a canvas awning and showed Elisabeth several crates. One, measuring about three feet long and two feet wide, was filled with personal possessions, mostly phonograph records. These he emptied onto the bed of the truck.

Elisabeth squeezed herself into the crate and the officer nailed down the top, warning her that, if possible, she should "try to stop breathing" whenever the truck was stopped at a Russian checkpoint. A sneeze, he cautioned, could spell disaster.

The most uncomfortable journey seemed to last just short of forever. All along the hundred-mile corridor there were checkpoints, and at every checkpoint the Russians opened up the back of the truck and probed about with bayonets. Each time Elisabeth held her breath until a gruff clearance order was barked out in Russian.

With all the stops, it took eight hours to reach Helmstedt in West Germany. There, at a British military base, the officer opened the top of the crate.

She was safe now, he said. She could get up and stretch. Elisabeth could not move. Laughing, the officer reached down and grabbed her shirt collar. He pulled her out of the crate as unceremoniously as if she had been a kitten!

Elisabeth was embarrassed by the telltale dampness of her skirt. But the officer was apparently unaware of it, and when she could walk, he escorted her to a canteen and offered to buy her dinner; but for Elisabeth even the thought of food was nauseating.

The officer shrugged at the strange uncommunicative girl who had to be coaxed to drink a glass of milk. His chatter died as he himself attacked a substantial meal of steak and eggs. When he had finished, they walked out of the canteen together. The officer asked if he could be of any further help, but Elisabeth assured him that she would be all right and thanked him for taking a personal risk on her behalf.

The officer now seemed at a loss for words. It was probably inconceivable to him that this slip of a girl, penniless and in patched clothes, could manage to return to her home in Switzerland. After an awkward silence he braced himself and saluted.

Elisabeth moved away into the darkness. She was so stiff that every step was an effort. As she walked past a streetlight, staggering soldiers spotted her and made obscene suggestions in English. She felt lonely and insecure, and suddenly terribly tired. As she passed a cemetery, more sinister-looking figures came out of the shadows ahead. She climbed a low wall and, with her eyes now accustomed to the darkness, found a flat tombstone.

Feeling sure she would be safe—for a cemetery was probably the only place where a young woman could feel safe in this rapacious territory—she took out her blanket, wrapped herself in it and lay down. But she hardly slept. The cold of the tombstone seeped into her bones.

At sunrise she was on the road again and hitched a ride to the wooded outskirts of Hildesheim. Now every muscle hurt so much that she had to rest. She walked a few hundred yards into a wood and lay down on a patch of leaves. In spite of the late September warmth of the sun, her whole body began to shake with feverish chills. She thought about building a fire, but in rising to her feet she staggered and fell. Three times she tried to muster the energy to gather wood, and three times she failed to do so.

She knew now that she was very ill. The fever had struck suddenly, alarmingly. She curled herself up in the blanket and rested her throbbing head on the knapsack. Disinterestedly, she watched an old woman gathering wood. Then she drifted into sleep.

For a short spell during the night she awakened, disturbed by a strange munching sound at her ear. Aware of movement, she peered into the shadows. A cow was standing almost on top of her. Elisabeth's tongue was swollen, her lips cracked from thirst. She vaguely thought of trying to milk the cow, but even the effort of raising her head cost her all the energy she still possessed.

She sank back again, this time into oblivion.

13

The Prodigal's Return

ELISABETH OPENED HER EYES. She had been unconscious for hours. It took her many minutes to understand that she was in a hospital. Her ward was long, bleak and overcrowded. She was desperately ill. The diagnosis (she was to learn) was typhoid.

How she had gotten there from the forest she had no idea. She learned later that she owed her life to the woman she had seen gathering firewood, who had found Elisabeth when she returned to the woods the next day, tried to rouse her, then summoned police.

The ward was occupied by the most gravely ill patients, several of whom were dying. The resident physician and three overworked nurses were drawn with fatigue. Elisabeth's immediate neighbor was a terminally ill young mother whose small twin boys, come to visit her, peered at Elisabeth through frightened eyes.

Days drifted into restless, fevered nights, and nights to sunless, dreary days as she clung to life. She was never quite sure whether she was awake or sleeping. The figures that moved about her bed and sometimes bent over her and spoke to her often seemed to be part of her dreams, the figures in her dreams more real.

In one vivid and frightening dream, she saw herself on a sled in strange company. A blizzard was raging, and she and her companions were wrapped up in furs and blankets. The emaciated horse pulling the sled strained and then stopped in its tracks, its thin legs unable to cope with the depth of snow. No shelter was visible, and the land resembled the steppes through which she had journeyed in the Gypsy caravan.

Suddenly out of the dark forest a pack of wolves loped toward the sled. The wolves howled and circled, always moving closer. One of her companions lighted a lamp, but to no avail. Unless the travelers could get the sled moving again, all of them would be torn to pieces.

Elisabeth awakened sweating. The nightmare remained so deeply etched in her mind that some years later she tried to interpret it. She believes now that the dream was a premonition, and that her life depended on continuing her journey. No matter how harsh the environment, how great the peril, she had to keep moving.

In more rational moments she was convinced she was dying. She wasn't afraid. Her great concern was to get a message to her mother. She desperately wanted her mother to understand that she, Elisabeth, had not thrown away her life. She wanted to tell her mother that although she had lived only twenty-one years she had lived fully and that she had no regrets. Were she to have the chance to live her life again, she wouldn't change anything. She was glad she had traveled to Poland. If her mother could only know about Janek, perhaps she wouldn't grieve too much.

She cried out, appealing for someone to write to her mother. Because she had been thinking of Lucima, she cried out in Polish. No one paid any attention. In fact some of the patients turned their backs to her.

A second time she called for help. Again no one responded. She felt hopelessly trapped, as if she were in a deep pit or a glacier crevasse and looking up at faces silhouetted against the light. But no one would throw her a rope.

She sank back into the bed weeping. She was too tired to try anymore. She was alone and deserted. She was ready to die.

Some time later in the small hours (or so it seemed), the muscles of her heart cramped into an agonizing spasm—the cruelest pain she had ever felt. Her body jackknifed to a sitting position as she clutched her chest. Her shriek awakened the ward. The resident physician came running. Seeing Elisabeth's distress, he asked what was going on with the *"kleines Schweizermädchen."*

She felt the prick of a needle and was conscious of the retreat of pain. Almost as if she were an observer of the fussing around her bedside, Elisabeth heard awakened patients asking if Elisabeth was truly a Swiss girl. She heard patients near her express surprise. Surely Elisabeth was Polish, she heard them say. Hadn't she spoken in Polish? Hadn't the doctor said that he had found Polish papers on Elisabeth?

One of the patients said, "Oh, we were sure she was just a Polish pig! That was why we refused to help her."

Elisabeth slept for a long time. When she again awakened, she found the other patients were now solicitous.

She asked incredulously how anyone could see her so sick, perhaps dying, and yet refuse to write a letter to her mother. Did they now want to bring her extra soup and puff her pillows simply because she was Swiss and not Polish?

Her anger simmered. It was this kind of racial prejudice that had caused the war, she thought, and there would surely be another war, another Hitler, if such prejudice continued. She knew she must live and escape from this ward, and then join others to help end the bitterness that still existed, even in a ward for the terminally ill. She thought a lot about Golda.

The coronary spasm she had suffered had apparently been the crisis of her illness. She continued to feel very weak, but the delirious dreams stopped, her pulse slowed and her fever abated.

A couple of days later she herself wrote a letter to her mother. She would be home soon, perhaps before the end of October. She had been ill, but she was getting well. She longed more than anything else in the world to be home again. She loved them all at home so very much.

With stern self-discipline she exercised her limbs. Amazed at how thin she was (she could not have weighed, she believes, more than seventy-five pounds) she took all the nourishment now offered her. Some of the visitors to the ward brought her flowers and writing paper. But when they asked for her home address and offered their own she began to suspect their motives. Some of the visitors, indeed, asked her to send them food parcels, especially coffee and chocolate.

She took every opportunity to talk about Lucima and Maidanek, about the gas chambers and the butterflies she had seen on the walls of the barracks. The dying mother of twin boys seemed to be the only one to understand the meaning of the butterflies. When the twins next came to visit, Elisabeth asked her ward companions how they would feel if these two young children of a dying woman were themselves condemned to die. She pulled from her knapsack the handkerchief of Polish soil and she told the story of Janek. The feelings of Polish mothers, she said, were no different from the feelings of German mothers.

In spite of the inadequate diet, the speed of Elisabeth's return to strength astonished the veteran physician. On her first day out of bed her legs crumpled, but each day after that she set herself longer distances to walk. At last, having heard of her whereabouts, the German branch of the International Voluntary Service for Peace sent her a train ticket that would take her home. (She had deliberately not asked her parents for help. She had resolved never to do this, because, she felt, it would have compromised her independence.)

In the last week of October, when she was strong enough to leave, an embarrassed hospital administrator presented her with a bill. Her physician suggested that she could pay it off by working for a few weeks in the hospital, and for a couple of days she did in fact empty bedpans and help to make beds. But when the physician saw how exhausted she became, even with light duties, he tore up the bill. The *kleines Schweizermädchen* must go home. That was where she should rightfully be, home with a mother to care for her.

The doctor himself drove her to the train station and saw her aboard a Basel-bound train. She was touched by his kindness and care. He had unquestionably saved her life. He was, she told him, the kind of physician she wanted to be one day. She cried when he pressed some cookies into her hand, gave her a hug and wished her a speedy return to full health.

Just as the old soldier at Ecurcey had done with his penciled note "from one human being to another," so now the Frankfurt doctor blunted the edge of her feelings about Germans—the Germans who

140

had built Maidanek and who in a hospital ward had had no time for a dying girl they thought was Polish.

After the frontier formalities, Elisabeth suddenly found herself in another world. Switzerland, after months in still devastated war zones, was no less astounding to her than Sweden. On the German side of the frontier the people seemed to her to move sluggishly through the miasma of defeat and hopelessness. The faces of even the young people were lined by hunger and stress, and their eyes were self-pityingly cast down. That was her impression—a montage of acrimony, resignation and starvation.

But on the Swiss side of the border the people walked with their heads held high and with purposeful steps. They all seemed so well dressed that for the first time in months Elisabeth was conscious of her own shabby clothes. On the platforms at Basel, small groups of people exchanged news and laughed among themselves. She couldn't recall hearing laughter in Germany.

At Basel, where she changed trains, there was time to leave the station and walk a few blocks down the streets. Everything looked so clean. Buildings glistened, and geraniums hung from window boxes against white walls. She passed a candy kiosk where she feasted her eyes on trays of chocolate. She had not seen candy displayed since she had been in Sweden. Her mouth watered, but except for a few virtually useless Polish bills, she had no money to buy even the cheapest candy. She considered seriously whether she might be able to sell her blanket for enough money to buy a bar of chocolate, but it was unlikely that anyone in the street would purchase her frayed and faded blanket, even for a dog's kennel—a blanket which for months had been her most valuable possession.

As the Zurich-bound train glided through the autumn-crisp Swiss countryside, Elisabeth became restless and excited, childishly leaping to the window at the prospect of her homecoming. Names were enthrallingly familiar—Brugg, Baden, Dietikon. She tried to picture the reunion with her parents and sisters. She could smell the pastries in her mother's oven. In the evening when the lights were lit, she would speak of her adventures. Then she would sink into her own featherbed warmed with hot water bottles. If her excitement could have fueled the locomotive, the train would surely have become airborne!

At seven o'clock in the evening—precisely on schedule—the train slowed for its approach to Zurich. She peered through the window, half expecting a member of the family to be there to greet her, although without enough money for a phone call, she had not been able to tell anyone the time of her arrival.

Elisabeth stumbled as she descended from the train. Her recent illness had left her with very little strength. She wanted to run up the hill to the Kübler home on Klosbachstrasse, but she was obliged to walk very slowly and stop occasionally to catch her breath.

However, the reunion at home was everything she had expected. Her father beamed on her. So the prodigal was home, he said. Her mother and sisters shed tears and expressed their horror over Elisabeth's loss of weight.

As it happened, the letter she had mailed from the hospital had never arrived—she assumed later that the stamp had been stolen by the patient who had volunteered to mail it—and the family knew nothing of her illness. From time to time they had received cryptic postcards from Belgium, Sweden and Poland. Otherwise, Mr. and Mrs. Kübler knew no more than that their maverick daughter had, for reasons they could not fully understand, given up a steady job to work in various countries which, they believed, could have coped very well without her.

She now told them about Belgium and Sweden and the hilarious train journey to Warsaw. She told them about Hanka and Danka and, proudly, of her surgical accomplishments. She related the story of Janek, and she produced from her knapsack the handkerchief full of Polish soil.

While Elisabeth spoke of these adventures, Mrs. Kübler bustled in and out of the kitchen with plates of hot food which Elisabeth, with her very limited capacity for nourishment, was only able to sample.

However, within ten days she had regained twelve pounds. She was not yet quite ready for skiing or mountain climbing, but she took long walks along the lake and felt her strength returning. There was plenty of time to catch up with all the family news. Erika proudly displayed her first story in print—a children's story that had been well received—and Eva had just secured a job as a ski instructor. Ernst's letters from India reported his business success. However, his comments about his servants and the social life seemed so irrelevant to Elisabeth, so distant from her own priorities, that she felt apart from him as she never had before. Even at the family hearth she found it hard to concentrate. The chatter of her sisters about clothes, parties and vacations was too remote from her own fresh memories. For all the joy of the reunion, it seemed to Elisabeth as if her own experiences had separated her from cheerful domesticity. She doubted whether even Erika or Eva would understand why she felt spiritually closer to a mining village in Belgium and to a peasant community in Poland than she did to old family friends who lived in comfort and security.

Shortly after her return she paid a call on Professor Amsler at the eye clinic. The old physician seemed overjoyed to see her and insisted that she tell him all about her adventures. His office schedule was disrupted by the visit, but he told her with a twinkle that he would soon catch up with his backlog of patients now that "the swallow had returned from the steppes!" It was his way of saying that her job was waiting for her. Elisabeth could have hugged him, but in spite of the mutual respect and affection between them, he was still her dignified mentor and employer. In all her long relationship with Dr. Amsler, he was always the "Professor."

She was amazed at how easily she slipped back into the routine of her work at the eye clinic. Dr. Amsler again invited her to watch him at eye surgery, especially when he had an unusual case. She continued to board at the Kübler home, and once or twice a month she spent a weekend in the mountains—skiing, climbing or hiking, according to the season and the weather.

On one winter visit to Furlegi, Eva introduced Elisabeth to her boy friend, Seppli Bucher, a champion skier who came from a large Catholic family in the heart of Switzerland and who was currently taking a business course in Zurich. That evening at Furlegi after the party of skiers had returned to the cabin, Elisabeth found herself next to Seppli. Without any stress or reserve the two of them shared their dreams and ambitions. It was the beginning of an extraordinary intimacy, deeper than ordinary friendship, different from, quieter than, the relationship of lovers.

Physically Seppli was a blue-eyed fair-haired Adonis who could outski and outclimb anyone on the mountains; yet he was not competitive. He seemed to accept his own strength and grace as providential gifts, an acceptance that gave him a natural humility. Seppli was a poet, sensitive and aware, and in his poetry he expressed a love of nature that captured Elisabeth's own feelings. Deeply religious and a practicing Catholic, he yet lived out a personal creed not limited by church dogma.

It was Seppli's self-assurance, his inner strength, that fascinated Elisabeth—this and his smile, which could light up a room. She had not felt more at ease in the company of any young man.

She saw Seppli only on rare occasions, when Eva brought him to the house for a family dinner or musical soiree, or when she joined Eva and others for a weekend in the mountains. Although she did not at the time deeply analyze her feelings for Seppli, she saw in him the exemplar-knight against whom she could measure the qualities of other young men. When Eva and Seppli became engaged, Elisabeth felt it was so right that he should become part of the family, eventually to claim the status of a brother.

Elisabeth worked at the eye clinic without a break until June 1949. In her darkened examination room she continued to be an uncertified therapist, refining her skills as a counselor, understanding when to speak and when to listen. Although she enjoyed her work and found it rewarding, she was constantly aware that it was only a stepping-stone to her ambition to be a physician.

She never discussed this ambition with her father. She knew that, having once made it clear that he would not support her financially, he would not go back on his word. Both Mr. and Mrs. Kübler intimated from time to time that the natural goals for all three daughters were to find suitable husbands and in good time to produce grandchildren.

Erika was the first, becoming engaged to be married to Ernst Faust, a young businessman. But Elisabeth never lost sight of her own citadel, saving her money for the day when she would enter medical school.

Considered rationally and objectively, her prospects were just as meager as they had ever been. Before even applying to a medical school she would have to take the Mature examination, which ordinarily required a minimum of three years of study. But something would happen, some gate would open, she convinced herself. She would know when and how to move forward to the fulfillment of her dream.

She continued too to keep in close touch with the Volunteers' office in Zurich and she often gave a hand with administrative work. Just when her vacation was due, a message was received at the office from a Volunteers' work force on the Italian Riviera. They were constructing an access road to a hospital, and they urgently needed a cook.

Neither Mr. nor Mrs. Kübler raised objections when Elisabeth told them she was off again to join a Volunteer camp in Italy. Mr. Kübler stated vigorously that so long as she wasn't planning to visit any countries behind the Iron Curtain she would have his blessing.

Elisabeth was about to retort that within a month she would be twenty-three years old, and that if she wanted to visit Moscow she would certainly do so. But anxious to avoid an unnecessary family dispute, she bit her tongue. It was a long time before she understood the depth of her father's feelings about the threat of communism.

As it happened, the road construction project in Italy took much less time than had been anticipated. Elisabeth worked as a cook for the Volunteers and took her turn with pick and shovel. Then, with time to spare, she made a quick tour of Italy, hitchhiking with a friend to Pompeii, Naples, Rome, Florence and Venice. In Venice she decided that she had seen enough stained-glass windows and statuary to last her for a long while.

She returned to Zurich and on her arrival reported immediately to the Volunteers' office. They told her that if she could leave that evening, they had a special assignment for her that would take up the slack of the last few days of her vacation. A Swiss woman married to a Polish national had left her two young children in Switzerland. The couple had now found a suitable home in a rebuilt suburb of Warsaw and they wanted their children to join them immediately. Would Elisabeth take the children to Warsaw? Railroad fares would be provided. Elisabeth said that she would be delighted to be the children's guardian and to return even briefly to a country where she had left part of her heart.

When she reached the Kübler home in the early afternoon, no one was there. She bathed, repacked her knapsack and left a note advising her parents that she was off to Poland on a special mission. The note was casually phrased, for at the time it never occurred to her how her father would react to her plans.

Elisabeth also went to the bank and withdrew all her modest savings; then in buoyant spirits she proceeded to the Zurich train station and met her young charges, a boy aged eight and a girl aged six. The Volunteer who had brought the children to the station proposed that since the train was routed both ways through Czechoslovakia it would be helpful if she took the opportunity to evaluate the needs of an orphanage in Prague from which the Volunteers' office had received a vaguely phrased appeal for assistance.

After an uneventful journey to Warsaw, Elisabeth handed over the children to the grateful parents. Once in Poland, she could not resist the temptation to revisit Lucima, to see how the community was faring two years later.

This time she traveled by bus. By happenstance, the priest who had blessed the school at the opening ceremony boarded the bus at Lublin. He recognized her at once and at Lucima proudly took her on a tour of the community. Many of the village people remembered her and overwhelmed her with offers of hospitality. At the schoolhouse the priest introduced her to the students as "one of the kind foreigners who had come from faraway countries to build their classrooms." The children sang Polish songs to their VIP guest and garlanded her with flowers. She felt, she told them, that she was back home again.

On learning from a teacher that the school was chronically short of books, pencils and other essential school equipment, she impulsively emptied her purse of all but a few coins. She possessed a return train ticket to Zurich and she was confident she could get home without money.

In Prague two days later she called on the orphanage that had appealed to the Volunteers for assistance. She immediately found herself confronted by communist bureaucracy and great suspicion. One of the orphanage staff warned her that she was being constantly watched by the secret police. A Communist Party official to whom she was referred told her contemptuously that "effete and patronizing capitalists" were neither welcome nor wanted in Czechoslovakia.

Elisabeth was incensed. She had wanted to do something for the or-

146

phanage, but all she could do, it turned out, was to empty her knapsack before she left. There would be some child who could make use of her spare pair of boots and her change of clothing.

So when she arrived next evening at Zurich's train station, all she possessed were the clothes she was wearing. She hadn't even pennies enough for the trolleybus fare.

Still she felt content, with a sense of mission accomplished. And she would be home soon enjoying one of her mother's fabulous meals, sleeping in her own featherbed.

But the front door of the Kübler home was locked, and the key was not in its usual secret place under a potted plant. From behind the drapes of the open dining-room window she heard the sounds of voices and dishes. She recognized a voice she had not heard in a couple of years or more. Ernst was home on leave from India and the family was obviously celebrating. Her arrival, she thought as she pressed the doorbell, was perfectly timed.

Unexpectedly it was her father who opened the door. After a second for recognition, Mr. Kübler asked flatly, "What do you want?"

Elisabeth laughed. She assumed her father was playing a game with her. He had sometimes played a deadpan game when she had been a young child. She was about to move toward him when he closed the door.

In a moment, thought Elisabeth, he would open the door again. He would laugh that deep familiar laugh. He would take her hands and draw her into the dining room and shout out to the rest of the family, "Guess who's arrived!" The family would leap from the table and rush to embrace her. That was the way it had been before. That was the way it always would be.

But the front door was not opened again—not after the expected few seconds, not after a minute. The realization slowly matured that her father had not been playing a game with her, that he had deliberately closed the door in her face.

From the dining room she heard the conversation resume, subdued now. She believed she heard her name mentioned. Then in a firm voice she heard her father call for a toast to Ernst.

14

First Steps to the Citadel

WITHOUT ANY SENSE of purpose or direction, Elisabeth walked slowly away from the Kübler home. The numbness caused by the initial shock of her banishment began to wear thin, and feelings returned; at first small waves of anger lapped her mind, and then a sweeping surge of pain and fury.

She tried to recapture the expression on her father's face as she had seen it in the light from the hallway, and she asked herself what he had expected of her. Could he possibly have thought she would plead for forgiveness and mercy because she had traveled behind the Iron Curtain against his wishes? He knew her better than that. Had Ernst played a role? Was her father attempting to demonstrate to him that he, Mr. Kübler, was still head of the family, still master of the home?

She was swept by another wave of anger. For God's sake, she was a woman, not a child! Not her father, not anyone could now dictate to her. She would never apologize, never, not for doing what she believed to be right! If the price she now had to pay for refusing to go hat in hand to her father was to have no place she could call home, then she was quite ready to pay that price. Her father would be the one to feel the guilt.

She thought of her mother and the hurt she must be suffering. She had never known her mother—or, for that matter, her sisters—to cross Mr. Kübler's iron will.

If she, Elisabeth, was the obstinate member of the family, as her parents had often accused her of being, then she had inherited this trait from her father. He had often talked of being a man of his word, but the phrase was sometimes a euphemism for stubbornness. Well, he would have no more claims upon her, nor would she ever again ask her father for anything!

She paused and looked up at a street sign. She had reached Seefeldstrasse. Suddenly she heard someone calling her name. Farther up the lighted street a young woman was waving to her. She did not immediately recognize her friend Cilly Hofmeyr, who had graduated as a speech therapist at the Canton Hospital at the same time Elisabeth had qualified as a lab technician. She and Cilly had once seen a lot of each other.

As they stood on the sidewalk under a streetlamp, Elisabeth explained her situation. She was without money and she needed a place to sleep.

Cilly pointed across the road to an apartment building. She herself had been looking for a suitable apartment. She had just found the ideal place on the top story, but the woman who owned the building had insisted that she also take a second room across the hall. Cilly had no use for the second room, which was very small. Perhaps it could at least be a temporary pied-à-terre for Elisabeth.

Two minutes later Elisabeth and Cilly were climbing the ninety-six stairs to the top of the apartment building. Cilly led the way to a large room, the one she was anxious to rent for herself, and then took Elisabeth across the hallway to a room so small that it might have been designed as a linen closet or storage room.

As soon as she opened the door, Elisabeth exclaimed with delight. With its sloping ceiling under the roof and tiny window, it was like a dollhouse. The rent was the equivalent of seven dollars a month.

Elisabeth paced off the floor. Against one wall there was just room

149

enough for a small bed. Against the opposite wall there was room for a table and hotplate. She flung open the window. By leaning far out she could see the lights on the lake. This meant that in daylight she would also be able to see the mountains. Off the hallway was a toilet serving the two rooms, and alongside the toilet was a cold-water sink. The fact that there was no bath did not dampen Elisabeth's enthusiasm. The room was perfect, she told Cilly.

They descended to the ground floor and signed the lease. They could move in immediately. Cilly cheerfully advanced Elisabeth the equivalent of twenty dollars. After they had had a meal at an adjacent café, Elisabeth slept that night on the floorboards of her new home, the first that she had ever been able to call her own.

Next morning Elisabeth phoned her mother, who came close to weeping with relief that her daughter was in such high spirits and had not spent the night on a park bench. Elisabeth briefly explained that she had found her own place. If the coast was clear—meaning that if her father was not at home—she would call and collect some clothes. She learned that Ernst was flying to England to join his wife and had already left for the airport. Her sisters had left for work.

When she reached the Kübler apartment, Elisabeth was told by her mother that Mr. Kübler could not be persuaded to rescind his banishment decision unless Elisabeth apologized for going against his wishes; then the family could be united once more. Elisabeth made it clear that she could not be so hypocritical as to apologize for something she did not regret. Anyway, she was delighted to have her own place. She collected some clothes in a duffel bag and her featherbed comforter. Balancing the featherbed and clothes on her head and ignoring the stares of people on the street, she walked back to Seefeldstrasse and up the ninety-six stairs.

Later in the day she bought a used hotplate, basic kitchen utensils, crockery and some provisions. She was in a hurry to make her room not only habitable but comfortable, for she was determined that she would not give her father the satisfaction of learning that she was living in squalor.

She bought some lumber, screws, wood stain, varnish and simple carpenter's tools. She had picked up the rudiments of carpentry at Ecurcey, and she had no difficulty in constructing a solid bed frame and a table that would serve both as a desk and for dining.

In the first flush of creativity she made drapes for the windows and started to weave a bedspread. On her second visit to the Kübler home her mother lent her two bedsheets, towels and a blanket. Elisabeth learned later that when her father heard about this loan he was incensed that his house was being depleted of, as he put it, "legitimate Kübler belongings."

However, later in the week when her sisters arrived for their first visit, the tiny apartment was beginning to reflect Elisabeth's personality. Erika and Eva were charmed by what Eva called "a room surely appropriated from one of Snow White's dwarfs." It may well have been the smallest human habitation in Zurich.

Erika had brought pastries, and Elisabeth brewed a pot of tea. The three sisters sat on the bed and reminisced. For a couple of hours they could have believed that they had turned back the calendar, that they were children again at Meilen, and playing at being grown-ups. They turned the pages of a family photo album and tried to guess who was Erika and who Elisabeth in some of the earliest pictures of them taken by their father. They recalled the scandal when Elisabeth had hurled her prayer book at the sadistic pastor, and they became almost hysterical with laughter as they remembered the pastor's shock.

Eva and Elisabeth even pouted their lips and tried talking in the language of Higaland. They were happy to find that they could still communicate as readily as they had done nearly twenty years earlier.

The visit strengthened bonds that had seemed to slacken as the sisters had pursued their own careers and interests.

There were few other visitors during the first few weeks, but Cilly looked in from time to time to check the progress of Elisabeth's work. The two young women sometimes shared hotplate meals. With her beautiful gold-blond hair, Cilly was so strikingly attractive that she was never short of male assistance for hauling heavy furniture up the flights of stairs or helping with the hanging of drapes or the painting of walls.

Once she had settled in, Cilly gave pride of place in her room to a small grand piano. She was an accomplished musician, the violin being her own instrument, and she designed her room to be a salon for musical soirees. Instead of chairs, she invested in a score of colorful throw pillows.

Elisabeth and Cilly were grateful for their mutual compatibility.

Both understood the need for privacy, yet each knew that she could count on the other for assistance.

While she built her furniture (a bookcase and window box had now been added) and decorated her room, Elisabeth thought through her plans for the future. Her father's obduracy was a spur in her flank. She would prove to her father not only her capability for complete independence; she would demonstrate that she had the mind, self-discipline and strength to be a physician. It was time to study for the Mature. She wouldn't boast about her intention. At this stage she wouldn't let anyone in the family know that she was doing anything more than holding down a job at the eye clinic.

When, however, she went to see Professor Amsler, who immediately invited her to rejoin his staff, she told him of her plan to start studying for the Mature. She would, of course, have to take a few practical classes in physics and chemistry at a technical college; but otherwise all her study would be done at home in the evenings, and she would work in the clinic full time.

Professor Amsler shook his head doubtfully. The Mature's requirements were formidable. He counted the exams off on his fingers: advanced mathematics, chemistry, physics, geography, history, Latin, German, French and English. She would be obliged to study the classical literature of the three modern languages.

Her only concern was Latin. She had never studied Latin, but she understood that if she gained top grades in the other subjects she could afford to fail one subject.

The professor then reminded her that for several years she would have very little time for social life. Not several years, she told him, but one! What normally took three years of study by a full-time student she would accomplish in twelve months.

Professor Amsler threw up his hands in a gesture of disbelief. But after a long pause, during which he studied her closely, he said softly that if a Mature record was to be set then he believed she would be the one to set it.

Elisabeth was not able to start serious study for the Mature for almost a year, for she was without funds and she needed to save up enough money to pay for courses and classes.

But from August 1950 the light in the smallest window on the top

152

floor of the apartment building on Seefeldstrasse burned long after the other lights in the building had been turned off. Sitting on a hassock (there was no room for a chair) and crouched over her small table, Elisabeth immersed herself in textbooks.

By day she held down the eight-hour job at the eye clinic. At night she found that all she needed was four, at most five, hours' sleep. She allowed herself a day in the mountains no more than once a month.

When she cooked for herself, her meals were very simple, always light. When her mother was certain that Mr. Kübler would be out of the house she would send a message to Elisabeth to call in and enjoy a fuller meal. From time to time too Erika and Eva climbed the stairs to her apartment to drop off parcels of food—sometimes food sent by her mother, sometimes pastries or other delicacies they had bought themselves.

Elisabeth occasionally saw her father on one of Zurich's streets. In these unplanned encounters he would nod to her as they passed, but he did not speak. On one occasion Elisabeth was visiting the Kübler home when her father arrived unexpectedly. She greeted him, but her father, taken by surprise, turned on his heel and left. His expression was not hostile, not even angry, but in character he was sticking to his guns. Insofar as he was concerned, since the day she had returned from Poland, Elisabeth had not been a member of his household.

In her room across the hallway, Cilly lived an active social life. On Saturday or Sunday evenings she usually entertained musicians. Elisabeth always helped out with preparing the supper and allowed herself an hour or two away from her textbooks to enjoy the concerts. Then she would slip away without being noticed.

On one occasion Elisabeth went to the Kübler home to "borrow" a couple of bottles of wine from her father's excellent cellar to contribute to the party. She had just collected them when Mr. Kübler arrived unexpectedly. She flung herself under her old bed, but in doing so she slipped, and one of the bottles crushed her ribs. As her father stomped about the house she remained mute in spite of the pain. Only when he had left the house again did Elisabeth emerge from her hiding place. Because of increasing difficulty in breathing and continuing pain, she reported later that evening to the emergency room at the hospital. An X ray revealed three cracked ribs.

Incidents like these, along with the occasional meetings in the streets, simply strengthened Elisabeth's determination to surprise her father with her academic achievement.

In mid-1951 she submitted her application to sit for the Mature, and in early September she took the examinations, which were held over a period of five days. She was confident of passing all but Latin, which she had virtually ignored. The Latin exam comprised both written and oral tests. The professor who examined her was puzzled by a student who, according to the record in front of him, had up to this point fared well in the Mature. When she seemed incapable of answering even elementary questions, he asked her if she was ill, and he actually apologized for having to fail her!

In failing Latin, by design, Elisabeth knew she had taken a grave risk, and that the marks for her other subjects would have to be well above average. On September 22, 1951, she returned home from a full day at the clinic to find a buff-colored envelope in her mailbox. Her eyes blurred as she read, "The examiners are pleased to announce that Elisabeth Kübler has passed the Mature"!

In the envelope was an additional note signed by the professor who had examined her in German. The professor congratulated her on obtaining the highest marks ever given to a student for her German composition. Her paper had been titled "Mind, Soul and Body of Human Existence."

She instantly thought of her father, and of the best way of telling him. It was his birthday on the following day. She went to a stationer's and asked for a 1951 calendar with blank day-by-day tear-off sheets. The clerk was puzzled, reminding her that it was late in the year. Didn't she perhaps mean a 1952 calendar? No, she did not. After a search in the back of the store the assistant found the kind she wanted. The tear-off sheets were attached to a plate painted with pictures of mountains. Returning home, she wrote on the first page the words "Happy Birthday!" and on the page for September 23 she wrote, "Passed Mature!" Not trusting the post office, she took the wrapped parcel to the Kübler home and pushed it through the letter box.

Next day she stood outside her father's office at the time she knew he would be arriving for work. He walked slowly, leaning heavily on a cane. Suddenly he saw her, his eyes narrowing in the morning glare. Slowly his mouth stretched into a congratulatory smile.

That evening Erika came around to her room. She brought an invitation to dinner at home. Mr. Kübler had asked his wife to prepare a meal to celebrate the academic achievement of the eldest of his triplets.

Elisabeth asked Erika if her father had said anything else. Yes, he had, over the breakfast table. Mr. Kübler had opened her birthday gift to him and torn off the pages of the calendar. He had remained silent for a long time while he stirred his coffee. Then across the rim of his cup he had pronounced gruffly, "Although Elisabeth is still very young, I'm damned if she's not as tough as I am!"

===15===
The Anatomy Room

ERIKA HAD NO SOONER left her room than Elisabeth experienced, as she now puts it, "a cold, gray, drained feeling." It was anticlimax, of course. She had known this emotion many times in the mountains. It came upon her when she had reached a crest after a rugged climb—first the euphoria of conquest, the joy of having tested her daring and resolve; then a sort of vacuum, a close cousin of depression, while she surveyed a higher peak yet to be vanquished, a longer, tougher climb to be essayed.

With the Mature diploma in her possession she could now attend any Swiss university, study for any profession. Where she would go and what she would study were already decided. She would, of course, enter the medical school of the University of Zurich.

Even the family dinner to honor her academic success did not completely lift her spirits. She looked across the table at her sisters, seeing the predictable pattern of their lives. Marriage, children, security, suburban homes, memberships in sporting and cultural organizations—these marked out the common course of the daughters of an upper-middle-class Swiss-German family.

Why couldn't she settle for this course herself? Whence came this flame that burned within her heart, this passion to strike out for a new frontier of knowledge, this restless gut-deep feeling to seek the truth?

Erika was now married to Ernst Faust and would soon move to Bern, where her husband had his business. Eva had become engaged to Seppli. In her journal Elisabeth wrote, "Seppli is the most beautiful, the cleanest, the most upright and most sensitive man I've ever met." Her absent brother, Ernst, also married, was now on his way to making a fortune. She alone was without the support or the prospect of a mate. As her father filled the wine glasses and called for a toast to her success in the Mature, Elisabeth felt an uncharacteristic temptation to follow the beaten path, the known way.

Although her mother had prepared a superb meal, and although the wine was from the best stock in the cellar, the atmosphere was never completely relaxed. Convivial phrases were exchanged, laughter punctuated anecdotes, but sudden silences indicated a barrier still remaining between the father and the eldest of his daughters. Only the traditional singing around the piano after dinner helped to ease the feeling of awkwardness and tension.

But if pride and obduracy had caused wounds too deep to be healed in one evening, Elisabeth's heaviness of spirit did not last long. In any case, her mood was less a melancholy than a time to catch her breath.

Since her father made no offer of financial assistance while she attended medical school—not that she expected him to do so; she was an adult as far as he was concerned, no matter how proud he was of her accomplishments—Elisabeth knew that she would have to stay on at the eye clinic. Professor Amsler immediately supported her proposal for a night-shift schedule. When she started her classes at the university, she could, he told her, work in the laboratory from four until ten o'clock and when necessary work on Saturdays. She could also make up time in her lunch hours and when she had free periods. The professor pointed out that many patients who had jobs might find it more convenient to be examined in the evenings and on Saturdays.

Although she did not immediately appreciate the fact, Elisabeth was about to enter the medical school of the University of Zurich during the school's most illustrious era. Almost all the departments were headed by men of international renown.

Professor Manfred Bleuler, whom Elisabeth had already met, was head of the department of psychiatry. The brilliant Professor Löffler headed up the department of medicine and Professor Fanconi was in charge of the famous children's hospital. Professor Schwartz, whom newspapers had named the "Swiss Sherlock Holmes" for his deductive skills, was the senior chairman of the department of forensic medicine. Professor Miescher was head of the department of dermatology. And of course there was Professor Amsler, whose research had broken new frontiers in ophthalmology.

However, it was to be another year or more before Elisabeth was to have these distinguished medical men for her mentors. Along with all students studying medicine, she was obliged first to pass the exam known as the First Propi. She must spend her first year studying physics, organic and inorganic chemistry, botany and zoology.

With the First Propi behind her, she would then work for two years studying anatomy, histology, physiology and pathology, and at the end of this period she would take the Second Propi. Then there would be four and a half years of clinical work before her final examination.

Elisabeth organized her new timetable. She rose at six, made herself a modest breakfast and reached the university by trolleybus at seven (eight in the winter) for her first lecture. At midday she ate a sandwich lunch (or occasionally went to the cafeteria) and hurried over to the clinic to work with patients for an hour. After school classes ended at five (four in the winter), she again hurried the few hundred yards to the clinic for additional appointments with patients and for writing her reports. She usually remained at the clinic until ten or eleven o'clock. She then caught a trolleybus to her lilliputian apartment, made a meal on her hotplate, and worked on her school studies. She usually studied until one in the morning, and felt she had indulged herself when she got more than five hours' sleep.

On weekends she was likely to spend most of Saturday at the clinic and then enjoy social activity on Saturday evenings (frequently one of Cilly's musical soirees). Sunday was the day when she could do her laundry, perhaps catch up with her school work, or go to the mountains.

It was a hectic schedule in which almost every minute counted. But in spite of a diet (most often snacks eaten when she had a spare moment) that defied every dietitian's rule book, she remained marvelously healthy and at a weight that was consistently within a few ounces of a hundred pounds.

All her expenses were covered by her small salary as a laboratory technician. The University of Zurich was heavily subsidized, and her school fees were minimal. She bought textbooks second- and third-hand, often for a few pennies. The only transportation she needed was a trolleybus, or a train on occasional trips to the mountains.

Her clothes were virtually limited to garments to cover her decently and in winter to keep her warm. She had no interest in them beyond the necessary. In summer she wore cotton print dresses, never possessing more than three at a time, and in winter her preference was for durable corduroy skirts and woolen sweaters she knitted herself. In her wardrobe closet (actually a misnomer, for it amounted to hooks and shelves alongside the sink in the hallway) she had slacks for the mountains, a raincoat and a heavy winter coat. She never wore a hat. Her two pairs of shoes were familiar to the cobbler down the street, and anyway, shoe leather was cheap.

Her social life improved, especially during school vacations. She got to know some of the young musicians who visited Cilly. Sebastian, a twenty-five-year-old pianist who had been a child prodigy and who had played in concerts in Vienna and Paris, fell mournfully in love with Elisabeth. If she had had time, she could have listened all day and half the night to his lyrical playing (he knew almost the complete pianoforte repertoires of Mozart and Chopin); but when he brought her love poems and billets-doux and sought her hand and shoulder, he was given no encouragement. His love for her was flatteringly reassuring, but he fell far short of having the qualities she might have looked for in steady male companionship even were she to have time to enjoy it.

Not only musicians came to the two rooms at the top of the apartment building. Zurich was a center for foreign students from a score of countries who had come to attend the university and technical colleges. Most of them were studying medicine, music, architecture or engineering, and most of them were impoverished. They were often lonely and depressed. By word of mouth on the campuses they discovered that, at least on weekends, they would find good company and a cheerful meal at the top of the ninety-six stairs on Seefeldstrasse.

Eighteen months after they had rented their rooms, Elisabeth and Cilly initiated a tradition of preparing at least one international meal a month for this cosmopolitan group. With inexpensive ingredients, they planned a Turkish meal, for instance, to which they invited Turkish students who did the cooking. The following month there might be a Norwegian dinner, or curry cooked by an Indian. Other dinners served in rotation included Polish, Russian, French and Austrian cuisines.

Because of her experience in cooking for the Volunteers, and because she thoroughly enjoyed cooking for large numbers, Elisabeth took on the major culinary responsibility. She rarely had to spend much time or money on marketing, because the students themselves brought most of the ingredients. It was rare to find a freeloader in their company.

If she felt that a meal might be enhanced by a good wine, she smuggled out a few bottles from her father's cellar. Since her father carefully and regularly inventoried his wine stock, he knew when bottles were missing and, she learned much later, guessed the name of the culprit. But he said nothing.

One special gain for Elisabeth from these international meals was her exposure to a broad spectrum of cultures, philosophies and politics. She and Cilly encouraged and often provoked their guests to be forthright, so that the restrained and courteous discussion in the earlier part of an evening invariably evolved into animated debate.

Music always played a part in the success of these evenings, as did the décor. Cushions were spread and candles lighted, and any student who played an instrument brought it along. When debates became too stormy, the students were invited to sing their national songs. The singing lasted into the small hours, and not infrequently the landlady would protest by banging the ceiling with a broomstick.

Looking back on these lively student get-togethers, Elisabeth acknowledges their role in offsetting the stress of her workaday week. The good company, relaxation, the music and laughter, proved the best mental therapy.

For her the mental therapy was serendipitous, but for many of the students it began to be planned. At first singly and then in larger numbers students came to the apartments not only for conviviality but to seek help with their personal problems. In her work in the darkened room at the eye clinic Elisabeth had found that many patients were ready to expose their souls—to talk about their fears, anger, guilt and grief. She had learned the art of listening and of counseling too. Now students with problems quickly recognized someone who empathized, and Elisabeth found herself listening to their difficulties and woes.

Cilly's fiancé was a postgraduate student specializing in psychiatry. He was able to call in friends who were psychiatrists and psychologists for those students who needed professional help. As the need arose, the Seefeldstrasse apartments became an improvised psychology clinic. The students—those who were lost, lonely, depressed and heartsore, and not infrequently suicidal—were never charged a fee for these expert consultations. The free psychology clinic lasted throughout Elizabeth's years at the medical school.

She took the First Propi in September, passing comfortably and gaining top marks in her favorite subject, chemistry.

The first year of medical school proper did not begin until March, so Elisabeth returned to a normal workaday schedule at the eye clinic. She spent much more time in the children's wards at the hospital and was sometimes given full responsibility for Professor Amsler's young patients.

Early in March she took a brief holiday in the mountains with a party that included Eva and Seppli. Watching Seppli skiing so superbly on the most precipitous slopes, and listening at night to his rich baritone voice, she realized that he possessed many of the best attributes of her father. But it was impossible to imagine Seppli behind a desk. She could only picture him, she told him in the wilderness, skiing, striding a high trail or, equipped with rope and pitons, scaling the faces of cliffs that no other climbers would dare to tackle.

Returning to the university in March, she registered and then spent her first hour in the medical school in some confusion. The first lecture was in anatomy. She assumed she had gone to the wrong auditorium, because all around her the students were speaking a foreign language. Puzzled, she got up from her seat in the front row and started to leave the room, but the tall arrogant professor called her back. What, he asked sarcastically, was this young woman doing upsetting his lecture? Elisabeth blushingly explained what she thought was her mistake. The professor sneered that if she was indeed a medical student, then he would agree that she had made an error, since young women could better spend their time studying homemaking, not medicine.

She soon discovered why the other students near her were talking a foreign tongue. They were a group of Israelis who made up about a third of the class. Switzerland had just concluded an agreement with the new Israeli government to teach their medical students because Israel had not at this time established preclinical classes.

Used to working rapidly, Elizabeth was often bored at the lectures. She took up the slack by helping to organize a drive by some Israeli students who were keen to raise funds for the more impecunious of their number.

For some reason the anatomy professor took strong exception to this extracurricular activity. The medical school, he insisted, was not to be used for charitable pursuits. When he learned that the Israeli student who was the prime organizer of the drive had defied his instructions to desist, he summarily ordered him expelled from the school.

Elisabeth fumed and, throwing caution to the wind, sent him a letter of protest. She demanded an interview, although several senior students warned her that she was risking expulsion, for Swiss professors have almost monarchal status and students tremble in their shadows.

When she entered the anatomy professor's office, he ignored her for about five minutes as he ostentatiously busied himself with papers on his desk. Eventually he looked up, frowning his contempt. He was seemingly taken completely off guard when Elisabeth launched her attack.

The Israeli students were not, she challenged, in any way interfering with the proper conduct of his class or the dignity of the university. The students who had organized the fund-raising drive, especially the student he was expelling, were moved solely by a desire to help their fellows. In deciding to become a physician, hadn't the professor himself solemnly pledged to give all possible aid within his skill and authority to his fellow man? In opening the Swiss medical schools to

162

foreign students, wasn't the Swiss government inspired by exactly the same motives as had prompted the fund-raising drive?

By the time she had finished, Elisabeth was panting, and her hands were white-knuckled as they gripped the desk. She had a sudden feeling that she had enacted this scene—or something so like it—before. She half expected the professor to react as her father would have done—to thunder for silence or to storm from the room. The professor did neither. He resorted to biting sarcasm.

Why didn't Elisabeth go back to her village and become a seamstress? Or perhaps her rhetoric would be effective in a fish market. He reiterated his contention that medicine was no profession for women. Women were too emotional, as Elisabeth had now clearly demonstrated.

He contemptuously waved her away and returned to his papers. Elisabeth lived through an anxious twenty-four hours in which she many times asked herself if she had thrown away all chances of becoming a physician. The first intimation that her protest had proved effective was when the Israeli student who had been expelled approached her, gleefully waving an envelope. He had received a note from the anatomy professor rescinding his expulsion order.

Elisabeth herself waited with a sinking heart for a letter bearing a different kind of message. But no expulsion order came. She had, however, made a powerful enemy in the medical school; and largely because of her continuing antipathy toward the professor she detested anatomy.

Some weeks later an incident in the anatomy class changed her life more radically. One morning the professor was late in arriving at the lecture hall filled with 150 restless students. To amuse themselves while they were waiting, she and a friend, Gerta, exchanged views, both caustic and flattering, about the male students. Elisabeth lightheartedly suggested that they pick out the men they would be most likely to marry.

Attractive Gerta giggled as she selected a tall blond Swiss student. Elisabeth's eyes then scanned the rows. Her eyes hovered and then sharp-focused on a handsome dark-haired man whose brown eyes, she thought, suggested both humor and serious intent. She pointed surreptitiously to her choice.

Both girls laughed. It had been only a game, and one surely to be forgotten as soon as the professor arrived. Elisabeth had no idea anyway who her chosen student was.

Some days later in the anatomy laboratory the medical students were allocated their cadavers. By design, the Swiss students were teamed up with foreigners, with five or six students assigned to each cadaver. Elisabeth found three American men in her group. She was surprised but not displeased to see that one of them was the handsome young man she had so casually pointed out in the lecture hall.

She now gave him a closer survey. Broad-shouldered, he stood about five feet eleven inches. He looked intelligent, a year or two older, or at least more sophisticated, than most of the men in the class. He caught her eye as she made her frank appraisal. She dropped her own eyes shyly.

The student smiled, put out his hand and with a New York accent said, "My name's Ross—Emanuel Ross."

16

The Man Who Came to Dinner

AN ANATOMY LABORATORY, with its shriveled cadavers stretched out on marble-topped tables, is not the most propitious setting for the development of friendship. But two hours a day spent dissecting human tissue, seeking the origins and insertions of muscles, and probing for blood vessels and nerves necessitated cooperative effort and communication between Elisabeth and Manny Ross. A major problem for Manny and for most of the other foreign students was their limited understanding of German. Elisabeth immediately found herself in her old role as interpreter.

In Swiss medical schools (as in most such schools in Europe) anatomy laboratories are accorded special sanctity, and the cadavers are treated with reverence. For students to speak much above a whisper comes close to sacrilege.

The three Americans (there were actually twenty-five Americans in the class) working with Elisabeth had been reared in homes and classrooms tolerating casual behavior. They were not aware that the smell

165

of formaldehyde in a Swiss anatomy laboratory was effectively the odor of sanctity. Elisabeth was horrified and alarmed by their casual conduct and their apparent flippancy.

While Manny himself was the reserved one of the trio, his two irrepressible colleagues, Bill Swemmer and Art Chemally, could not be restrained by Elisabeth's cautions. One morning she looked up over the cadaver to find them holding a length of human intestines and laughingly suggesting it would make a good jump rope! Before the professor's cold eyes could swivel in the direction of their table, Elisabeth snatched the intestines and stuffed them back in the cadaver.

This was only one of a number of similar incidents. Before long, as interpreter and self-appointed guardian of the Americans, Elisabeth gained their affection and gratitude—especially Manny's.

At first all three young men, and then Manny alone, paid their debt to her by taking her to the school cafeteria or occasionally to a cinema. Neither Manny nor Elisabeth sought anything beyond student companionship. In any event he was regularly taking out another Swiss girl, and both he and Elisabeth had set their goals. Both were studious and self-disciplined, and they had very little time for social contact. When they occasionally had an evening together, they enjoyed each other's company, and this in spite of, or perhaps because of, the difference in their personalities.

One evening about three months after they had first met, they went to a film together and then to a restaurant for coffee and pastries. Perhaps prompted by a medley of American tunes played by a palm court orchestra, Manny started to talk about his upbringing. He was born in Brooklyn, New York, the third child of poor Jewish parents who were both deaf mutes. His father had died when he was six years old, and he, his mother, his sister, who was four years older, and his beloved brother, Charles, eight years his senior, had moved down the street into the home of a taciturn uncle, almost as poor as his mother.

Manny's recollections of his early childhood were primarily memories of a silent home and extreme poverty. He was five years old before he received his first toy. His father had taken him to the hospital for a tonsillectomy and left him with a balloon in the shape of a tiger. A nurse admired the balloon and said she wanted to show it to her colleagues at the nursing station. She left the ward with his first and last gift from his father. He never saw it again.

He laughed as he recounted this childhood episode, but Elisabeth could see how deeply hurt he had been, and she told him of her own childhood trauma when she had been obliged to take her favorite bunny, Blackie, to the butcher.

Manny went on to relate how his brother had left high school early to enlist in the navy, mainly to help support the family. It was Charles who had insisted that Manny graduate from high school and who persuaded him to join the navy.

This was in 1946, and Manny had signed on for two years. He was assigned to Norfolk, Virginia, and served as a medical corpsman on an auxiliary repair ship that never raised anchor. His interest in the science of medicine and the patronage of a naval surgeon saved him from succumbing to boredom. On his discharge from the navy he took advantage of the GI Bill and entered New York University, graduating in 1951 with a BA in biology. He applied to a number of medical schools, but by then they were choked with World War II veterans, so on the advice of a close friend, and because he had studied German in high school, he applied to the University of Zurich. Zurich could accept him in March 1952.

He filled in the nine intervening months working as a waiter in a Florida hotel. Arriving in Zurich, he found accommodation in a pension near the university. In addition to the language problem, he admitted to Elisabeth, he had serious financial concerns. Funding under the GI Bill would run out in two years. His brother was sending him a small allowance every month. But he would probably have to go back to America and find summer vacation jobs to augment his budget.

Elisabeth and Manny continued to see each other in the classrooms, but, in a mutual understanding that did not need to be articulated, they made no serious effort to seek each other out when the classes were over. Anyway, on five afternoons a week Elisabeth gathered up her books after the last class of the day and ran straight to the eye clinic.

However, she and Manny were always aware of each other and exchanged smiles whenever they caught each other's glances. One Friday afternoon before a long weekend she impulsively invited him to join a skiing party. He had never skied, he told her. It was time to start, she retorted, laughing, if he was ever to understand the Swiss.

167

She borrowed her father's skis and boots and watched with amusement as Manny struggled on the slopes. Later Seppli was to become Manny's instructor, and in a very short time he was tackling the slopes for advanced skiers.

With the approach of the Second Propi examination, general student anxiety increased. Elisabeth herself was struggling with anatomy, essentially because she had no interest in the subject. For her, anatomy was largely a matter of memorizing names, and it made no demands upon her creativity. Her nemesis would be the examiner, and she was convinced he was unlikely to have forgotten her fiery defense of the Israeli student. However, squeaking through in anatomy, Elisabeth passed the Second Propi examination (as did Manny); then she joined her family on a summer holiday in the mountains. Her brother, Ernst, and his English wife were home on leave from India and spent a few days with them. She and Ernst now had little in common. She deeply resented what she called his "British colonial attitude" toward the Indians. Ernst, on his part, seemed to find little to interest him in her experiences with the Volunteers or in her student life.

However, for a few days Seppli brightened the family circle, and Erika's husband, Ernst Faust, arrived as well. Elisabeth was fascinated by the contrast in personalities between Erika's husband and Eva's fiancé. They presented, she realized, the different facets of her father's character—athletic Seppli, her father's love of the outdoors and of nature, and Ernst, her father's meticulous, logical and pragmatic traits and his strongly conservative attitudes.

Manny had returned to America, at the start of the university vacation having been offered through a friend well-paying jobs, first at a resort hotel in New Hampshire and then, in the late summer, at a hospital in the Bronx. In spite of the cost of the round-trip voyage, he was able to save nearly $2,000 toward the time when he would have to be self-supporting.

After her own vacation, Elisabeth returned to the eye clinic. She was impatient for the start of the fall semester, because at long last she would be at the feet of the giants, the renowned professors of the Zurich medical school, and be allowed to work with patients instead of cadavers.

When students begin their clinical studies in Swiss medical schools, they do not, as they do in medical schools in English-speaking countries, follow the teaching professors around hospital wards. In Switzerland almost all clinical teaching is given in lecture halls. A volunteer patient is brought to a dais, where his symptoms are discussed and diagnosis and treatment are debated.

The clinical lecturer would usually pick out students at random. To help them arrive at an accurate diagnosis, he would encourage them to ask the patient questions and to use, when necessary, a stethoscope.

The advantage of this demonstration method of teaching in an auditorium setting is that it allows every student to see the patient and hear the exchange. In the confined space surrounding a bed in a ward, only those students at the shoulder of the professor or teaching physician can be sure of what has transpired.

Elisabeth had her favorite subjects and her favorite professors. She was deeply impressed and influenced by Professor Manfred Bleuler, head of the department of psychiatry and an internationally famous figure. His seemingly infinite patience with psychotics reminded her of the extraordinary courtesy of Professor Amsler. But the classes she enjoyed most were conducted by Professor Schwartz, the head of the department of forensic medicine.

Professor Schwartz often handed out gruesome relics of a murder or suicide and significant pieces of tissue from a corpse. He advised the students that they now possessed all that they needed to deduce accurately how the victim had met his end.

What fascinated Elisabeth was the challenge of this scientific investigation. In a classic instance, the professor might present the students with tissue from lungs, liver and brain, and instruct them to find out whether the victim had been murdered or died from suicide or by accident. The solution might well be that the victim had been poisoned and then submerged in a bath by the murderer in an attempt to give the impression of accidental drowning.

Elisabeth surprised herself by proving to be the class super sleuth. She loved chemistry, and this kind of investigation usually demanded precise and delicate chemical analysis, as well as the keenest microscopic observations.

One afternoon after triumphantly coming up with the correct solution to an especially challenging case, Elisabeth impulsively told Professor Schwartz that she was ready to make a career of forensic medicine. Chuckling over her enthusiasm, he suggested that her deductive skills could be effectively used in any branch of medicine. Anyway, he added, there would be time enough for her to decide on her specialty.

But one specialty that she knew would never capture her interest was gynecology and obstetrics. Again it was a professor who provoked her antipathy. His aloof and grossly insensitive attitude toward his patients enraged and disgusted her.

Elisabeth's short fuse of tolerance was ignited on an afternoon when a fastidious, delicate middle-aged woman of her acquaintance was wheeled into the auditorium. Insofar as the professor was concerned, the patient might have been a tailor's dummy. Elisabeth appreciated that patients were needed for demonstrations, but felt they should retain their dignity as human beings. Instead, the professor permitted no fewer than forty of the students to make vaginal examinations.

Trembling with anger, Elisabeth stormed from the lecture hall and scribbled off a furious letter of protest to the insensitive professor. She suggested that he himself should volunteer to go to the auditorium's examining table and submit to a rectal examination by forty students!

Fortunately her temper cooled in the writing, and the letter was never mailed. If it had been, she knew she would almost certainly have been expelled. Once she was a physician, she would campaign against all those professors and physicians who failed to treat patients as sensitive human beings. She would wait.

She had known Manny Ross for more than two years, seeing more and more of him. In disposition they were polar opposites. Where she had mood swings which carried her to peaks of excitement and exhilaration, and to troughs of sadness and depression, he seemed to be even-keeled. Where her imagination raced and soared, he was stolid, practical, demanding proof and distrustful of intuition. If she was an Ariel and a rebel spirit, then Manny was earthbound. His ability to sit back and calmly evaluate a situation was a counterweight to her own impulsiveness.

The opportunity to introduce him to her parents came at Christmastime. She was distressed that Manny and his two friends would not be spending the holiday in a family setting. A week before Christmas she asked her parents if she could invite them to Christmas dinner.

It was a request that called for serious parental consideration, because in Switzerland, perhaps more than in any other country, Christmas dinner is traditionally an exclusively family affair.

Mrs. Kübler naturally deferred to her husband. Elisabeth had rather expected that her father, the traditionalist, would shake his head no; he had not been much impressed by other foreign students whom Elisabeth had from time to time brought to the house. However, perhaps because he had had little contact with Americans, or because he was touched by her plea, he agreed that his daughter could bring her student friends to the house on Christmas Day.

Mr. Kübler was always at his best as a host. He received the Americans as if they were royalty. Just before dinner he went to the cellar and exchanged the wine he had originally selected for the best vintage he possessed and a rare brandy. The convivial atmosphere at the table was like old times at Meilen, and Mrs. Kübler outdid herself in the kitchen.

Elisabeth marked with interest and some pride that her parents seemed to be specially drawn to Manny. Mr. Kübler appeared to be particularly impressed by his grasp of international affairs, but conversation ranged comfortably from politics to Picasso, from life in Brooklyn to Beethoven.

It had been a long while since Elisabeth had seen her father so animated. He found in Manny a sympathetic listener to his stories of mountain climbing.

What captured Mrs. Kübler was that while the two other guests lingered over their cigars and brandies, Manny offered to help with the dishwashing. While he stacked the plates, she told him that he was the first guest ever to make such an offer.

The evening stretched into the small hours, with Mr. Kübler introducing Manny and his friends to his library and stamp collection. It was obvious to Elisabeth that Manny relished being in a home of culture and comfort. She was impressed by his natural charm and courtesy. She found herself thinking of the time in the anatomy auditorium when she had pointed out the man she would choose to marry.

After the Americans had finally left the house, Mr. Kübler remained expansive. As he closed up his stamp albums, Elisabeth thanked him for entertaining her friends. He responded that he had much enjoyed their company and then added, "That young man Manny is by far the most admirable of all the young men you have brought to this home."

Elisabeth paused. She had not intended to indicate that Manny was a special friend, but she now said deliberately and evenly, "And just imagine he's a Jew!"

Her father had just struck a match to relight his cigar. He held the match poised until it died as he studied Elisabeth's bland expression. She guessed how his mind was running. Although her father had been firmly anti-fascist and never admitted to being anti-Semitic, she knew that he had no affection for Zurich's Jewish community, among whom were his principal business rivals. She guessed he was reading into her remark more than she had intended to convey. She guessed he was struggling to digest the prospect of an American Jewish son-in-law.

Mr. Kübler stood up, pushed the unlighted cigar into an ashtray and flicked out the desk lamp. His face was perhaps designedly in shadow when he said quietly, "You may bring that young man here whenever you like."

17

"You Are Now a Physician!"

ELISABETH SLEPT in the Kübler apartment that night, and at breakfast next morning her parents suggested that she close down her tiny apartment on Seefeldstrasse and move in with them. It would be a saving of expenses for her, they reasoned, and now that Erika was married and in her own house there was plenty of room. Eva too would be getting married soon, and then there would be three spare bedrooms.

The move back to the Kübler home was accomplished with some feelings of sadness over leaving an apartment that held such happy memories. It was, as she put it to Cilly, "like yielding up your own castle and kingdom." It was in this room that she had gained the landmark victory of total independence. It was essentially here, by candlelight, that she had gained the Mature—the first major advance toward the fulfillment of her dream.

At the medical school her studies progressed according to schedule, and in 1956 she began her penultimate year as a student. At the eye clinic Professor Amsler treated her as a professional colleague. Although he had not said as much, he seemed to be hoping and perhaps even assumed that when his technician was qualified as a physician she would make her career in ophthalmology.

However, Elisabeth resolved to live a day at a time and a month at a time. Certainly the future would take care of itself. In her head, if not so confidently in her heart, she knew there could be no shortcuts. She was on guard against diversions, but a growing affection for Manny made her defenses vulnerable. Manny now had an open invitation to the Kübler home and arrived unannounced for dinner two or three times a week, sometimes when Elisabeth wasn't home. He was treated by Mr. and Mrs. Kübler as a member of the family; so warmly was he received that Manny often laughingly spoke of Mrs. Kübler as "my mother-in-law." When Eva married Seppli in the chapel attended for generations by the family Manny was included in the bride's party.

With the approval of her parents, Manny and Elisabeth joined another couple on a ten-day vacation and drove down the west coast of Italy in a rented car. One of the main purposes of the trip was to visit Manny's brother, Charles, stationed at a naval base in Naples. On this trip Elisabeth shared with Manny her dream of practicing medicine in Africa. But he made it very clear that he would never consider being party to "such an impractical, romantic notion." No, he was going back to America, and nothing could dissuade him from this intention.

Not even marriage? she asked. He shook his head. Then if he refused to go to Africa, would he consider staying in Switzerland? They could establish a husband-wife practice in the country. She would never go to America—never, never. When he laughed at her passionate outburst, her resentment destroyed the moment of intimacy, and it wasn't until they arrived in Naples that her anger cooled.

It was Charles Ross who lifted her spirits. Physically he was like Manny, a little taller and heavier and, Elisabeth thought, very handsome in the uniform of a chief petty officer. He, his wife and their three young boys gave her and Manny a warm welcome, Charles seeming to assume that Elisabeth was already a sister-in-law. She understood why Manny almost worshiped his brother, and she came close to telling Charles about her own feelings, but something held her back—perhaps the thought that her fears about America would sound irrational and childish.

Meeting Charles weakened still further the barricade she had constructed to protect her independence and her resolve to fulfill her dream of a pioneering medical career. If only Manny would understand how deep-rooted were her convictions that there was a very special task for her to fulfill, and how impossible it was for her to link this task—undefined and nebulous though it remained—with permanent residence in what she contemptuously regarded as the world's most materialistic nation, she would be ready to marry him the next weekend. For there was no denying her love.

Meanwhile, she would wait for pointers. There had always been some promptings to help her reach conclusions, some intuitive nudging.

What seemed to be a signpost of sorts developed out of an appeal by Professor Amsler to come to the aid of one of his more unusual patients. An Indian youth had been sent to the Zurich Canton Hospital by a Swiss philanthropist who lived in New Delhi. The young man, who came from a remote village at the foot of the Himalayas, had been bitten in one eye by a rat. He had completely lost the sight of his eye, and sympathetic ophthalmia had developed in the other. He was completely withdrawn, blind and refusing food; and no one at the hospital had been able to communicate with him.

Elisabeth suggested that one of the Indian students at the university might be able to find out what was troubling the youth so deeply. With the professor's approval, she sought out a group of engineering students who had been to one of the apartment soirees. She took them to the patient's bedside, where a distraught nurse advised them that the youth had refused all nourishment for five days. The Indian was almost catatonic, but after he had been gently questioned in Urdu it seemed clear that the cause of his depression was abject loneliness.

Permission was obtained to induce the patient to eat by preparing an Indian meal. The students cooked curry and rice in the kitchen of their lodging house and brought the meal to the ward, where it was heated up. An aroma of turmeric and other spices permeated the whole floor. Suddenly the patient raised his head and sniffed. When

175

the curry was placed beside the bed, the youth dipped in his hand and devoured it.

Twice a day under Elisabeth's supervision the Indian students prepared familiar meals and brought them to the ward. The boy quickly regained strength, and although he remained almost completely blind, his spirit responded to this special care. When he was able to get out of bed, Elisabeth spent her lunch hours with him and wheeled him into the sunshine.

Shortly before the patient was discharged, when plans were being made to send him back to the care of a brother, a goodwill visit was paid to Switzerland by Jawaharlal Nehru, then Prime Minister of India, and his daughter, Indira Gandhi. Nehru was told of the successful struggle to save the Indian youth's life, and Elisabeth received an engraved invitation to attend an embassy reception in Bern. She phoned the embassy and was given sanction to bring with her the half dozen Indian students who had worked with her on the ward.

One of the students gave her a silk sari, so she was dressed for the part when she arrived at the embassy with her friends. Indira Gandhi spoke to Elisabeth about the urgent need for physicians in her country. Somebody as caring as Elisabeth, she suggested, would be sure to find a very fulfilling life in India. Nehru himself said some kind words to her too and readily signed a copy of his autobiography.

Before leaving the embassy reception, Elisabeth collected an armful of literature about India and the names of various groups who were taking modern medicine to Indian villages. It was glamorous reading; perhaps, she thought, it was not in Africa that she would find her holy grail but in India.

Impetuously she shared this new enthusiasm with Manny. She could try it out—go for six months perhaps or a year. It could be just the work she was looking for, the fulfilling of an urgent need. Just imagine, there were millions of people whose lives could be saved and extended by medical care. She would write him full reports of the work. She would yet convince him that practicing medicine in America would be dull and vapid compared with work in India, where the need was so great.

She pointed out that the timing of the opportunity seemed to be perfect. Manny was one semester (effectively one-half year) behind

176

Elisabeth, primarily because of his difficulty with the language. So there was no immediate need for him to come to a decision.

Manny had watched her closely while she had been speaking. When she paused for his reaction, he looked away, his forehead furrowed, his jaw working. He said in a flat, unemotional voice, "I had hoped very much to return to America with you." That was all.

After this exchange they avoided each other for several weeks. To deaden her own feelings, Elisabeth threw herself even more vigorously into her own work. She breezed through her clinical studies, and although textbooks bored her, she found that she could memorize clinical procedures almost photographically. She could remember not only the faces of patients she had seen eighteen months earlier but repeat almost verbatim the dialogues between patients and professors.

When, for instance, a professor asked her to describe the symptoms of multiple sclerosis, her mind visualized a Mrs. Schmidt, saw the green color of her eyes, the little scar on the side of her nose, remembered her hesitant speech, her expressed fear for the well-being of her family, recalled the way the woman's lips had trembled when she was asked to speak about her difficulties in managing the farmhouse. Because of this facility for almost total recall, Elisabeth rarely needed to refer to her notes, notes taken many months earlier. To the professor's questions she simply quoted the remembered dialogue and subsequent diagnostic conclusions.

In their senior year for short periods Swiss medical students are encouraged to take a full responsibility for general practices. These experiences are the equivalent of compulsory hospital internships in America. Opportunities for "locum tenens," as they are called in Europe, result from the annual drafting of Swiss male doctors for several weeks of military service. The students usually have some choice in selecting a locum tenens, either in urban or country practice.

In the fall of 1956 Elisabeth was ready to take on a temporary practice, and she naturally chose a country setting. Her practice was in Wäggithal, and it served seven small villages inhabited mostly by farm families and their Italian-speaking farmhands.

She arrived at the home of the local physician an hour before he was due to leave for military camp. He was a fairly young, enthusiastic man casually dressed in tweeds smelling of strong tobacco. He

177

quickly explained his primitive filing system and underscored the names of patients needing special attention. He demonstrated his ancient X-ray apparatus and showed her the dispensary where he prepared his medications, such as cough mixtures, suppositories and drug capsules. He also showed her his laboratory, where, he reminded her, her hospital experience would come in handy in testing blood and urine samples. Then, with minutes to spare before he had to leave for the train station, he nonchalantly introduced her to his only means of transportation for traveling around his widespread practice. It was a vintage motorcycle.

Elisabeth had never driven anything more sophisticated than a bicycle. She did not possess a driver's license. He dismissed this inexperience with a wave of his pipe. So long as she could kick-start the machine and knew the difference between throttle and brake, she would, he promised, be just fine.

Relishing the adventure of this new challenge, she mounted the machine, and was just mastering the art of changing gears when the office telephone rang. The doctor kissed his wife and four children goodbye and left Elisabeth to answer the phone. It was an emergency summons from the farthest of the seven villages. She strapped her medical bag to the motorcycle and set off toward the sunset.

The mist-cooled autumn air beating against her face carried the smell of burning leaves. The motorcycle was proving much easier to handle than she had expected. She was excited at the thought of visiting, unsupervised, her first Swiss patient. It was twilight by the time she saw the village silhouetted against the sky at the top of a very steep hill.

Not appreciating the power of the machine beneath her, she assumed that the only way she would be able to scale the hill was to tackle it at top speed. She turned the throttle hard over, and the evening air was filled with the sound of thunder.

What she had not observed was a large pothole in the middle of the hill. The motorcycle bucked like a mule. Elisabeth miraculously held on, but her medical bag was flung from the machine. Aware of something amiss, she turned her head. That was her second mistake. The motorcycle hit another pothole, this time throwing her into the dirt. The riderless machine then continued for another fifty yards and almost gained the top of the hill before collapsing with its wheels still spinning.

The village people had been advised on the phone that the new "young lady doctor" was on her way. Elisabeth was not aware of being watched by almost the whole community until she heard a roar of laughter. The villagers ran to pick her up and dust her off. They helped to collect and sort out instruments and vials scattered from her medical bag. A couple of men straightened the motorcycle's twisted handlebars. Then they led her to the patient, an elderly man suffering from angina and fearing another occlusion. The patient made no effort to conceal his initial alarm on seeing what appeared to be a schoolgirl with torn stockings and a bloodied chin.

The story of the mishap spread through the villages, and Elisabeth was thereafter treated with affection and shouts of encouragement whenever the sound of her motorcycle shattered the peace of the valleys. She herself had not been happier since her time in Poland. She allowed herself occasionally to dream of setting up her own country practice.

The best part of the day was the time for house calls. The village people were appreciative of the diminutive young woman who was ready if need be to sit with a patient through half the night. She soon learned to conserve time and distance by starting her house calls at the farthest village and working her way homeward.

Three patients were terminally ill, and she noted that their behavior and attitudes were quite different.

One was a wizened woman in her eighties who, though poorly educated, seemed to possess the wisdom of the ages. The woman was completely at peace as she talked with humor and pride about her grandchildren, about her husband, who had died thirty years earlier, and how she looked forward to meeting him again. The old woman knew she was dying; but living each moment, she became animated at the sight of the birds on her windowsill and the changing colors of the autumn landscape.

After an hour or so spent with her Elisabeth always felt refreshed. Although the patient had few material possessions, she seemed, as Elisabeth noted in her journal, "so full of riches."

Elisabeth found a completely different situation when she called on a man in his thirties, a blacksmith by profession, who was dying of lung cancer. He was angry and rude, and the family was particularly distressed as he even cursed God. On her first visits Elisabeth was uncomfortable with the blacksmith and distressed by his discourtesy and crudeness. Then she began to see that the intensity of the man's feelings came from his bitterness at being struck down in his prime. On her third visit she allowed the blacksmith to rage against his sickness and incapacity, and then said gently that she was trying to understand just how tough it was for him. Had he been struck with one of his own hammers, he could not have looked more amazed. Suddenly he burst into tears and poured out his soul. It was his wife and young children that he was concerned about. How, he asked, could there be a God of love out there, a God who would so cruelly deprive him of his strength and his future?

In subsequent visits the blacksmith's attitude was quite different. He had not gained the peace—the acceptance of death—achieved by the old woman, but he had moved much closer to it.

The third terminally ill patient was a teenage girl suffering from leukemia. She was in deep depression. Nothing Elisabeth said evoked any response. She realized finally that this patient did not want to talk, that she was in a state of grief, "preparatory grief for her own death," as Elisabeth was to phrase it later.

She continued to visit the girl and to sit silently with her. It was only through the pressure of the girl's pale hand that Elisabeth understood how much she appreciated not being deserted.

These times spent with terminally ill patients gave Elisabeth her first understanding of the different stages of death, and she stored the experiences in her mind. Recalling them later, she saw the three patients as her "thanatology kindergarten teachers." One lesson she learned was that a dying patient gained nothing from the stereotypical bedside manner, the jolly approach and hypocritical pleasantries: "How much better we're looking today!" and "We'll soon have you up and about again!" The eighty-year-old woman would, she was sure, have laughed at her had she said that, and the blacksmith might well have thrown her out of his house, while the teenager would have turned her back.

That Elisabeth was both young and a woman were factors not always appreciated. One evening when she was cleaning up the dispensary, she heard a car pull up and then the ring of the doorbell. A well-dressed man confronted her and asked immediately for the resident doctor. She explained his absence. The man became uncomfortable, shifting his feet and shaking his head. He seemed to be about to turn away when Elisabeth asked him his problem. He came, he said, from a distant village not within the boundaries of the practice. He had seen the doctor's name in the telephone book.

Puzzled, Elisabeth asked why he had traveled so far. After another awkward pause he told her that he had an infection in his private parts. He very reluctantly agreed to be examined. It was her first case of gonorrhea. Ashamed of his disease, the man had deliberately sought out a physician in a distant community. Elisabeth maintained a clinical expression as she made the examination and took a smear. The patient's only concern was that she should not report the disease to the health authorities, as the law prescribed. He was a man of political ambitions, and he feared such a report might get out. She promised that if he was honest about his contacts and reported regularly for shots of penicillin, she would not advise the health authorities. Satisfied that there was only one woman involved and that this woman could be advised by mail to go for treatment, she agreed to stretch the law. When the lab in the nearby town confirmed what she had already diagnosed as gonorrhea, her grateful patient turned up regularly for his shots.

Although the country practice kept her busy seven days a week from sunup to well after sundown, Elisabeth sorrowfully counted the days to the physician's return. Her only worry was that she was putting on so much weight. Thickly sweetened coffee was on the stove of every home she visited, and an apple pie was in every oven. She grew to love these country folk, and they apparently had full confidence in her, for soon the waiting room was barely big enough for the number of patients who arrived before 8:00 A.M. The younger women always came first, followed by grandparents and children; and then, giving the community's final stamp of approval to the young physician, the men arrived. The men demanded priority attention, as they had to go to work. When the town's physician returned, his patient roll was doubled.

She was to have other locum tenens experiences, but for excitement and enjoyment none could match her first.

Early in the new year Elisabeth began her final exams. Swiss students are examined individually over a period of six months on both the theory and practice of medicine. The exams cover the four years of clinical study, encompassing surgery, internal medicine, ophthalmology, diseases of the ear, nose and throat, gynecology, obstetrics, dermatology, neurology, psychiatry, cardiology, pediatrics, forensic medicine, orthopedics, and other subjects such as allergies and public health. Throughout the years of clinical studies, Swiss professors evaluate the personalities of their students. In the final assessment, when a student's graduation or failure is decided, as much store is put in character as in academic grades. The system aims at eliminating "commercial physicians"—those students pursuing a medical career for profit or because of its snob appeal.

Two subjects gave Elisabeth serious concern. These were obstetrics/gynecology and cardiology—the first two because of her continuing antipathy toward the teaching professor, and cardiology because the diagnosis and treatment were essentially technical and because she never could master the old-fashioned skills of auscultation (listening for body sounds).

The six months of examinations are a period of considerable stress, because until the last of the exams has been taken no indication is given of how a student is faring.

After being examined all day in internal medicine, Elisabeth felt particularly drained. Needing to unwind, she went to visit Eva and Seppli in their small rented apartment. She had not seen them in several weeks, and she knew they could always be counted on to cheer her up. She flopped into a chair in their living room and told them about the three patients in the examination room whom she had been instructed to "work up," and how she had coped with the professor's penetrating questions.

When Eva turned on a lamp, Elisabeth noticed that Seppli was looking pale and thin. She asked him how he was feeling, and he admitted to not having felt well for some time. He had, however, visited a physician, who had taken stomach X rays disclosing an ulcer. He was now on a strict diet and that was doubtless the reason why he had lost weight.

Ulcers? Seppli? It was absurd! Before leaving the apartment, Elisabeth took Eva aside and told her that there had to have been a misdiagnosis, for ulcers were caused primarily by worry, and Seppli's personality was the calmest in the world.

What then, asked Eva, could be wrong with her husband? Elisabeth had what she now calls "a flash of certainty, a sudden knowingness." She hesitated to share her conviction with Eva, but reflecting that she and her sisters had never concealed anything from one another she said quietly but firmly, "I believe Seppli has cancer."

Next day, with Eva's concurrence, Elisabeth got in touch with a prominent surgeon, a part-time professor at the university whom she greatly admired both for his professional skill and as a humanitarian. She explained why, in spite of the evidence of the X rays, she was not satisfied with the diagnosis. The professor agreed on the need for exploratory surgery. On Eva's urging, Elisabeth herself took Seppli to the hospital, and was astounded when the surgeon asked her to scrub up for surgery. She was, so far as she knew, the first student he had ever invited to assist him, and she was at the operating table when Seppli's stomach was opened up.

The surgery revealed that Seppli did indeed have an ulcer, but behind the ulcer, and not shown on the X rays, was a virulent, inoperable cancer. There was nothing to be done. Elisabeth phoned up Eva and said simply, "My diagnosis was right." Seppli was twenty-eight.

In shock and sorrow, Elisabeth herself experienced two of the stages of death she had seen in the dying patients during her country practice. She raged over the injustice of a mortal illness striking a man so young in whom she could find no fault, a soul she loved unconditionally. For a few days too she went through a period of "preparatory grief" for the inevitability of Seppli's death. In this period she withdrew into herself and sought no company.

She was grateful now for the pressures of her life. At night she continued to work at the eye clinic, and by day she faced the stress of final medical examinations. In some weeks there were two or three exams, then perhaps two weeks would pass before the next ordeal.

Her stress was compounded by a fresh surge of ambivalent feelings about marrying Manny. Playing her own devil's advocate, she raised or created reasons for not marrying him or not living in America. Derogatory stories about America published in the Swiss press reinforced her doubts.

She had met Americans whom she liked, the Quakers among them, but were they not the exceptions? What about the "ugly Americans" she had encountered? She recalled an incident in Frankfurt on the day she had been driven by the German physician from the hospital to the railroad station. On that drive she had seen a group of brash young GI's carelessly back their jeep onto a sidewalk and knock down an elderly woman. The woman had not been hurt, but her basket of vegetables had been scattered in the gutter. The young American soldiers had made no effort to help the woman. Indeed they had laughed and driven off. She remembered stories told by patients in the ward of the Frankfurt hospital—stories about young girls being bought for bars of chocolate by soldiers of the occupying army. Weren't these soldiers, and not the Quakers, the more genuine representatives of America?

She recalled another incident too, when she had been living at the Seefeldstrasse apartment. There had been a possible opportunity to visit America. She had applied for a visa and had been told to report to the office of the United States Foreign Service in Zurich, which was authorized to investigate applicants for visas.

At the agency she had found herself confronted by four dour men who, to her amazement, knew much about her personal life. They knew she had been behind the Iron Curtain and intimated that a young Swiss woman could hardly have escaped what they called political contamination.

It was the Joseph McCarthy period, and her inquisitors had obviously done their homework, for they knew about the student visitors to the apartment. Elisabeth protested that foreign students had simply been lonely, some of them hungry, most of them poor. Certainly, she admitted under questioning, they had discussed political and ideological issues, but these discussions did not make her a convert to communism.

The inquisitors demanded to know the names of the students who had gone to the apartment. Elisabeth refused to name them. The visa application had been turned down.

In the early fall of 1957 Elisabeth took the last of her medical exams. After the final oral test she waited in a hallway, along with half a dozen students still to be examined. Tension was high and no one talked. She felt no tension at all, merely an empty feeling, waiting for a door to open and for someone she barely knew to come out and tell her the outcome of her seven years of study.

There was one brief warm moment when Manny, on his way to class, looked around a corner and gave an encouraging wave. Then a tall, stooping gray-haired man entered the hallway and called her name. When she responded, he peered at her over his pince-nez. He referred to a white card in his hand and repeated her name. "Elisabeth Kübler?" A faint smile and an outstretched hand, cold and bony. "Congratulations! You are now a physician!"

18
Poems and Priorities

THE HAND of the university official was withdrawn, and its owner shuffled back to his office. The hallways suddenly emptied, and Elisabeth was quite alone. "Congratulations, you are now a physician." Was this really her moment of triumph? she asked herself. Was this what she had been struggling and striving for all these years? Her heart should be leaping. She should be shouting, crying, laughing. There should be someone to hug!

But the feelings wouldn't stir. She had felt like this on learning that she had passed the Mature. Another mountain had been climbed, another peak scaled; but beyond and piercing the mist were higher peaks. Would they always be there?

She walked slowly along the corridor, down a flight of stairs, out into the courtyard. Conscious of little flutters of guilt because she had not immediately sought out Manny or rushed to a phone to tell her parents of her success, she walked the few hundred yards to the eye clinic. The priority of the exams had made her late with her ophthalmology reports. She knocked first on Dr. Amsler's office door. Per-

186

haps he could stir those feelings she ought to be having. Dr. Amsler would talk about his special "little swallow" and ask what new migratory thoughts were occupying her mind.

But the professor wasn't there. He was probably at the medical school examining students.

Her own office at the eye clinic had recently been moved out of the basement to a newly added wing of the Canton Hospital. The lab had a small foyer with windows opening up to a view of a garden. She stood at the windows contemplating the garden ablaze with chrysanthemums. Just below her a gardener was sweeping the fall of leaves. She could, she thought, be completely happy tending a garden for the rest of her life.

She began to think of her childhood conviction that her life was meant to be spent as a researcher and explorer of untrodden frontiers of human knowledge—words she had written in her sixth-grade essay. She recalled other phrases she had written with such assurance: "I want to study life. I want to study the nature of man."

Turning her back reluctantly on the window and its autumnal view, she went to work for a while on the reports. But before she left the clinic that evening, she wrote a letter to the Indian medical group of which Indira Gandhi had spoken. She said that she was now qualified and ready to join them for a time.

Although she couldn't raise any real enthusiasm for the adventure, she thought that going to India would give her the time to think about her future, about marriage and the prospect of living in America. In any event, Manny would not graduate until the following summer.

After a brief holiday in the mountains—the first winter snow had fallen and the skiing was good—Elisabeth returned home to find a letter from the Indian medical group, headquartered at Sitapur, southeast of Delhi. The group was reorganizing, said the letter, and creating medical teams that would travel to outlying villages. They were delighted that Elisabeth was ready to volunteer her services. They would shortly send her money for a passage to Bombay.

Elisabeth began to get ready for the voyage. She gave away all her winter clothes and ski equipment. Within a few days she had reduced her possessions to what could be packed in a couple of suitcases.

When no follow-up letter arrived from India, she sent them a reply-paid cablegram saying that she was packed and ready to sail. Two days later she received the reply. The whole project had fallen through and the group could not after all make use of her services at this time.

Before showing the cablegram to Manny or to her parents, she went for a walk along the lakefront. She re-examined her motives and painfully acknowledged that in planning to go to India she had really been running away from the prospect of living in America. Yet how could the "new frontier" she had dreamed about since childhood possibly be found in the most technically advanced nation on earth?

There had to be an answer to this confusion. It came through an unexpected source. When she returned home, there was a visitor in the Kübler apartment. She was Betty Frankenthaler, an American nurse married to a Swiss businessman. The Frankenthalers, good friends, had been introduced to them through Manny. Betty invited both Elisabeth and Manny to dinner.

After the dinner, Elisabeth poured out her feelings, speaking of her deep concern about living in America. Finally Betty said softly, "So, Elisabeth, you are determined to work in a jungle?"

Elisabeth nodded vigorously.

"Then," said Betty more firmly, "why don't you work in the most savage jungle in the world? It's called New York!"

This was an entirely new thought. A jungle in America—a vast sprawling city where the stars and the sun were often concealed by smog, where the din of traffic never ceased, and where people lived in towering egg-box apartments! Somewhere deep in her heart the words struck a responsive chord. To go to such a jungle, with its values so foreign to her own, suddenly seemed the ultimate challenge.

Zurich's medical school had an office to advise students about job vacancies. The woman who ran the office checked Elisabeth's file and found a letter from the physician at Wäggithal, who paid glowing tribute to the manner in which she had handled his practice while he had been on military service. The woman told Elisabeth that only that morning her office had received an urgent plea from a country practice near Langenthal, about forty miles northeast of Bern. The letter, written by the young widow of the local physician, who had died very suddenly, said that her husband had been known locally as "Dr. Pestalozzi" because he never sent out bills to impoverished patients. The now untended practice badly needed another Pestalozzi.

The employment placement officer looked at Elisabeth over the top of the file and exclaimed, "Perhaps you're the new Pestalozzi!"

Elisabeth laughingly replied that that was the name her father had often given her. She could start at once, but there was one problem. The letter pointed out that the practice covered a large farming area and that it was essential for the new physician to be an experienced driver. Elisabeth bit her lip. She had never driven a car, still had no driver's license. However, this shortcoming could be remedied without delay.

After two hours of driving lessons, and against the advice of her instructor, she reported to Zurich's motor vehicle licensing office for a test. The stolid Swiss inspector was clearly ambivalent after Elisabeth had driven him for half an hour through busy streets. When he expressed his concern about her proficiency, she spoke up for the first time on her own behalf. Couldn't the inspector understand that a whole valleyful of patients near Langenthal was awaiting her arrival? Couldn't he understand that she would be driving in a district where the most serious hazards were likely to be a hay wagon or chickens crossing a country lane? The inspector issued her a license but growled that he was motivated in doing so by his hope that he would never again be obliged to sit beside her in a car when she was at the wheel.

The widespread Langenthal practice was no rest cure. Physically Elisabeth was as strong as she had ever been, and she exulted in her ability to cope with an eighteen-hour working day. In many ways, especially in the attitudes of patients and their gratitude for her ministrations, the practice was similar to her first locum tenens. She and the physician's young widow got along very well, and the most conservative of the country folk eventually put aside their concern over exchanging a beloved doctor for a newly qualified young woman who, as several reminded her, looked as if she should still be carrying schoolbooks.

At Christmastime she put up an OFFICE CLOSED sign and took a train to Zurich. At home she learned that Eva was away for Christmas and that Seppli was alone in a furnished room near the hospital where he was being treated. The thought of his loneliness, especially at this time of the year, appalled her. She went out at once and bought a small Christmas tree, candles and traditional Swiss tree ornaments.

She found him thin and frail—physically a shadow of his former self—but was amazed and overjoyed to see her. They hugged and laughed in the doorway of the bleak little room, but even helping to move the Christmas tree to the small hearth sapped all his strength. She made him rest in the only comfortable chair while she decorated the tree. Before sitting down, he took out his violin, and while she attached the tree ornaments he played Christmas music, reserving until she lighted the candles his playing of their favorite carol, "Silent Night."

It is this moment, with the candles lighted and during the hauntingly beautiful melody, that remains indelibly fixed in Elisabeth's mind and, as she now puts it, "seems to me to be suspended in time and space by threads of tranquillity and harmony."

In her heart she carried the beauty and peace of that evening back to her hectic practice at Langenthal. At the center of her calm was an inner assurance that her life was most caringly in charge and that she was moving, as if on the crest of a strong current, inexorably toward the destiny for which she had been born.

The prospect of marriage, with its inevitable sacrifice of total independence, no longer frightened her. She was confident that in due course she would be given the reason why she must go to America to live. Elisabeth does not now recall Manny's formal proposal or her acceptance. Marriage now seemed to be part of the unfolding of natural events. But their decision to be wed in a civil ceremony almost immediately had a very practical reason. The American Embassy advised Manny that it would take possibly three months for his wife to obtain a U.S. entry visa. A marriage certificate would be required well ahead of the sailing date.

In spite of Elisabeth's promise to her parents that she was prepared to have a formal wedding in the summer before she and Manny left for America, her mother insisted on a wedding banquet after the civil ceremony. Elisabeth protested in vain that she had hoped to take only half a day off from her practice for what was, after all, simply a registry office formality.

Resentfully she spent the morning of the day she married Manny in a beauty shop. The ceremony itself, held in a drab office in front of an official suffering from a heavy cold, could hardly have been less romantic. What makes the day memorable for Elisabeth was a downpour of rain that thoroughly soaked the wedding party and guests as they ran from their cars to a plush restaurant. Elisabeth was particularly glad to be able to wipe the smudged rouge and mascara from her face. Her costly hairdo was ruined. All formality was abandoned, and with the help of vintage Veuve Cliquot champagne the carefully planned program of toasts and speeches dissolved into a hilarious party.

A very special guest at the ceremony was Seppli. He had delayed his return to the hospital for this event. Although he was in obvious pain, his face remained radiant. The day after the ceremony he entered the hospital, knowing he would never walk in the outside world again.

Elisabeth hardly regarded herself as married. So far as she was concerned, she had merely signed papers to qualify for an American visa. Manny was totally occupied with studying for his final examinations, she with her Langenthal practice. He was, however, so confident of passing his exams that he applied to the Glen Cove Community Hospital on Long Island, New York, for internships for himself and his wife. Manny had originally planned to intern at the Bronx hospital where he had taken a vacation job, but sensitive to Elisabeth's antipathy toward city life, he chose the suburban appointments instead.

One morning a few weeks after the civil marriage, when her Langenthal waiting room was crammed with patients, Elisabeth received a telephone call from Seppli. Could she, he asked, come to see him as soon as possible? She had been stitching the leg wound of a child patient when the telephone had rung. She breathlessly explained the complications to Seppli, told him about the full waiting room, and said that she still had a dozen house calls to make. However, she added, she would make arrangements to leave the practice and take a train to Zurich on the weekend. Saturday was only three days away. It was a hurried phone call. The injured child on the examining couch was crying. There was hardly time to say goodbye.

Through the remainder of the day Elisabeth could not get her mind off Seppli. Thoughts of him intruded even while she was treating patients. As she drove into the countryside on her house calls, she reflected that he had never before asked her for anything. But except for Christmas and for the marriage ceremony she had not closed her practice for a single day. She must, she told herself, fulfill her proper responsibilities to her practice. Her reflections did not console her; her depression remained.

Next morning there was another telephone call from Zurich. It was Eva to say that Seppli had died in the small hours. Elisabeth experienced the greatest grief and guilt she had ever known.

On the spiritual level she had felt closer to Seppli than anyone else in her life. Now she would have given all she possessed to recall the lost opportunity to have been with him when he was dying, to have been with him when he most needed her.

She attempted to find excuses for not having gone to Seppli immediately, but finally accepted what she knew to be true—that there are some human priorities beyond all other claims, and that she should have been with Seppli when he died.

On the weekend, when she traveled to Zurich for the funeral, she was puzzled by the fact that although Seppli was a staunch Catholic the service was to be a Protestant one at the Küblers' family chapel. Eva explained why. Her husband had not been forgiven by his priest for marrying a Protestant. Seppli had even been denied the last rites and could not be buried in a Catholic cemetery.

Elisabeth's indignation helped to blunt her grief, for she had seen Seppli as a paragon of what a Christian should be. That his own priest had not recognized the qualities of the man hardened her heart against denominational religion.

Back at Langenthal, there were times when she felt Seppli was at her shoulder. Often she was almost physically conscious of his presence, especially when she was traveling in the country. He would, it seemed, urge her to stop the car and look at a sunset or examine the perfection of nature in the shape and color of a wildflower.

In such moving and unexpected moments Elisabeth started to write down free-flowing thoughts reflecting the sudden liftings of her spirit.

Typically, one evening while driving along a rutted country road to a distant farmhouse, she stopped at the sight of a cluster of wegwarte, the tiny blue flower that grows in such profusion in Switzerland. In her journal she wrote:

> I have a special affinity for the color of the wegwarte and the valorous way it defies the dirt and the dust. How appropriately it is named—a name that means "the one who waits at the roadside." The wegwarte seems to thrive in the driest places and blooms where there is little or no beauty all about. This brave flower never seems to wither, and surely blossoms solely for our joy!

On another day a gnarled and dying oak tree caught her eye and suggested to her a natural parable. In her journal she wrote:

> So like a monster in the half-light, this tree trunk reaching out its twisted arms against the skyline. How frightening it must seem to children, and yet within its aged and rough exterior it gives safe harbor to small birds. I suppose the way we see this dying tree depends less upon the tree's shape and light and shadow than it does on who we are. If fear dominates our lives, then we see only the sinister contorted limbs, and we fail to notice that tiny birds fly swiftly to the tree for shelter.

Captured by a blush of wild roses clinging to a farm fence, Elisabeth noted:

> Some will observe you as roses, some as spreading and thorned weed. But your beauty will be given proper tribute when a bee or butterfly touches your petals. Weeds can become roses when they are lovingly touched!

A sparrow that hopped to her bedroom windowsill provoked a tender memory of her childhood. She took her journal from the nightstand and wrote:

> Meisli [Little Sparrow] was what my father sometimes called me when he loved me as a unique and tiny creature of God. Recollection of those rare, especially loving moments with my father helps me to face the storms when they rage—memories that sustain me in those hours when no sparrow would dare to spread its wings.

At times when she wrote in her journal, it seemed as if the words were not her own—as if her hand were grasped, as if the thoughts came from elsewhere. It was then that she felt the nearness of Seppli,

193

or if not of him then of some presence, some guardian angel. Usually when she felt his closeness, she was in the sunlight, for in her mind she always saw Seppli out of doors, bronzed, graceful and daring.

An excerpt from her journal, a poem written while she was sitting in a splash of sunlight, reads in translation:

> Sun, my golden sun,
> Have we worshipped you in long gone days?
> Have we prayed to you in temples
> And sung to you in Inca times?
> Does the source of my love
> Stem from the Maya kingdom?
> Or Atlantis, or Egypt?
> Sun, my golden sun
> Whether you rise on a mountain
> Or sink into a lake
> My love for you is ancient, deep and true.

Elisabeth now thinks that these and other meditative journal entries written at this time suggest a period of emotional growth, of deepening spiritual consciousness. The rote learning required in the medical school, the pressures and hard driving demanded by her years of study had forced her to a tight-jawed determination to achieve. From time to time there had been chances to relax, brief weeks in which to ease the tension, but overall she had not dared to slacken. Nor, except with Seppli, had she ever fully shared her deep feeling of a special life mission, for she was sure that anyone less understanding of her nature would misinterpret her conviction.

In the late spring Elisabeth set about finding the right buyer for the Langenthal practice, not only for the sake of her patients but because she felt obligated to the widow of the "Pestalozzi."

Fulfilling her promise to her mother, she agreed to a religious wedding in the family chapel on June 3. Ten days before the date, a physician fitting the Pestalozzi mold signed a purchase agreement for the practice, and on the following day Manny was told he had passed his final medical examinations.

Events were moving along with such perfect timing and so without strain that Elisabeth noted in her journal her gratitude for "divine manipulation."

On the May morning when she was due to leave Langenthal for

194

home—the new physician having arrived and taken over her responsibilities—she glanced through her bedroom window to see a flight of geese arrowing toward the north. If the birds were migrating, she thought their flight was out of season. Perhaps, then, the geese were a sign that her own life was on course. She made a last Langenthal entry in her journal:

> How do these geese know when to fly to the sun? Who tells them the seasons? How do we, humans, know when it is time to move on? How do we know when to go? As with the migrant birds, so surely with us, there is a voice within, if only we would listen to it, that tells us so certainly when to go forth into the unknown.

With a few days to spare before her wedding and her departure, Elisabeth paid a visit to Meilen. It was not so much a sentimental journey as an opportunity to be alone for a while in an environment she loved. She walked down the main street of the village, nodded to acquaintances, greeted friends, smiled at strangers. She felt no hankering for bygone days, just gratitude for remembered joys, for disciplines and growth, but mostly for hopes generated here, and dreams that made life purposeful. She visited the Sundance Rock. A field-scented breeze winnowed her hair as she raised her arms Indian fashion and murmured a prayer of thankfulness.

At the hospital in Zurich, Professor Amsler and the nursing staff gave her a farewell party. For the first time since she had known him, the professor seemed ill at ease. She learned the reason for his agitation when he confessed to being troubled about what to give to Elisabeth as a parting gift. In the course of the party he darted from the room several times, always returning with gifts, ranging from leather-covered bottles of aged slivovitz to an ophthalmoscope that he himself had designed.

On her formal wedding day her sisters were her matrons of honor. She had her hair curled, but she turned down her mother's plea to apply makeup. When she was ready and dressed, her father embraced her with a warmth that she had not known since her childhood. She was, he assured her, marrying a good and reliable man who would care well for her.

She nodded agreement and held back tears. It was a very special moment shared between them.

Ernst had flown in for the wedding, and it was one of the last times that the whole Kübler family was together.

Just as most of her life had been untraditional, so was her honeymoon, because next day Mr. and Mrs. Kübler and Ernst traveled together with Elisabeth and Manny for a week at the world's fair in Brussels. Elisabeth recalls little of those seven days beyond her own impatience to be on her way to America.

Ernst left them in Brussels, but Mr. and Mrs. Kübler accompanied the newlyweds to Cherbourg, France. There Elisabeth and Manny boarded the liner *Liberté*, bound for New York. As they said their farewells at the top of the gangway, Mr. Kübler pinned to the lapel of Elisabeth's dress a corsage of wegwarte.

19

The New Immigrant

SHE WASN'T PHYSICALLY ILL, but Elisabeth soon discovered she was an indifferent sailor. The *Liberté*'s lavish menus had little appeal, and she had no inclination for deck tennis, at which Manny excelled, or for evening parties. But, having for years filled every minute of every hour, she found it hard to cope with shipboard idleness. In spite of her low spirits, she finally "adopted" two small children whose guardian had succumbed completely to the rolling Atlantic waves. She taught them the songs of the Swiss mountain men and introduced them to the guessing games she had played at Meilen. She hoped, she told Manny, that they would have at least six of their own.

In Zurich Manny had warned that New York at the end of June would almost certainly be steaming, so Elisabeth had packed only summer clothes in her cabin bags. The night before their arrival she pressed her favorite dress, a silk creation, sleeveless and floral-patterned; and because she wanted, for Manny's sake, to make the best possible impression on his relatives, she spent an unusually long time setting her hair, a cosmetic chore that she always detested.

On the last night at sea she had such a vivid dream that she shared it with Manny. She was dressed as an Indian squaw, riding a horse across scrub desert country dotted by cactus and strangely shaped rocks. The sun was beating down on her. The horizon was vast, and she was quite alone but so marvelously content that, as she told Manny, she had a sense of "sort of coming home."

Grinning, Manny told her to put aside romantic notions of America; unfortunately he had not been able to arrange for Indians to meet them at the dock. She would have to be content with the local natives, including his kin and loquacious cab drivers; and, he added, if she wanted to see the fabulous New York skyline lit by the rising sun, they would have to get up to the top deck immediately.

However, there was neither sunrise nor skyline as the liner steamed toward the Hudson River. It was the start of the coldest and wettest June day recorded in New York in a quarter of a century. Even the Statue of Liberty was invisible.

Manny and Elisabeth were the last passengers to be cleared by customs. By the time all their crates, trunks and suitcases had been inspected, it was after one o'clock. They had had nothing to eat since dawn and were separated from Manny's relatives by a security fence. The suspicions of one of the customs officers had been aroused when he discovered some morphine ampuls in Elisabeth's medical case. She had been given no warning that medicinal morphine, legal in Europe, was contraband in America. A further delay was caused when other officials arrived and rechecked all their baggage with a Geiger counter.

When Manny eventually introduced his bride to his deaf-mute mother, his uncle Anschel and his sister and her husband, Elisabeth's hair hung as limp as seaweed, her dress was wrinkled and her shoes were black with dockside oil. Under the critical gaze of the relatives she knew she looked awful, and she felt as bad as she looked. She had hoped so much that Manny's brother, Charles, would be there. As an old friend, he would have been an instant ally. Now, while everyone fussed over Manny, she watched and listened. She liked the two men—Uncle Anschel, small, wiry, quiet and a "park-bench philosopher," as she later described him in a letter home; and Manny's brother-in-law, Milton Arnold, a dentist, whose handshake and greeting had been genuinely warm and solicitous. She could not understand her mother-in-law, who spoke in the toneless manner of the born deaf, and she took an immediate dislike to her sister-in-law, to whose Long Island home they were now driven.

The house was ornately furnished, so heavily draped that she felt shut in. A lavish welcoming dinner, delayed by the problems at the dock, was on the dining-room table. When they sat down, Elisabeth was asked if she would like anything to drink. Because she was chilled and felt an outsider, she would have loved a brandy, but in the hope of making a good impression she blithely asked for a glass of milk.

Conversation died in mid-sentence, and Manny kicked her shin under the table. But only when her sister-in-law returned from the kitchen holding the glass of milk as if it were a long-dead fish did Elisabeth realize her faux pas. By asking for milk at a strictly kosher meal, she lost whatever credit she had possessed.

She and Manny remained at his sister's house for a difficult week, the tension relieved only when Manny took her on sightseeing tours of New York. They also hunted for an apartment near the Glen Cove Community Hospital, where both of them were due to start their obligatory year of internship. Their principal concern was to find a place they could afford on their joint income of $205 a month. Finally they noticed a FOR RENT sign in the window of a house on a quiet tree-lined side street within a quarter of a mile of the hospital. The owner, big-bosomed, beaming Austrian-reared Mrs. Fischer, welcomed them with the broadest smile and showed them a pleasant furnished room on the first floor overlooking a lovely walled garden. Elisabeth pronounced the apartment, which had a neat kitchenette and tiny bathroom, perfect, although the rent of $100 a month would leave them little more than $100 a month for food, transportation, laundry and anything they might need. As he tested the springs of the pull-out bed, Manny worriedly asked Elisabeth if they could really live on four dollars a day. She had once, she reminded him, survived on pennies. Four dollars a day would be plenty. Besides, she added, as she pointed to the garden, they could grow all their own vegetables. Little did she know the pressures of an American internship. There would never be enough hours for adequate sleep, let alone pastimes.

The Glen Cove Community Hospital, a fairly typical suburban

hospital of 350 beds, had seven interns, and on the recommendation of the administration, it was agreed that Elisabeth and Manny, being one of two married couples, should work together on alternate weekends, when they would have full responsibility for the entire hospital. From Monday through Friday all interns were on duty for ten-hour shifts.

They coped well enough through the weekdays, but on their working weekends, which began on Friday morning and ended on Monday evening, they counted themselves lucky if they managed six hours' sleep. With the whole hospital in their charge from Fridays at 5:00 P.M. until Mondays at 9:00 A.M., they tried to divide the wards and the hours between them. But their loose arrangements went by the board when, as often happened, an ambulance pulled up at the emergency room just as a baby was being delivered in the maternity wing or an elderly patient suffered a cardiac arrest.

Whenever Elisabeth had a choice, she chose duty in the emergency room. On Saturday nights in particular, when the ambulances backed up the ramp and unloaded the shocked and mutilated victims of road wrecks and assaults, she found her fatigue lifted as her adrenaline flowed. She discovered that she enjoyed surgery and was capable of making cool and quick life-and-death decisions.

But where she felt she had a special gift was where the need was greatest. Patients arriving in screaming ambulances were invariably terrified and confused. Pain—even the pain of broken limbs and gunshot wounds—was usually the lesser problem. It was fear that seized the victims—fear of death, fear for their families, fear of losing their jobs, fear about such simple domestic issues as who was going to feed the baby. So while she stanched hemorrhages and sutured wounds and administered analgesics, Elisabeth talked to the frightened casualties—and listened too. When she touched a cheek or held a hand and assured them all was going to be all right, she saw the fear retreat. She wondered sometimes whether her foreign accent helped. A smile always did, a smile of confidence and empathy.

Elisabeth's first impressions of America were mostly negative. Later she could appreciate that many of her feelings stemmed largely from cultural shock and different values, but initially she was often appalled.

200

She was especially shocked, for instance, by the casual attitudes and behavior of the Glen Cove medical staff. Swiss nurses with whom she had worked were, by and large, as dedicated as nuns, middle-aged vestal virgins wed to the healing arts. But at Glen Cove the nurses looked like Hollywood starlets in white uniforms. She could not conceive that the glamorous young women with their perfume, lipstick, enameled fingernails, their chatter about boy friends, tennis and movies, could possibly be as competent and reliable as the seemingly sexless nurses in her homeland.

The physicians she divided into two groups—the pompous and the playboys. After she witnessed a surgeon flirting with a nurse while performing an operation, she swore to Manny that if she ever had appendicitis or even needed to have a toenail removed, he was to pawn everything they possessed and fly her back to Zurich.

However, after a few months of working at Glen Cove, she was obliged to acknowledge, albeit at first reluctantly, that the efficiency of the glamorous nurses and the competence of most of the doctors matched the professional capabilities of the medical staff in Zurich.

Elisabeth and Manny had very little time for social activity, but they occasionally accepted invitations to cocktail parties. She hated them. In a letter to Erika she wrote:

> The cocktail party is the most barbaric of American rituals. You find yourself pushed into the corner of a crowded room where you are expected to sip a perfectly foul drink and eat tiny artificially flavored sausages off toothpicks while having to listen to a neurotic woman tell you how she has fallen in love with her therapist. It's a world I don't know. ... Life is made more complicated by my failure to understand idiomatic English. Last evening I spent ten minutes trying to understand what a nurse was talking about when she invited me to attend a baby shower! Why should I want to look at a bathroom constructed for infants? It turns out that a baby shower is a gift party for a pregnant woman.

A more amusing linguistic misunderstanding, and one that proved hard to live down, occurred one day when she was assisting at surgery. Disapproving of the flirtatious dialogue between the instrument nurse, one of the "Hollywood starlets," and the surgeon, she nudged the nurse out of the way and took over responsibility for passing the instruments to the doctor. Unexpectedly, the patient started to hemorrhage. The surgeon peered into the open wound and shouted, "Shit!"

Elisabeth searched the instrument tray, spread her hands in perplexity and innocently asked, "Which one is shit?"

The operating theater exploded in laughter. No one volunteered to explain the cause of the hilarity, and when that night she related the incident to Manny, he laughed himself off the bed.

Yet it was perhaps this incident, or at least this one as much as any—for it was related all through the hospital—that helped break down the barrier of mutual suspicion between herself and the medical staff, who had interpreted her shyness, coupled with her initial judgmental attitudes, as aloofness.

She and Manny had quickly gained respect for their professional competence. In fact Elisabeth had been aware almost from their arrival that the nurses always paged Manny or herself whenever they had a special problem or needed extra help. But the laughter over what Manny lightly called Elisabeth's "banana skin episodes" now gained her affection as well.

What won over the nursing staff even more surely was Elisabeth's care for a senior forty-year-old nurse who, after having her first baby, developed septicemia. As the nurse grew worse, Elisabeth took every opportunity to sit with her. On the day she died, it was for Elisabeth she asked. The nurse was a woman much loved by her peers, and the staff was grateful for the sustaining and sustained presence of their young Swiss intern at her deathbed.

At Christmastime a wave of nostalgia swept over Elisabeth. To her family she sent hand-knitted sweaters and scarves, and in a letter to her mother she wrote:

> How horrified you'd be by America's commercialization of Christmas. You cannot believe how hideous are the flashing electric lights they use to decorate their houses, and the plastic Christmas trees—oh God! I plan to decorate our tree with real candles and homemade ornaments. ... Christmas here seems to be an opportunity to bully people into buying presents they cannot afford. In this neighborhood the kids are so greedy and demanding! They're smothered with more toys than we received all through our childhood. Manny and I will be on duty on Christmas day, and perhaps that is just as well.

Living hand to mouth on their pittances, all Elisabeth and Manny could afford for dinner at eight o'clock on Christmas night was a couple of steaks and a bottle of cheap wine. Because she was so exhausted and because Christmas in Switzerland (with the one exception at Romilly) had always been associated with what she called "old-fashioned happiness," Elisabeth's spirit ebbed to the point where she seriously thought of fleeing America. Her dark and desperate mood continued into the following day.

Then at the hospital the woman in charge of the medical library noticed Elisabeth's dejection and inquired about its cause. Elisabeth told of her woes—her homesickness and fatigue, her yearning for the Yuletide spirit. The librarian listened sympathetically to the outpouring of feelings, and then invited the two doctors Ross to be her guests at dinner that night.

The meal was quite elaborate, and included homemade strudels. The librarian and her husband were warmly welcoming, and, to Elisabeth's amazement and delight, the Christmas tree was lighted up with real candles.

In her next letter home, she wrote, "Without that real Christmas tree and without the wonderful caring and sharing of our new friends, I really believe I could not have faced the New Year. . . . In the darkest night I found my little candle."

Two or three times a month Elisabeth and Manny visited with Manny's relatives, occasionally at the Long Island home of his sister, more often in the modest Brooklyn apartment of his mother and Uncle Anschel. If these visits often were difficult for Elisabeth, the young couple were grateful for the nourishing meals that invariably were part of them. Elisabeth had too little "free" time to shop economically or to cook.

Fatigue was her constant companion; and indeed her principal memory of her year at Glen Cove Community Hospital is one of bone-deep weariness, the like of which she had not experienced even at Romilly. In the new year, a grateful patient who had theatrical connections gave Elisabeth and Manny expensive tickets to a long-sold-out performance by the Bolshoi Ballet. They dressed for the occasion and drove to New York. Elisabeth vaguely remembers seeing the opening curtain, but her next memory is of Manny awakening her. She slept through the whole performance.

In the new year too she had to decide what she would do in July, when their internships ended. Manny had already decided. Although he loved his patients and had a good rapport with them, he was not interested in private practice. He was so meticulous that he would spend an hour with a patient whom Elisabeth could handle in five or ten minutes. Where she was intuitive, he was painstaking and logical, at his best with a microscope; indeed, in Zurich he had proved himself better at pathology and histology than anyone else in the class.

Manny decided firmly that his forte was pathology, and since Montefiore Hospital in the Bronx had a renowned neuropathology department, headed by perhaps the leading American neuropathologist, Professor Harry Zimmerman, it was Montefiore that was his first choice for a residency.

Elisabeth was tempted to aim for a general practice. There would, she reasoned, be little difficulty in opening such a practice wherever Manny eventually found a position as a pathologist. The immediate issue, then, was what she should do to prepare while Manny was fulfilling his three years of specialist residency.

An incident in a children's ward at the Glen Cove hospital helped to bring her to a decision. She happened to be on the ward when a mother arrived at the bedside of a convalescent child. The small boy, sulky and spoiled, gave her no greeting but immediately whined that he had not been brought a present. Appalled, Elisabeth watched as the child-battered mother scurried to the hospital gift shop and returned apologetically with an outsize teddy bear.

Elisabeth realized that she disliked these overindulged children, whom she described to Manny as "the most deprived minority" she had ever encountered, so cushioned and cosseted were they against reality. But how, then, could she think of going into general practice, where a large proportion of her patients were likely to be members of this "deprived minority"? If she were going to have to cope with spoiled brats, she would have to overcome her antipathy, work closely with children, and perhaps find a few answers for them and their parents. As a necessary preparation for general practice, then, she should specialize in pediatrics.

Her supervisor at Glen Cove suggested she apply for a residency at New York's Columbia Presbyterian Medical Center with its famous "Babies Hospital," although he cautioned that her chances were very slim, since the hospital was besieged by applicants. There were only about twenty available pediatric residencies offered each year, and foreigners were likely to be shuffled to the bottom of the list.

Undaunted, Elisabeth sent in her application and was summoned for an interview. Behind the desk was not the supercilious administrator she had expected, but a kindly, grandfatherly physician, Dr. Patrick O'Neil, who was chairman of the hospital's medical board. She immediately felt at home with him, and they talked together for two hours about many things, including her relief work in Europe.

Elisabeth's frank admission that she could not tolerate the behavior of American children amused him. It was the first time in his memory, he told her, that anyone had admitted to choosing pediatrics for such a negative reason. Toward the end of the interview he advised her that since residents would be on duty every second night for two years and since the residency was extremely demanding, the hospital had ruled that pregnancy was a disqualification. She told Dr. O'Neil that she and her husband were not planning to have children in the foreseeable future.

On her train journey back to Long Island, Elisabeth was elated, confident that she had gained the residency despite the fact that she was a foreigner and not a graduate of an American medical school.

As she waited anxiously for word, Manny's letter of acceptance from Montefiore arrived. He would begin his pathology residency in July. Still she waited. Finally the slim envelope arrived, on one of the off-duty days, when they were about to begin an eleven o'clock breakfast. Elisabeth slit open the envelope and excitedly waved the acceptance letter under Manny's nose. So much for gloomy prophecies!

Then suddenly she was overwhelmed by nausea. It was excitement, of course, she told Manny. Or perhaps the dubious fish they had had last night.

But the same nausea hit the next morning as she was getting out of bed, and on the day after that. To rule out a possible pregnancy, Elisabeth had a frog test. The results were positive.

Before writing to Dr. O'Neil to decline the appointment, Elisabeth spent a long time sucking her pen. After all, it would be another three months before it would be obvious that she was pregnant. Surely Columbia Presbyterian wouldn't expel her once she was enrolled.

But at the thought of the kindly old physician, who must have pleaded her case to gain her acceptance ahead of the American applicants, her conscience pricked her. He had trusted her; she could not let him down. She wrote to ask him if she could see him.

At their second meeting Dr. O'Neil sadly shook his head. Grateful as he was that she had leveled with him, there was no way he could waive the rules. He could only promise that he would see to it that she was granted the coveted residency again the following year.

But it wasn't the following year that concerned her. What was she going to do when her internship ended in June? With a baby on the way, she and Manny would not be able to live on his salary alone. She needed a job, and she needed it quickly.

It was Manny who pointed out that the only place where she might hope to gain a residency on such short notice was in a state hospital—a public mental institution—considered the least desirable place for even psychiatric residencies by America's young doctors.

Among the testimonials she had brought from Switzerland was a letter from her professor of psychiatry at Zurich, Dr. Manfred Bleuler. Armed with this letter she went for an interview at Manhattan State Hospital, a huge ugly prisonlike building on Ward's Island.

She was as unimpressed by the dispassionate man who interviewed her as she was by the building and its environment. However, before she left the hospital she was told that she could take up a research fellowship beginning in July. She was not sure what the job entailed. There would be time enough, said the physician, to explain the work when she reported for duty. The salary would be $400 a month.

On Elisabeth's return to Glen Cove, she found Manny beaming at her from the driver's seat of a shiny new turquoise Impala convertible. He opened the passenger door and invited her to come for a drive. He laughed off her anxious inquiries about the car's cost. Physicians, he assured her, were considered the best credit risks. Besides, he was not going to have his pregnant wife running for trains. With two salaries it would be easy to pay off the car over the next thirty months.

Stifling her doubts, Elizabeth accepted the job at Manhattan State. With both of them now assured of jobs in New York, they went to look for a new home more convenient to their new places of work. They located a one-room ground-floor apartment on East 96th Street in New York City. It wasn't the place Elisabeth had dreamed about, but at least it had a garden. It was bleak and barren when they first looked at it, but one day the following weekend Elisabeth hauled in a load of topsoil from Long Island and planted the seeds of vegetables and flowers. A garden, she told Manny, who was amused by her industry, was her only guarantee of survival if she had to live in New York City.

Perhaps because she had overexercised in planting the seeds and in lifting shovels of soil, or perhaps because she was simply overtired from working at the hospital for up to eighty hours a week, two days afterward she nearly fainted in the operating theater. An hour later she herself was a patient in the Glen Cove maternity ward—the reason, a miscarriage.

Her sadness was deepened by the calls to mothers over the public address system to "prepare to feed your babies," and she returned home to Mrs. Fischer's house only to learn that Mrs. Fischer's daughter had come to stay with her own newborn baby. That night, when Elisabeth heard the cry of the baby from the room across the hallway, she sobbed into her pillow. It was to be a long time before her grief left her. And only years later was she to understand and accept how the advent of an infant that never drew breath played a critical role in her career, preventing her from becoming a pediatrician or, perhaps, from going into general practice, and instead directing her to psychiatric research.

An annual valedictory custom at the Glen Cove hospital was for both patients and staff to vote for the year's best interns. Elisabeth and Manny jointly received the highest number of votes. However, the senior medical and administrative staff claimed veto rights, and on the excuse that the honor was instituted and reserved specifically for American graduates, the award was given to the third-placed intern, an American trained in the U.S. Only when many nurses and patients protested, was an attempt made by the senior staff to salve consciences by giving Elisabeth and Manny letters of "the very highest recommendation."

Because their internships ended on this sour note, Elisabeth and Manny emptied their hospital lockers without regret and, after making the rounds of all the wards to say goodbye, returned to Mrs. Fischer's house. The kindly landlady had prepared a special Viennese dinner, but the celebration was dampened by a penciled letter that had arrived that day from Mr. Kübler. He was hospitalized with a pulmonary embolism and close, he felt, to his end; he desired nothing more fervently than to see Elisabeth and Manny.

That night when they went to bed, they agreed they had to go. Elisabeth recalls gratefully how Manny unhesitatingly proposed to sell his treasured Impala convertible to pay for the tickets. Within forty-eight hours the car was sold, the airline tickets bought, and they were on their way to Zurich.

At the airport Erika and Eva told them that as soon as Mr. Kübler had been given the news of their coming, he had started to recover. In fact, when they arrived at the hospital he was out of bed, and a few days later he was once again presiding over his own dining-room table.

Elizabeth spent many hours alone with her father. Though he was eager to know details of life in America, he often turned the conversation to religion and philosophy. She was aware that he was earnestly seeking answers to questions about the meaning of life, and that he was not happy about the narrow, exclusive dogma of his own church. She bought him books—a volume by the theologian Paul Tillich; *Exodus* by Leon Uris; the works of the Indian philosopher-poet, Rabindranath Tagore. She herself, she told him, was also searching and she had found these books helpful.

One day Elisabeth told her father how Manny had sold his car to raise the money for the air tickets. Mr. Kübler, deeply touched, struggled to find words. He was alive, he insisted, because she had come to him. If only she and Manny lived in Zurich, then surely he would live to be a centenarian! Even as he spoke, she knew it would never be. There was no going back. She could only promise that if ever he really needed her she would come to him.

When they returned to New York and moved into their new apartment on East 96th Street, New York was hot and sticky. Manny talked nostalgically of the clean air of Switzerland. Laughing, Elizabeth reminded him that this was, after all, his jungle.

It was she, however, who was about to enter the jungle's depths.

The Kübler triplets on their first birthday, July 8, 1927

Dressed for the festival of Sechseläuten, in Zurich, marking the end of winter

The Kübler family on skis, when the triplets were eight. It was rare for Erika (next to her father), frailer than her sisters, to join such outings.

Elisabeth in Belgium,
hard at work hoeing

On the boat from Sweden to Poland, Elisabeth meets four physicians, each of whom comes from a different East European country

Patients young and old wait for treatment at the impromptu "clinic" in Lucima, Poland (1947)

With the Gypsy woman, in the Russian border town of Bialystok, on the way home from Poland (1947)

Elisabeth with her friend Cilly Hofmeyr, with whom she shared her
first home away from home after her father banished her from the
Kübler house

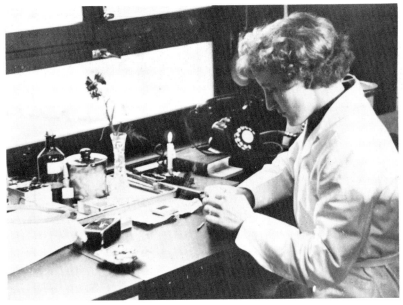

At work by candlelight in her beloved darkroom laboratory in
Professor Amsler's clinic-hospital

Seppli Bucher, Eva's husband, a year before his death in 1958. "He is the most upright and sensitive man I've ever met."

Medical student Manny Ross, soon after he and Elisabeth met

Off on a house call, as a young locum tenens in a Swiss country practice

Elisabeth's wedding dinner (1958). Professor and Mrs. Amsler beam at her.

Young interns Elisabeth and Manny Ross (right) with colleagues at the Glen Cove Community Hospital (1958)

Kenneth Ross, a few days old, with his parents in their Bronx apartment

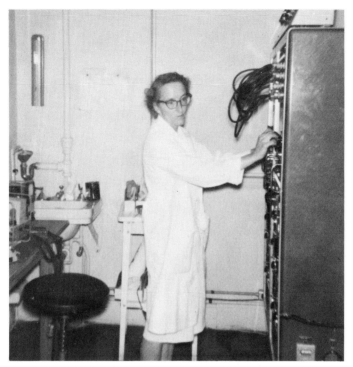

Elisabeth at work in Dr. Sydney Margolin's psychophysiology laboratory in Denver

Barbara and Kenneth wait at the Marynook railroad station for their mother to come home from work. This was their first home in Chicago.

The Rosses take Mrs. Kübler on a trip across the United States

Work with the dying. Elisabeth talks with young leukemia patient Eva behind a one-way window. *(Leonard McCombe, Life Magazine © 1968, Time, Inc.)*

Elisabeth today, at Shanti Nilaya *(Anne Ring)*

20

Into the Jungle

ON THE FIRST MONDAY of July 1959, Elisabeth rose before dawn, watered her garden, fed a crust of bread to some sparrows and brewed two mugs of coffee. She took the mugs to the bed, where Manny calmly glanced at his watch. Why so early? he asked her. They could have had another hour's sleep.

Not on this day, she responded, puzzled that he wasn't as excited as she about starting their new jobs. Ninety minutes later they went their separate ways—Manny to Montefiore Hospital in the Bronx and Elisabeth to Ward's Island and the forbidding fortress that was Manhattan State.

The place reminded her of Maidanek concentration camp, and she referred to it in her journal as "a nightmare of bedlam."

She had come to America expecting to find the world's most advanced medical care, a blend of the best of technology and the healing arts. What she found was an institution that seemed to belong to an earlier century—"a place where," she recorded, "the mentally sick are often treated like animals, freaks or human guinea pigs."

One of the unit chiefs, a middle-aged balding man with a deeply lined face, a voice that trailed incomplete sentences and a smoker's cough, gave her a hurried tour. He pointed out the administration offices at the center of the institution, the laboratories where biochemists worked on new drugs, the medical and surgical wards, and a dreary spread of wards for psychopaths, schizophrenics, manic depressives and convalescent psychotics. About half the patients were black; the remainder mostly Puerto Ricans and indigent whites.

The unit chief took her eventually to a room measuring fourteen feet by ten feet, furnished with a small desk and rickety wooden chair. This would be her office, he told her. The hospital was as seriously overcrowded as it was underfunded, and office space had necessarily been sacrificed.

Sitting on the desk, with his back to a grilled window opaque with grime, he outlined her duties. Elisabeth would work on a unit for female patients, some of whom were being treated with a variety of experimental drugs. He did not name the drugs, and it was much later that she learned that they included LSD, psilocybin, mescaline and other hallucinogens. One of her main responsibilities would be recording psychophysiologic responses to the drugs administered by him and the biochemical research staff. With a mirthless laugh he added that since the drugs were supplied free by the pharmaceutical manufacturers, they were about the only thing not in short supply. It soon became clear that the patients were regarded as *non compos mentis*, and their consent was not required for treatment. Should patients protest, they were given sedatives or deprived of privileges. Surely, Elisabeth objected, she should know what drugs were being given to her patients. The doctor waved his hand. No, she would merely be informed on whatever was essential to the studies.

Most of her patients, he continued, were not rated as potentially dangerous, but Elisabeth would naturally have to be on constant alert. Any patient who got out of hand should be given Thorazine or electric shock treatment, or reported to him immediately.

Together they toured the wards. The patients slept in cubbyholes about the same size as Elisabeth's office. At the end of one corridor the doctor opened the door on what was known as the recreation room. As she stepped inside, she was almost overwhelmed by the stench of

210

urine. The room was filled with patients, most of whom were half dressed, some lying on the floor in puddles of their own urine, some hugging their knees, others sitting on stained couches or rigidly upright in hard chairs. None looked up at the visitors. Some cried aloud, others rocked to and fro. Eight or nine mangy cats—the pets of the head nurse—contributed to the odor and the hellish scene.

Elisabeth never saw the unit for so-called uncooperative patients, but the nurse on duty there carried a wooden stick, she was told. Alongside the "punishment ward" were "therapy baths"; it had proved effective to tie down recalcitrant or violent patients in the "therapy baths" for several hours.

On a later reconnaissance tour Elisabeth was obliged to press herself to a wall in order to allow space for two orderlies who were forcibly dragging away a screaming patient scheduled for electric shock treatment. The spectacle horrified her; she was ready to run, ready to admit a dreadful mistake in ever coming to the state hospital. She couldn't believe that outside a concentration camp such degrading conditions could exist.

Before leaving her, the unit chief introduced her to some of the staff on her floor. The only other physician was a young bean-pole-thin sandy-haired French Canadian, Dr. Philippe Trochu. He seemed very quiet, taut and somber, but he expressed his understanding of Elisabeth's revulsion over what she had seen. He had been on the unit for quite a while, he told her, and the fact that he lived on the premises made his life even more depressing. She was conscious of Dr. Trochu's innate compassion. She liked him.

Another staff member with whom she gained immediate rapport was a black social worker, Mrs. Grace Miller, a woman in her midthirties, competent and cool, who in spite of the grim working conditions managed to retain a sense of humor. Mrs. Miller's brown eyes sparkled as she shook Elisabeth's hand and bade her welcome. How much she was needed! Working together, they could help so many patients return to the outside world. To this task Mrs. Miller was completely dedicated.

Elisabeth saw a glimpse of hope and with it a new sense of purpose. She would dedicate herself to helping the women in her charge get well and flee this dreadful place. Surely that was why she was here;

211

that was the goal that could make her work meaningful.

She also met several of the nurses who worked on the unit. Six of them, she sensed, would be cooperative in the reforms she was determined to make. They were motherly women, kindly and caring. The others were there to earn a living, secure in state employment from which they could be fired only for the most flagrant misconduct.

Still having to cope with problems of custom, culture and language—and trying to comprehend the dialects of Harlem was like having to learn new languages—Elisabeth spent her first few months at Manhattan State acquiescing to rules and authority. With her background of respect for and total obedience to Switzerland's godlike professors, it was not easy ever to contemplate challenging her seniors.

But with increasing experience, Elisabeth's assertiveness also increased. She pushed aside her psychiatry textbooks. What was most urgently needed in these outdated wards was not textbook psychiatry, she decided, but simple basic care and the creation of an atmosphere of trust among patients and staff.

Conscientious about her research duties, she sat with patients who had been given hallucinogenic drugs and recorded for the members of the senior medical staff the fantasies, usually horrendous, of patients who had been given them, almost always unwillingly. Her heart bled as her patients wrestled with the monsters conjured up in drug-distorted minds.

Elisabeth resented most bitterly the fact that the patients were rarely if ever consulted about the powerful chemotherapy and shock treatment to which they were subjected. She herself stolidly refused to send patients for shock treatment or to prescribe hallucinogens, but she could not prevent others from doing so. All she could do was to comfort the patients as they traveled through their private hells. At least, she resolved, they would know that alongside them there was someone who really cared. Patients began to respond to the small woman who reached for their hands when they cried out in anguish.

Elisabeth's first major reform was to clean up the "recreation room." She argued that so long as the patients were not motivated to look after themselves, to dress properly and to practice decent hygiene, they would continue to lie about helplessly like zombies. She and her Canadian colleague issued firm instructions that the daily allocation of cigarettes and Cokes would now have to be earned. These luxuries would no longer be automatically handed out to patients who wandered about with their stockings slopping around their ankles or who sprawled about the floor or in chairs in wet pants. If they wanted cigarettes and soft drinks they would have to dress themselves properly and make proper use of the bathroom. They would have to comb their hair, brush their teeth and put on shoes.

The results were almost immediate. Even the more seriously ill psychotics soon understood that it was worth their while to conduct themselves with some modicum of dignity. As the cats were gradually removed from the wards, the stench of urine began to lift and, with its lifting, something of the miasma of fear and degradation. Patients who a few weeks before could barely be recognized as belonging to the human race began to look like people. They stood in an orderly line at 9:00 A.M. to go to an adjacent building where, as "therapy," they packed thousands of eyebrow pencils into boxes. If the work was mindless, it was better than sitting about the ward, and the recompense allowed them to buy the Cokes and cigarettes.

Elisabeth learned that psychotic patients are hypersensitive to the attitudes of those who look after them. Because a confined mental patient's world is shrunk to the dimensions of ward and recreation yard, he becomes as alert as a wild animal in hunting season. He instinctively knows whom to trust, who is hostile and who really cares.

In one revealing incident, Elisabeth noticed some patients actually cower against a wall when a member of the kitchen staff approached. She spoke to this staff member, who admitted hating her job, hating her colleagues and, above all, possessing an almost paranoiac suspicion of patients. Elisabeth was able to talk her into finding a new job.

In the evenings at home Manny and Elisabeth continued to share their day-by-day experiences. Manny had bought another car, and on weekends they usually drove into the countryside, but otherwise their lives took on a routine. With the advent of winter and shorter days, Manny was particularly concerned about Elisabeth's need to travel through Harlem to get to Ward's Island. On returning on dark evenings, and changing from the bus to the subway at 125th Street, or sometimes, by choice, waiting for a second bus, she often found herself the only white person around. Elisabeth does not recall ever having

213

been afraid or feeling threatened, even when approached by drunks or bums, and she turned down Manny's suggestion that she drive herself to work in their car.

One day in the spring, when arriving at the hospital, she noticed a young white woman she had never seen before sitting alone on a bench in the recreation yard. With her dark hair and skin like porcelain, the woman, in her early twenties, was stunningly beautiful. Her eyes stared into space. Elisabeth greeted her, but she made no response.

Each day when Elisabeth walked through the yard, she found the girl sitting still as a statue in almost exactly the same position. Each day she greeted her without receiving a response. Eventually Elisabeth inquired about the patient and learned that her name was Rachel and that she was a catatonic schizophrenic. No one could recall when she had last spoken, and her condition was said to be "completely hopeless."

Would it be possible, Elisabeth pleaded, to take Rachel into her own charge and see if she wouldn't react favorably to more individual treatment than she was probably getting at the moment?

Elisabeth's superior told her she was talking like a child wanting to adopt a stray puppy, that she would never make a good psychiatrist unless she were completely objective in her relationship with patients. Elisabeth's anger flared. She believed, she told him, that impersonal staff relationships with patients were precisely the reason patients didn't make progress. Many of her own patients had begun to respond to therapy only when she had gotten to know them, when she had begun to probe their backgrounds, to talk about their families, their feelings, fears and hopes. What was needed was simply human care, not textbook answers, not experimental drugs, not shock treatments.

She bit her tongue. She had said more than she had intended to say. But her outburst had a constructive result. With a gesture of dismissal, the unit chief growled that if Elisabeth wanted to make a complete fool of herself she could have Rachel transferred to her ward for a limited period.

It could in any event, Elisabeth realized, be for a limited period only, for she planned to leave Manhattan State in June and take up her postponed residency in pediatrics at the sophisticated Columbia Presbyterian Babies Hospital. She took Rachel into her ward at once.

214

Then in May Elisabeth found she was pregnant and once again was obliged to advise Columbia Presbyterian that she could not take up her residency. She elected to remain at Manhattan State, which was chronically short of staff. In midsummer she had another miscarriage; for the second time an embryo that never matured had changed the course of her professional career.

Two times a week, for one-hour sessions, she spent time alone with Rachel. There was no dialogue, because Rachel never uttered a word. At times Elisabeth almost believed that the authorities had been right after all, and that Rachel, in withdrawing within herself, had passed some point of no return. Yet just when she was about to despair of Rachel's recovery, she would detect a gleam of understanding in those sorrowful, beautiful eyes. And so she persevered.

Rachel's birthday brought an especially promising moment. Elisabeth had baked and frosted a cake, and as the candle was lighted and a choir of patients sang "Happy Birthday," she was certain that she saw a flicker of a smile move a face that ordinarily looked as if it had been exquisitely carved in marble.

But then in December the unit chief bluntly told Elisabeth that she was wasting her own time and thus the hospital's time in attempting to help a patient who, as he had pointed out earlier, was a totally hopeless case. Elisabeth was being pigheaded and he would tolerate no more of her farcical therapy. Rachel must be returned to the ward for the incurables.

Elisabeth was obliged to acknowledge some substance in the argument. Perhaps she was merely being stubborn; it was true that there never seemed to be enough time to give adequate attention to every patient. Her colleague, the young Canadian, was himself becoming increasingly depressed and was frequently absent on sick leave. Was it fair to spend time with Rachel when more responsive patients needed her too?

Yet her conviction remained that Rachel's condition was not hopeless. Her hopes for Rachel were intuitive and not supported by evidence. Yet she believed that Rachel had learned to trust. Once again she pleaded for more time. Her sardonic superior was adamant. The transfer of Rachel had to be made at once. But Elisabeth refused to leave his office until he agreed to allow Rachel to remain in her care at least until after Christmas. Reluctantly he acquiesced. But if the patient had not spoken at least one word by Christmas Day, Elisabeth was to have nothing more to do with her. That was his irrevocable decision.

For the next two weeks Elisabeth arrived at the hospital an hour early each day in order to have more time to spend with Rachel, but Rachel remained mute.

Christmas approached all too swiftly. Elisabeth was heartbroken. There would now have to be a miracle. One day during lunch hour she took Rachel into the recreation yard. There had just been a fresh fall of snow, but the clouds had cleared and the sun suddenly broke through. Elisabeth brushed away snow from the bench where she had originally seen Rachel nearly nine months earlier and they sat down. She had learned that Rachel had been a successful artist, so she talked to her about the beauty of the snow, about the shadows and sunlight, the crystal air and how the scene brought back memories of Switzerland. Then she turned and held Rachel's shoulders.

"All you have to do," Elisabeth pleaded urgently, "is to speak one word, and then we'll travel together until your health is fully restored. If you understand what I'm saying, answer me with one word. Simply say, 'Yes.'"

Rachel's face and body contorted with anguish, and her shoulders shook under Elisabeth's hands. She opened her mouth and from, it seemed, the depths of her soul, she uttered a sound—the first word she had spoken in three years. The word was distinctly "yes"!

Elisabeth hugged her patient and pressed her face—now unashamedly wet with tears—to Rachel's cheek.

Convinced that no one would believe a claim that Rachel had spoken, Elisabeth made no immediate report. Instead, she took her patient to two of the most caring and sensitive members of the staff—the occupational and art therapists, the former completely dedicated to her work, and the latter a volunteer and a sophisticated woman of culture. Elisabeth gives credit to the patience and skill of these two women for Rachel's continuing progress.

On Christmas Eve Elisabeth asked the unit chief to visit the occupational therapy rooms. Rachel's lovely face was bent over a canvas. Elisabeth urged the physician to ask the patient about her still unfinished painting. Rachel looked up at him, smiled and said huskily but distinctly, "You like it?"

Rachel traveled courageously the long road to full recovery, and today from her studio in New York, where she is a successful silk-screen artist, she still keeps in touch with Elisabeth.

Elisabeth was determined to give her patients an unforgettable Christmas Day. Most of them had no known relatives or had been completely abandoned by them, so early in December she toured the wards as a surrogate Santa Claus, asking the patients what they would like as presents. Almost all of them wanted clothes, one a green coat, for instance, and another a plaid skirt, and so on. Armed with a list of requests, she traveled on the next two weekends to Long Island and visited the wealthy homes of her former Glen Cove patients. She was quite specific in her requests. The green coat had to be a size twelve, the plaid skirt a size fourteen. Families with well-stocked wardrobes were pleased to help.

The social worker and the nurses assisted in wrapping up and labeling nearly sixty parcels, and on Christmas Day Santa Claus proved to be extraordinarily accommodating to patients in the experimental chemotherapy wing. In almost every instance, they received the gifts of clothing they had specifically ordered, even to color and size, and at no cost to anyone.

Festooned tables in the recreation room groaned under the weight of sodas and of cakes and cookies baked in Elisabeth's apartment— naturally to Meilen recipes. Carols were sung, toasts were drunk and, strictly against hospital rules, candles were lighted. For a few merry hours patients and staff forgot about the bars on the windows.

By spring the social worker, the occupational therapist, the Canadian physician and Elisabeth were working as a genuine therapeutic community and felt, as she phrased it, "family close" to the ever-improving patients.

And Elisabeth was pregnant once again. In spite of earlier miscarriages, she felt confident that this time she would carry the baby to full term. In fact, through the spring and early summer, she never felt healthier. The work was marvelously satisfying. The evident return to mental health of patients was its own reward for the long hours she spent in the bleak environment of the hospital. She continued to work through the last months of her pregnancy and, to Manny's consternation, continued to take crowded subways and buses for the forty-five-minute journey each way to and from Ward's Island. She thrived even

217

when temperatures soared to a hundred degrees and when the humidity came close to saturation.

She constantly refined and individualized her therapeutic techniques. When different treatments were discussed at staff meetings, some of the physicians spoke of the effectiveness of her Freudian, Adlerian, or Jungean therapies. She laughed and protested that she was guided only by common sense. Her therapy was, she told her colleagues, "what felt right." Some of the staff began to express interest in her unorthodox approach. Dr. Ben Israel, who was in charge of the interns, was particularly interested in the recovery rate, the large number of patients now ready for discharge. In Elisabeth's view, Dr. Israel was the only outstanding teacher at the hospital. She saw in him a man of empathy and wisdom, and persuaded him of her conviction that whatever success she had had was a direct result of and in proportion to the time she was able to spend alone with patients in her tiny office. Only when she had found the cause of a mental breakdown could the course of treatment be tailored to meet the patient's needs.

One could, she submitted, no more effectively treat patients en masse than one could effectively treat a community epidemic of conjunctivitis by throwing eye ointment onto a crowd from a balcony. Dr. Israel encouraged her to continue to go her own way.

One paranoid schizophrenic patient with whom Elisabeth spent a great deal of time was a powerfully built black woman, Sarah. Elisabeth slowly drew from Sarah the story of how as a child she had been farmed out as an unpaid servant in so-called foster homes. On three occasions the girl had been forced to flee these homes after being sexually attacked by white "foster fathers." Sarah had been committed to Manhattan State following a court conviction for stabbing a white man who had attempted to rape her.

In a breakthrough session, Elisabeth seemed to persuade Sarah that there really were people who, regardless of the color of their skin, genuinely cared for her. She assured Sarah that she, Elisabeth, would always have her office door open and be available whenever Sarah wanted to talk about her problems.

Shortly after this session, Elisabeth was in her office speaking to another patient, who was recovering but still withdrawn, when Sarah appeared at the door. Waving Sarah away, Elisabeth failed to notice the anger in her eyes as she backed out of the office.

A quarter of an hour later, when Elisabeth was alone, Sarah returned and, without speaking, sidled up to the desk and grabbed her throat. Unable to cry out for help, Elisabeth attempted to slide under the desk, but was prevented from doing so by her pregnancy-swollen abdomen. Her head was beginning to swim when she saw Rachel at the office door. Later Elisabeth learned how Rachel had run to the nurses' station and dragged a nurse to Elisabeth's aid.

After the paranoid Sarah had been subdued, she was marched off to the punishment cell, from which she emerged looking like a bruised zombie. Elisabeth was furious and stormed into her superior's office. Couldn't he understand, she protested, that Sarah was at the point where she was beginning to trust people once again? Couldn't he see that Sarah had attacked her only because she had felt she was being rejected by someone to whom she had so painfully poured out her life story? Couldn't he understand that the unwarranted punishment would set Sarah back by many months, perhaps years?

No, he could not understand. He pointed to the bruises on Elisabeth's neck. She was very lucky to be alive. Indeed, she was to blame for failing to take adequate precautions against being closeted with a criminally insane patient. Did she want to get killed? Did she want a public inquiry into the incident—the last thing the hospital wanted?

On the contrary, shouted Elisabeth, a public inquiry into conditions at Manhattan State was just what was necessary. What was more, unless the sadistic nurse in charge of the punishment ward was fired, she herself would tell the press about the overcrowding, the understaffing, the experimental drugs, the sadistic practice of dragging screaming patients to electric shock treatments. She would tell everything.

For the first time in his relationship with her her superior seemed to be shaken by her outburst. He stiffly quoted regulations protecting staff against dismissals, but he promised to take some remedial action. Elisabeth gained a partial victory when a directive prohibiting violence against patients was issued by the hospital administrators.

Today Elisabeth sees the most gratifying part of her work at Manhattan State as her opportunity to help patients who had long been cut off from it to readjust to the outside world. She and her social worker, Grace Miller, instituted "open-house day." Together they visited Harlem and other areas of the city and persuaded families to "adopt" patients and to visit them regularly. It was often the poorest families that were most eager to cooperate.

This adoption program resulted in an extraordinary incident. An elderly patient, Alice, who had spent nineteen years in the hospital had recently responded so well to therapy that she was ready for discharge. Alice had no knowledge of the whereabouts of her relatives. When she had first been committed to the hospital her young children had been told that she had died. Mrs. Miller was able to track down the children—now, of course, grown up—and without telling them that Alice was their mother she arranged for the children to adopt "a lonely old lady" who had the same name as their own.

The children turned up at an open-house day and immediately struck up a warm friendship with the old woman, who reminded them of their mother who had "died."

Elisabeth does not recall exactly how the children of Alice finally discovered that their mother had "returned from the grave," but shortly after this meeting they took Alice back into the family circle.

Working closely with Mrs. Miller, Elisabeth organized field days for patients ready for discharge. One test of this readiness was the ability of patients to handle money and balance their budgets. It was tempting for those who had been in the hospital for any length of time to spend money recklessly. To help them learn to spend wisely, and not feel lost in the big city, small groups of convalescent patients shortly before discharge were taken on shopping expeditions.

Macy's was the popular choice, and the shoppers and counter staff at the store must have been puzzled by the sight of a small woman with a foreign accent giving basic lectures on merchandising and domestic economy to an oddly assorted group of adults. They could hardly have guessed that until comparatively recently, some members of the group had been expected to spend the rest of their days behind the barred windows and high fences of a mental institution.

Reviewing the two years she spent at Manhattan State Hospital, Elisabeth today reflects gratefully on how much she learned, mostly from the patients themselves. She discovered that with patience and trust it is possible to visit and to understand the private worlds of psychotics, and she believes that without this understanding, which can be gained only through genuine compassion and care, most attempts at treating the mentally ill are likely to be a waste of time.

220

She learned that psychotics must be encouraged and motivated to break free of the shackles of their own fears, especially the fear of being unable to cope with the real world, the bustling, competitive, often harsh workaday world from which they have been sheltered. The mentally ill begin to turn to the road of recovery once they start to recognize that life is a challenge and not a threat.

She learned from Rachel, among others, that unless there is some organic reason for mental illness, no case should be considered hopeless.

She learned that not everyone in the healing professions is psychologically suited to have charge of the mentally ill, that this branch of medicine requires a special quality of the heart. In her eyes, only two of the physicians in a hospital of 2,000 patients qualified unequivocally.

She was persuaded that tranquilizing agents such as Thorazine, though they have their place in therapy, were frequently overused, not for the gain of the patient but for the convenience of the medical staff, who were not prepared to give the necessary time and energy to difficult patients.

She learned that if professionals were only to take the time to listen to patients instead of following literally textbook treatments advocated by different psychiatric schools, they would be much more likely to arrive at correct therapeutic answers.

She learned that no two patients are exactly alike, and that every patient should be individually treated.

Elisabeth had the authority to articulate these convictions because more than three-quarters of the patients originally put into her care were well enough to be discharged by the time she left Manhattan State—most of them capable of leading normal lives. In the hospital's history these recovery figures for patients labeled "chronic schizophrenics" were unprecedented. And she took special satisfaction in the medical team she had put together, particularly the nurses and two or three physicians converted to individualizing therapy by her successes and beliefs.

It was time now, she knew, to move on to new work, but there were still a few months in which she could consider her next advance. The immediate issue facing her was a purely domestic one—the birth of her baby.

═══ 21 ═══
Life and Death in the Family

In june 1960, two weeks before Elisabeth's baby was due, Mrs. Kübler flew in from Switzerland, arriving in time to help pack up the apartment on East 96th Street and to complete the move to a three-roomed one in the Bronx. The new apartment was in an almost exclusively Jewish neighborhood; Elisabeth seemed to be the only Gentile in a building complex that housed about four hundred people.

At first she was disenchanted by what she protested was "this egg-box existence without even the compensation of a garden." Manny had chosen the apartment because of its proximity to Montefiore Hospital and because it had an extra room for a nursery.

However, one compensation Elisabeth did find was the extraordinary friendliness of her new neighbors.

Erika had beaten her in giving birth to the first Kübler grandchild—a son. Elisabeth wrote to congratulate her sister, and in the course of her letter said:

I've never encountered such incredibly hospitable people. There's a tap on the door, and I find complete strangers bearing gifts—fruit, perhaps, or salted herring, even hot pies. When it comes to giving away food, I think the Jews must be the world's most generous people. Perhaps it is this kind of support for each other—and they must think I'm Jewish being married to Manny—that accounts for the way they have survived millennia of persecution. Actually, no one has asked me my faith, but I have a feeling of being part of a huge family. . . . I'm so unused to having any spare time that I've again taken up photography as a hobby. I've converted the kitchen into a darkroom and I'm developing my own prints. . . . I'm well overdue with the baby. Schnäggli [her mother's pet name] and Manny are eying me critically and obviously impatient for me to pop.

In July, when the baby was three weeks overdue, Manny resorted to a non-medically approved measure to expedite the happy event. He took his wife for stop-start drives, seeking out the bone-rattling potholes on New York's streets. Yet the baby would not be hurried. And when the birth was almost a full month overdue, her obstetrician decided over her protests to induce labor.

Because she felt so healthy and because of the lively kicking within her, she had no qualms about the well-being of the unborn infant on the day she entered the labor room at Montefiore Hospital.

What amazed and offended her was that all the women there—except the blacks who couldn't afford the procedure—were having or were about to have a labor induced not for medical reasons but for the convenience of obstetricians or for their own trivial family reasons. One mother sentimentally confessed that she wanted the birth of her child to coincide with her wedding anniversary, and another woman frankly admitted that she was expediting labor so that her husband could go on a golfing holiday! Elisabeth was no less astonished and shocked to learn that almost all the mothers delivered their babies under general anesthetic. She could not understand women who were so ready to deny themselves intimate knowledge of the richest of all human experiences.

But after fifteen hours in labor she too was denied the chance to witness the birth of her child. Cautioning her that it was now too late for a caesarian, her obstetrician insisted on giving her a general anesthetic for a low-forceps delivery.

Elisabeth was still half doped when an eight-pound son was put into her arms. She took little heed of her obstetrician when he told her that her cervix had been torn during delivery. All that mattered to her at the time was that she had a healthy baby, already crying for sustenance.

Manny had earlier decided upon the name Kenneth. Elisabeth had protested that she had never known anyone of that name; and in any event, since she had trouble pronouncing the syllable "th," she doubted their child would ever heed her when she called him. Nevertheless, Kenneth was the name given to the baby, who, Elisabeth still claims, was the most beautiful infant she has ever seen.

Before their marriage Elisabeth and Manny had agreed that they would not rear their children in either the Christian or Jewish faith. Kenneth would neither be baptized nor undergo ritual circumcision, and in due course the child would be encouraged to make his own choice of religion and cultural tradition.

However, Manny's mother and uncle, who, though not Orthodox, were steeped in Jewish tradition, felt strongly that the eldest child of a Jewish father should be ritually circumcised. When he arrived at the ward with an armful of flowers, Manny told Elisabeth that out of regard for his relatives he had arranged to have this done.

Elisabeth was upset. What she feared was that a ritual circumcision would lead inexorably to a bar mitzvah and to Kenneth's being channeled without his own sanction into the Jewish faith. But to avoid spoiling a happy day with an argument, she prayed for help and guidance. Her prayer was immediately answered, for a few minutes after Manny had left her to find a rabbi to perform the operation, a hospital pediatrician came to see her with the advice that since Kenneth was having difficulty urinating, he should be circumcised without delay. Elisabeth signed a consent form. By the time Manny returned with his mother and the rabbi, Kenneth had been non-ritually deprived of his foreskin and was healthily wetting his diapers.

Mrs. Kübler remained at the apartment for another two weeks and helped Elisabeth cope with the newborn baby, but she could not understand why her daughter would want to continue working now that she had a child to rear. Wasn't the care of Kenneth her priority? she asked. Elisabeth laughed away her mother's concern. Had she had triplets, she might have considered spending a year or two at home, she said, but she had not spent all those years at medical school in order to be a full-time mother. Of course, Kenneth, and any other children she had, would always have her first attention. And, of course, she would employ a full-time nursemaid. Mrs. Kübler was mollified. In fact, she had in mind a very capable young Swiss girl, the daughter of a Zurich couple, who was anxious to visit America and to learn English.

Two days after Mrs. Kübler returned to Switzerland seventeen-year-old Margrit—homely, tall and pink—arrived in New York. She proved to be just as capable as Mrs. Kübler had promised.

The Bronx apartment turned out to be quite adequate for the Ross family. Margrit and Kenneth had their own big and sunny bedroom, while Elisabeth and Manny shared a king-sized pull-out sofa bed in the living room. They ate most of their meals together in the large kitchen. For the first time there was room to accommodate all their wedding presents, to hang pictures of the Swiss mountains and to decorate tables and shelves with distinctively Swiss knickknacks. She had no garden, but Elisabeth saw to it that the apartment was never without flowers and plants.

Margrit took full charge of Kenneth, whom she adored, and after a month of maternity leave, Elisabeth had no misgivings about returning to work at Manhattan State. She had come to a decision on her future while nursing Kenneth. Her two years as a research fellow were the equivalent of two years' residency in psychiatry. All she needed now to become a full-fledged psychiatrist was one more year of residency. It would be folly, she reasoned, to abandon psychiatry when she was in sight of the end. She finally put aside all ideas of going to Columbia Presbyterian.

She had now proved herself competent in treating psychotics. In fact, as she told Dr. Israel, in this area of psychiatry she felt "supergood." But in treating neurotics she was woefully inexperienced. She had no intention of spending the rest of her professional career in a mental institution. But the thought of spinning out her years listening, as she phrased it, "to the whines and tribulations of overindulged neurotics" of the kind she had encountered at Long Island cocktail parties had even less appeal. Were she to go into general practice—a possibility still uppermost in her mind—neurotics and not psychotics were likely to make up the bulk of her neuropsychiatric patients. What she needed was to round off her third year of training in psychiatry in a general hospital, where she would encounter a broader spectrum of patients.

Montefiore was the obvious choice. If she could gain a residency in psychiatry at Montefiore, she and Manny could graduate in their specialties at the same time from the same institution. Because the apartment overlooked Montefiore, commuting time would be saved; and, more importantly, she would be only three minutes from home and Kenneth and would be able to have lunch with him every day.

On arriving for her interview with the head of the Montefiore psychiatry department, Elisabeth gazed with amazement at an office that contrasted sharply with any medical office she had ever seen before. It was paneled and furnished as if it were the office of a top business executive. Her shoes sank into the thick pile carpet. Behind the huge carved desk sat a suave-looking man in a dark custom-tailored pinstriped suit.

After the usual introduction, the interview began. The psychiatrist looked at the ceiling and asked what she knew of Meierian psychology. Elisabeth frowned. She had never heard the term and told him so.

He pursed his lips, tapped a gold-filled pencil on a snow-white blotter and reflected that surely Professor Meier's theories were recognized in Switzerland. Elisabeth brightened. Professor Meier, of course! Yes, she had indeed studied Meier's work.

Her interviewer made a note, looked up again and suggested that Elisabeth might like to state her views on menopausal depressive neurosis. She shook her head and said blithely that she had no views to express. He made a note with his gold pencil. In that case perhaps she would discuss Reichian variations.

Elisabeth gaped. The head of the department stroked an aquiline nose. Would Elisabeth care to state her views on the shift of the libido to earlier stages of personality evolution?

Insofar as Elisabeth was concerned, her interviewer might have been speaking one of the lesser known dialects of New Guinea. But she had had enough. Whether she gained the residency or not, she would tell this man who looked to her like a tailor's dummy what she had been doing over these past two years and how many manic depressives and schizophenics in her charge were now leading normal lives. For ten minutes she poured out stories of Manhattan State Hospital. Her eyes blazed and her face was flushed by the time she rose from her chair and turned to leave. She was certain she would be turned down for the residency, but at least she felt she had justified her existence and her work.

A couple of days later, to her astonishment, Elisabeth received a letter granting her a residency position in the department of psychiatry at Montefiore Hospital.

In June 1961 she left Manhattan State and in July started at Montefiore, where she was put to work in the psychopharmacology outpatient clinic. The man in charge of the clinic allowed her a free hand. Elisabeth's only complaint was that she .was underworked. To sit around waiting for patients and to take a sixty-minute lunch break when all she needed was a sandwich proved quite intolerable. What she had hoped for and what she wanted to do most was to get into the wards. She applied for and was granted two additional jobs. In the afternoons she evaluated psychiatrically ill children, and, to fill out her day, she undertook psychiatric consultations in the surgical and medical wards.

The unorthodox views and methods of the new resident psychiatrist were soon the subject of debate in the physicians' staff room. Most of the psychiatrists held strongly partisan opinions on the different schools of psychiatric thinking and techniques. If Elisabeth held to any school at all, it was strictly her own, or at best a hodgepodge, protested her critics, of the thinking and methods of the masters. Her techniques, she was told by one senior psychiatrist, were altogether too simplistic. How could she prescribe therapy without hours of free association and dialogue with patients?

Elisabeth answered this kind of criticism by referring to her hunches and intuition. She always acted upon gut feelings. And no matter that her peers and seniors were critical of her techniques, they were obliged to admit that her results were extraordinary.

For example, there was a certain wealthy and neurotic patient who was everyone's adversary, including her own. Almost everyone in the hospital knew her and, when possible, avoided her. She had gone from psychiatrist to psychiatrist with her tales of woe, and she was eventually shuffled to Elisabeth's office. Before she arrived, Elisabeth briefed herself on the patient's file.

The woman had hardly settled into her chair than she began to complain about the deteriorating quality of the hospital staff. Indeed, she was sorry that she had ever endowed a ward at Montefiore because the hospital was now actually admitting "foreign pig doctors."

Elisabeth lifted an eyebrow. The patient prattled on about just having shared the elevator with a physician whose apron had been grossly blood-spattered, and who had spoken with one of those ugly Middle European accents.

Deliberately exaggerating her Swiss accent, Elisabeth confessed to being "another of those new foreign pigs." The woman's mouth sagged open, but Elisabeth did not let her off the hook. Perhaps, Elisabeth suggested, it was precisely because she had such irrational prejudices and because she was so prone to making hasty judgments that she was now without friends and apparently incapable of communicating with her own family.

Elisabeth referred again to the medical file on her desk. Speaking firmly, she said that it was hardly surprising her patient alienated everybody by her negative behavior and arrogance, through which she attempted to cover up her deep sense of inferiority and loneliness.

The woman's eyes boggled. No one had ever dared to speak to her like that. It was outrageous! She would report this consultation at once to the head of the department. Elisabeth smiled her understanding of the patient's anger. Since no one ever smiled at her, she remained in her chair. After allowing her a moment or two to catch her breath, Elisabeth suggested that she possessed the courage to salvage her family life. She could begin by making a "laundry list" of all the things she disliked in other people. On this list she would find most of the shortcomings of her own personality. Once she understood her own deficiencies, she would know how to tackle them.

An unusually subdued and thoughtful patient left the office. Elisabeth saw her again several times and marked her progress. About five weeks after the first interview Elisabeth was summoned by the head of the department, who wanted to know what therapy she had used on the hospital's *bête noire*. The woman had once been his patient and he had had very little success with her. However, that morning she had actually smiled agreeably at him and had talked of making another donation to the hospital.

Elisabeth mentioned her "laundry list" technique; she was unable to resist adding that she did not believe this technique was referred to in Meierian textbooks!

She was not always successful in convincing colleagues of the value of her "gut-feeling" diagnoses. Nor were her hunches invariably on target. But she was absolutely convinced of the correctness of her diagnosis when in late August she was invited by a neurologist to give her opinion on a young man suffering symptoms of progressive paralysis and extreme depression.

The neurologist was certain that the symptoms were psychosomatically caused, and that all the patient required was a tranquilizing drug until he was over his morbid preoccupation.

Elisabeth found the patient paralyzed up to his chest and deeply depressed. She talked with him for an hour and left the bedside feeling certain that the young man was dying and that he knew it. She wrote out her findings on a consultation sheet, and recorded that the patient was in "preparatory grief." She believed that the patient suffered from amyotrophic lateral sclerosis (A.L.S.), not some psychosomatic paralysis, and that his death could be expected shortly.

The neurologist scoffed. How could a patient anticipate his own death with any accuracy, and who had ever heard of anyone grieving for himself? He reiterated that once the patient's morbidity was effectively countered by tranquilizers, his physiological condition would improve.

Three days later the patient died. The neurologist avoided Elisabeth and never again invited her to a consultation. As a result of this incident she began to understand that many physicians regarded the death of a patient as a personal affront and failure. She suspected that the neurologist had really accepted the accuracy of her diagnosis but had refused to acknowledge it because of his own fear of death or of his own unresolved grief. Other incidents in other wards strengthened her uneasy feeling that physicians seemed to have more difficulty facing up to a poor prognosis than did their patients.

These were feelings only, not yet convictions, but they puzzled and nagged her. Why was death—the one certainty about life—such a taboo subject? Paradoxically, it seemed the more sophisticated the society, the more the subject of death was avoided.

Then suddenly death moved to the inner circle of her own family.

On an evening in September a cable from her mother in Zurich reported that her father was seriously ill in the hospital and that he was asking for Elisabeth.

She was in a park near the apartment giving Kenneth an airing in his stroller when Manny brought the cable to her. Elisabeth remembers the moment well, remembers the sudden lull in the sound of traffic, a little whirlwind of fallen leaves at her feet, the concerned expression on Manny's face and her own certainty that this would be her last opportunity to see her father. She and Manny went straight from the park to a Western Union office and sent off a cable to say that she would be arriving in Zurich as soon as she could arrange a flight. Next morning she asked the head of the psychiatry department for a leave of absence and gave her reasons. He warned her that a break in her residency when she was only a few weeks into her work could jeopardize her chances of qualifying as a psychiatrist in nine months' time. She told him that she would take that chance, that she had given a promise to her father: If he ever needed her, she would go to him.

Manny, they agreed, would not travel to Switzerland this time, but she decided to take Kenneth with her. Her father had written earlier to say how anxious he was to see his grandchild.

She and Kenneth took a night flight and arrived in Zurich early the next morning. Erika met them at the airport and explained what had happened. Mr. Kübler had developed a bursitis in his elbow, and a simple surgical procedure to ease it had been botched. Inflammation in the elbow had developed into septicemia. The sisters drove straight to the hospital, where Elisabeth first consulted with the physician in charge of her father. The prognosis was poor. Mr. Kübler was not responding to antibiotics. He had developed a number of abscesses, and his strength was failing.

Arriving at her father's sunny hospital room, Elisabeth pressed her face to his sunken cheeks. In spite of the indignities of his helplessness and the noise of the suction machine drawing off pus from the abscesses in his abdomen, Mr. Kübler appeared at first to be in good

230

spirits. But soon his brow furrowed and he spoke urgently of the matter uppermost in his mind. He wanted to die at home.

Elisabeth evaded his plea, for she could see how sophisticated were his nursing needs. He required round-the-clock attention. But then he confessed to something he had never spoken of before—of how, when his own father had become totally incapacitated by a broken spine, he had put him into a nursing home, where he had died. In those days it had been accepted to take dying people home, there to be cared for by relatives and friends. Mr. Kübler had failed his father in this, and the memory of what he had done now surfaced and deeply disturbed him.

Elisabeth kept her first visit brief, for the emotion of the reunion had tired her father. At home she found her mother exhausted by worry and the strain of traveling for two weeks to and from the hospital. Mrs. Kübler knew of her husband's request to die at home and fully supported it if he could be given proper nursing care.

The hospital's senior physician, however, stated vehemently that if Elisabeth were to move her father, his life would be in her hands. Surely she as a physician understood that her father was being given the best possible care in the hospital. To take him home would be madness.

She discussed her father's pleas with Erika and Eva, who lived some distance from Zurich and who were unable to offer advice. Besides, as a physician Elisabeth was the only member of the family who would know what was best.

Alone, Elisabeth took Kenneth in his stroller for a walk in a park. The weather was cold with a sharp wind stripping the first leaves from the trees. The sight of children at play stirred memories of Meilen and of being with her father in the mountains. She thought of the time when she and her father, roped together, had crossed glaciers and how, as he had gone forward and probed for treacherous snow bridges, he had trusted her with his life. His trust in her now was not so dissimilar. He was helpless and calling on her to come to his aid.

What was it then that was holding her back? Was it not, perhaps, she asked herself, her own fear of taking responsibility? Was it concern over her own ability to care for him adequately?

As she faced up to these fears, she knew what to do. She telephoned a hospital equipment store and rented infusion and suction apparatus to be installed in the master bedroom of the Kübler home. Then she ordered an ambulance.

She herself helped to lift her father from his hospital bed. She wheeled him through the corridors and into the ambulance. Hospital officials glowered, but her father's face stretched into the biggest smile.

Half an hour later Mr. Kübler was lying in his own bed, the same bed in which she and her sisters and Ernst had been conceived. She hooked up the wheezing suction pump, but decided against the infusions, since he was able to swallow fluids. He rejected her offer of morphine and asked instead for a glass of wine.

Surrounded by those he most loved and by familiar things—pictures of the mountains, skiing trophies—and able from his pillows to see the same view of the church he had seen on waking for so many years and to hear the ringing of the clock bells, he expressed his complete content.

Elisabeth brought in a day nurse to help cope with the sophisticated nursing, but her father reacted against the woman's clinical, business-like ministrations, and Elisabeth seldom left him except to tend Kenneth. In spite of his wasted frame, in spite of the noise of the suction machine, the smell of pus, and his helplessness, he had about him a sense of dignity and belonging—feelings totally absent in the sterile ward of the hospital.

A couch moved into the bedroom served for Elisabeth's own catnaps whenever her father slept. However, when he was alert he was anxious to talk, and his mind was much occupied by spiritual matters. They discussed some of the philosophies in the books she had given him three years earlier—the creeds of Buddhists and Zoroastrians, the writings of the Dead Sea Scrolls, the faith and struggles of the Jews, as well as Christian beliefs. She was astounded by the breadth of his philosophical and religious reading, by a new tolerance and by the humor that suddenly broke through when they were discussing the most profound issues.

The rigid dogmatist of her childhood seemed far removed from this unprejudiced and non-judgmental man.

He resolutely refused all pain-killing drugs. His sense of peace and

232

his quiet acceptance of his grim physical condition seemed to lift him above pain. He declined food, for his stomach was now as pitted as a sieve, but he occasionally asked for wine, naming the vintage and where the bottle could be found in the cellar. He chuckled as he told Elisabeth that he had always known who had taken those bottles from his cellar when she lived in the Seefeldstrasse apartment.

For short periods her mother took over the bedside vigil, but her distress was clearly communicated to Mr. Kübler; Elisabeth realized it was not possible to conceal from the dying the sense of discomfort and feelings of unease of those who kept them company.

On the evening of his second day at home the pace of life's ebbing quickened. Mr. Kübler no longer struggled against currents carrying him toward the end.

On the third day he began to speak to someone not in the room. Elisabeth realized after a while that he was speaking, as if in dialogue, with his own father. Yet he remained quite rational, always conscious of her presence. Suddenly he would break off a dialogue with his long-dead father, turn to her and ask her to adjust a pillow or to draw a drape.

He was not hallucinating, of this Elisabeth was convinced, for the unseen entity was as real to Mr. Kübler as she was herself. This was her first experience of what later she was persuaded was the ability of the dying to communicate with the dead—almost invariably the dead most loved by the dying.

On the third night there was no doubt that her father's life was drawing peacefully to its end. She slept fitfully in the cot alongside him, awakening each hour to listen for his breathing or to attend to his comfort. At first light she got up and kissed him. He was too weak to speak and so she sat beside him, holding his hands. His face now seemed translucent, freed of lines of pain and anxiety. In another hour the hired nurse, starched, efficient and insensitive, would arrive. Elisabeth wished for her father's sake that she had not hired the woman. She bent over and kissed him, feeling for him a full tide of love, tenderness and gratitude.

From the door of the room she murmured that she was slipping out for a cup of coffee. She spoke to her mother and Erika, who had just arrived. She told them that her father was very close to death, but she encouraged her mother and Erika to take Kenneth for a walk. She was quite alone in the house when she returned to the sickroom. From the door she observed immediately the stillness of the figure in the bed. In the few minutes she had been out of the room her father had died.

She stood at the bedside for perhaps a quarter of an hour and reflected upon how this man, so strong, so proud and independent, had died in character. Physically, surely, no one could have suffered more—until he had been granted his final wish, until he had come home. But once he had set the scene and the timing of his dying, the torment of his body ceased, the spiritual turmoil calmed.

When she had briefly left the room, their farewells completed, she had left upon the bed a man she respected and loved. Yet the corpse she now saw was no more her father than his winter coat hanging in the closet, no more the veteran mountaineer than his skis and his boots gathering dust in the basement. Within the time taken for the exhalation of one breath a metamorphosis had occurred. The cocoon was left; the butterfly had flown.

The hired nurse arrived, and Elisabeth was grateful that someone her father had resented having near him at his dying, someone lacking in empathy, had not been there at the end.

Suddenly the idea of the woman touching the corpse was repugnant to her. She told the nurse to leave. Just as she was being assailed by a wave of weariness over having to undertake postmortem duties, the telephone rang. It was a woman physician, Dr. Bridgette Willisau, whom she barely knew. Elisabeth told her that her father had died a few minutes earlier. Dr. Willisau said that she had somehow sensed she would be needed. That was why she had called. She would leave for Zurich at once, and would arrive within the hour.

With efficiency and sensitivity, Dr. Willisau helped Elisabeth wash the body of her father. They dressed him in his favorite suit and changed the bedsheets and the pillows. Then, as required by law, Dr. Willisau informed the city health authorities of the death. (In Switzerland local authorities supply without cost casket, hearse and mourners' car.) Shortly, two city employees arrived and officially confirmed the death. The officials pointed out that because of the nature of Mr. Kübler's illness it would be necessary to remove the corpse immediately. (In the normal way, a corpse would be left in a house until the funeral for viewing by relatives and friends.)

Elisabeth was touched when one of the men suggested she might like to place a flower in her father's hands. Although she knew Mr. Kübler would have regarded such a gesture as sentimental, she was surprised that a public servant should care enough to suggest it.

She went downstairs and out into the yard, where she plucked chrysanthemums and placed them in the body's folded hands. The men carried it down the stairs, and she watched from the balcony as they placed it in the hearse, and long after the hearse had driven away.

Elisabeth had time for her private grief before her mother and Erika returned; by the time they got back the house was clean, the odor gone. She explained how the corpse had to be taken by the city officials to a special "cool room," not a morgue, adjacent to the chapel where the funeral would be held. Mrs. Kübler had her three daughters with her while she grieved.

Three days later, in the small chapel where the Kübler family had so often worshipped, and where Elisabeth and her sisters had been married, a host of friends and relatives paid final tribute. As Elisabeth joined in singing one of her father's favorite hymns, she felt the deepest gratitude for his life so perfectly rounded off, even to the smallest detail.

That night she wrote in her journal, "My father truly lived until he died."

22

"I've Lived Here Before!"

Elisabeth now finds it hard to believe in that full year at Montefiore Hospital and in the Bronx apartment, because for the first time in her life—at least since leaving school—her working days were governed by calendar and clock. There were times when she felt guilty that her evenings and her weekends were free.

Her most important and certainly her most rewarding work at Montefiore was with mentally disturbed children. She discovered her natural gift of almost immediate communication with children, even those labeled psychotically withdrawn. In one of her letters home she spoke of working therapeutically with children as "being like cooking from an old and familiar recipe." Family dynamics—the interplay of home relationships—fascinated her, and the only aspect of the work that she disliked was the necessity of working up diagnostic evaluations. When the pathology was so obvious, all the paperwork seemed such a waste of time, as did the endless discussions at staff meetings.

"Children are not cured by paperwork and professional suppositions," she argued, "but by listening, understanding, winning confi-

236

dence, sometimes with laughter and hugs, and sometimes by shedding a tear." She learned to delight in the children who came to her office, all from middle-class or wealthy homes. They were not by nature the brats that she had once thought them. Most often brattishness, when she came across it, was obviously caused by inadequate parenting.

She tolerated the elaborate workups, staff meetings and paperwork when she saw it all as an exercise in patience (never one of her virtues) and in logical thinking. The young patients she loved, almost without exception. To Erika she wrote, "When I see real progress with these kids I'm reminded of the Volunteer work we did in the coal-mining village in Belgium when children climbed up to the playground on top of the leveled mine dump—climbed out of the suffocating dust and grime and into the sunlight that is rightfully theirs."

In spite of being underworked, at least by her own yardstick, Elisabeth appreciated her spare time as a bonus, for it was time she could spend with Manny and Kenneth—time to cook more elaborate meals and entertain, time to explore the countryside, make new friends, and time to enjoy her hobby of photography in the makeshift darkroom she had created in the kitchen.

Her workday routines were almost as precise as the minute hand. Returning from the hospital at five minutes after five, she took Kenneth to the nearby park in a stroller. Manny sometimes accompanied them. They got to know a number of neighbors, including several mothers, with whom she discussed diet, diaper rash and teething. Not that Kenneth had any problems beyond an occasional sniffle or two. Indeed, Elisabeth was persuaded that were she to enter him in a baby contest he would be the runaway winner for first place.

The proprietor of the mom-and-pop store at the end of the street became a rather special friend. Because he too was a new immigrant from Europe, he and Elisabeth felt a common bond. He spoke to her in Yiddish and Elisabeth invariably replied in Swiss-German, yet they somehow managed to communicate—to the great amusement of Manny and others in the store. The grocer never allowed her to leave his establishment without stuffing her shopping bag with the black radishes much favored by Manny.

She and Manny entertained at home at least once a week. The most frequent guests were Japanese postgraduate students in neuropathology who had been attracted to Montefiore by the international renown of Professor Zimmerman. (The professor was subsequently given an order of merit by Emperor Hirohito in gratitude for the number of Japanese students he had trained in neuropathology.)

Elisabeth was particularly delighted with her Japanese guests, and she contrived for them a variety of Oriental meals. After dinner, while Manny and his Japanese colleagues discussed their specialty, she moved between the male guests and their wives and served desserts, including her own homemade Swiss chocolate cake. Kenneth's first playmates were Japanese children.

In a letter to Eva, Elisabeth spoke of "now living a thoroughly bourgeois life in which the spectacular length of Kenneth's eyelashes can keep a conversation moving for ten minutes. Even allowing for the fact that I'm a prejudiced mother, he's the most handsome child on the block! With capable Margrit looking after him, it's motherhood without tears. . . . Manny is trying to educate me in opera. We go to the Met again next week to see *La Traviata.* . . . Thrilled at the thought of seeing you soon."

Eva was engaged to be married again. Her fiancé was Peter Bacher, who accepted employment with Swissair in New York so that the wedding could take place in the United States, thus avoiding sad memories of Seppli. The bridal couple planned to spend their honeymoon on a world tour.

In November, Eva arrived for her wedding at the Connecticut estate of her godfather, a wealthy Swiss-born industrialist. Elisabeth and Manny drove to Connecticut for the wedding, and after the ceremony arranged to guide the couple back to New York, from where they would start their world tour. While they were driving, there was a sudden heavy downpour. Manny, driving the lead car, slowed, and the Bacher vehicle, skidding, crashed into the rear of the Ross car.

Manny and Peter were unscathed, but Elisabeth was knocked unconscious for several minutes, and Eva's face was lacerated by flying windshield glass. Although Elisabeth experienced spells of giddiness, she and Manny were pronounced fit at a hospital emergency room. Eva spent some days in a hospital, and then recuperated for a couple of weeks in the Rosses' apartment—by now, after a spate of visitors, known to the family as the "Ross Hotel." Eva's face eventually healed almost without a scar following cosmetic surgery performed by a brilliant plastic surgeon.

After the delay, Eva and Peter eventually set off on their honeymoon tour. When Elisabeth returned to her work, however, she could barely move her neck. Even more distressing to her than the whiplash was her frequent memory failure.

Puzzled and frustrated that she couldn't recall the names of her patients, she saw a hospital physician, who ordered traction for her neck and back pains but who insinuated that her memory lapses were imagined—"perhaps to impress an insurance company."

Since her new brother-in-law was responsible for the accident, and since he had not in fact been insured, Elisabeth was infuriated by the suggestion that she was playing some sort of game in order to make money—a common and profitable American pastime, she was told by a friend.

She wrote to her mother:

> I'm really beginning to feel more at home in America, and some of the things I felt so critical about when I first arrived I have now adopted. For instance, I now actually enjoy supermarkets, hamburgers, hot dogs and processed breakfast food. You'll be happy to hear that I don't yet chew gum! Don't be too shocked to hear that I wear pants as often as I wear a skirt, even when I go out visiting. . . . But one thing I don't think I'll ever get used to is the importance given here to money. America is a sort of "dollar-ocracy." If people have money, they are considered important and successful. If they don't they're not. . . . After the accident some people tried to cheer me up by saying I could claim a lot of money out of a stiff neck and concussion. Can you believe it! . . . Enjoy your trip to India, and remember it's our turn to have you in the summer.

The letter's reference to India concerned her mother's planned visit to Ernst. After Mr. Kübler's death, Elisabeth, Ernst, Eva and Erika agreed among themselves to invite their mother to their homes at regular intervals. They encouraged her to keep her home on Klosbachstrasse as a family pied-à-terre. With its three bedrooms, the apartment was obviously too large for an elderly woman living alone, but Mrs. Kübler was promised that the rooms would be filled from time to time with her children and grandchildren. Elisabeth, her brother and sisters believed strongly too that their mother would accommodate herself more easily to widowhood if she remained in a familiar environment and continued to be mistress of her home. The further promise was given that Mrs. Kübler would have no financial problems.

Elisabeth and Manny hoped to find specialist appointments in the western United States, and they wanted Mrs. Kübler to join them that summer on a sightseeing visit to that part of the country, which none of them had yet seen. When they started job hunting in January, however, they found that this was a harder process than they had expected: first, because Manny's specialty was a rather rare branch of medicine with few openings in the teaching hospitals; and second, because they obviously needed to find appointments in the same community. They received a number of responses from medical schools and teaching hospitals wanting a neuropathologist but not wanting a psychiatrist, or vice versa. Eventually a tentative offer of double appointments was received from the University of Colorado. They were invited to travel to Denver in May for interviews.

They were saving money to buy a house, and they calculated that it would be cheaper for the four of them—Kenneth and Margrit included—to travel west for the interviews by car rather than by air. Setting out on a Sunday, they took three days and two nights to reach Denver in their Oldsmobile convertible, economizing by staying at cheap motels and sustaining themselves largely on hamburgers.

At the University of Colorado's medical school they found that Manny's interviews were well set up for Wednesday, but because of the temporary absence of professors in the department of psychiatry, Elisabeth's interviews were delayed until Friday. They had not calculated on the delay, and Elisabeth was especially conscious of the importance of reporting for duty at Montefiore Hospital on the Tuesday following the Memorial Day weekend, because she did not want the head of the department to be reminded once again of the number of days she had been absent from work because of her father's illness and death. Manny was in a better position because he had a good friend and admirer in Professor Zimmerman.

Finally, on Friday, Elisabeth was interviewed by an acting department head whose mind seemed to be on a fishing vacation. In Elisabeth's view, his questions were irrelevant, and she was quite sure that he didn't really listen to her answers, which were much fuller than the answers she had given at her first interview at Montefiore. She was also seen by one of the administrators of the university's medical center, and she left the university unimpressed and uninspired. If it hadn't been for the beauty of the Colorado mountains and the fact that Manny was so full of confidence that he had gained just the appointment he wanted, Elisabeth would have been ready to look elsewhere.

The drive home, which they began Friday afternoon, increased her frustration, for they found themselves caught up in traffic heading for the Indianapolis 500 auto race. Highways were jammed, hotels and motels full, and when it seemed certain that Elisabeth would not arrive in time to report for work on Tuesday morning she boarded a New York-bound plane at Indianapolis, leaving Manny, Margrit and Kenneth to complete the journey by car.

Elisabeth has a very clear memory of the three evenings she spent alone in the Bronx apartment, for it was the first time she had been entirely alone in more than three years. There is a long entry in her journal on the "liberating feeling and absolute necessity of having one's own space." The journal goes on:

> I know that if I'm really going to find the cause and purpose of my life, I've got to find the place and the time to be absolutely alone—my own mountaintop where I can think and listen to the inner voice. I still don't know why I am in America, but there has to be a reason. I know that there is a frontier out there, and that sometime I shall be traveling into the unknown territory. But if I'm going to discover the frontier, I'm going to have to isolate myself from time to time and find the signposts.

On the night before her family returned, she had a repeat of the dream she had had on the night before she first arrived in America. She saw herself in Indian dress, riding a horse across a desert land toward a pueblo set against a distant horizon. She identified again distinctively shaped rocks and the reddish-colored mesa. Once again it was an extraordinarily satisfying dream, and she awakened refreshed and with all feelings of frustration quite lifted.

At the end of May, Elisabeth fulfilled the residency requirements for psychiatry and the University of Colorado advised her and Manny that they had both been accepted for faculty positions, Manny as assistant professor of pathology, and Elisabeth as fellow in psychiatry in the school of medicine. Both would be on the staff of the university's medical center. Manny would lecture on his specialty and be the hospital's neuropathologist. Elisabeth would have two jobs. In the mornings she would work in the therapeutic community for psychotic patients, and in the afternoons with mentally disturbed children at the child psychiatry clinic.

Manny took out a bank loan and flew back to Denver to find a house. Impatient, he signed the purchase agreement on the first one he saw. It was an oldish clean-looking brick house on 17th Avenue. When he returned to the Bronx, Elisabeth anxiously urged him to describe their first real home—her particular interest was the size of the garden—and Manny struggled to remember the dimensions of the living room, kitchen, the three bedrooms, the condition of the lawn in front and the large yard at the back. The house was on a quiet tree-lined street not far from the university, he assured her, and the neighbors looked friendly.

Mrs. Kübler arrived in New York in June, laughingly protesting that her invitations significantly seemed to coincide with house moving. They packed the furniture into a rented U-haul trailer. A little crowd of Bronx neighbors, including the friendly grocer and the Japanese postgraduate students and their wives, turned out to see them on their way. At the last minute, room had to be found in the trunk of the Oldsmobile for gifts ranging from a Japanese kimono to a sackful of black radishes.

With five aboard and a swaying U-haul behind, Manny took it easy at the wheel, and the only untoward incident on a journey that took them through Pennsylvania, Ohio, Indiana, Illinois, Missouri and Kansas occurred when Manny was ticketed for driving too slowly and holding up traffic.

When they arrived in Denver, they found their house was still occupied and they were unable to move in, so they decided to continue their exploration of the western states. On the following day they were driving through Monument Valley, near the junction of Colorado, New Mexico, Arizona and Utah, when Elisabeth suddenly became conscious of familiar territory. It was a strangely exciting, enigmatic feeling, for she had never traveled this far west before. On the excuse that it was time for a picnic lunch, she asked Manny to stop the car. Then she walked alone some three hundred yards off the road.

This was the place of her two vivid dreams. Here were the red-earthed flatlands leading to a far heat-hazed horizon. She recognized the pueblo in the middle distance, and the distinctively shaped rocks. Her dreams had in effect been photographs of this vista—an exact copy. Everything about this stretch of arid land—the blaze of the sun in the metallic blue sky, the sight and smell of desert flowers, the shadows cast by sand cones—was known to her already.

For some minutes she stood transfixed. She only then noticed, perhaps a quarter of a mile away, an Indian girl riding a horse. The reins of the horse were loose, and the girl looked neither to her left nor to her right as she headed toward the pueblo.

It was as if she, Elisabeth, were watching herself, dressed in Indian clothing, riding home.

A feeling of peace she had not known before, a sense of harmony embracing time and space, man and nature, totally engulfed her. Then the moment was broken by the shouts of Manny and her mother. She turned about and, as she recalls the experience, had to compel herself to re-enter her family's reality.

As Elisabeth arrived at the car, her mother asked what was the matter. Why was she looking so strange? She couldn't explain. How could she tell them that she had traveled through ten thousand yesterdays, that she had certainly been here before, that the scent and sound of the wind, the shapes and shadows of the rocks, the sweep of the mesa, the heat of the sun, were as familiar to her as the face of her husband, the cry of her child? How could she speak to Manny, the scientist, of an experience that surely had no scientific explanation? What were the odds that she should find herself in a place that was an exact replica of a dream? It seemed to her too that she had memories, albeit misted, that stretched beyond her dreams. Surely she had lived here before. She had come home.

Later in the afternoon they visited a pueblo and watched some Indian dancing. Her feelings of "belonging" remained with her. Though she had been born in a faraway land, she was akin to these people. Their art and artifacts seemed familiar, the steps of the dances, the haunting monotonous sound of the singing so well known to her that she sang along with the Indians. She watched three children playing in the dirt alongside an adobe wall. She felt sure that were she to call to them, they would look up and recognize her.

They drove on to the Grand Canyon, and in her hotel room that night she lay awake into the small hours pondering what she referred to in her journal as "this ultimate vision of harmony and oneness with nature, those moments of total happiness and peace." A further entry reads:

> I know very little about the philosophy of reincarnation. I've always tended to associate reincarnation with way-out people debating their former lives in incense-filled rooms. That's not been my kind of upbringing. I'm at home in laboratories. But I know now there are mysteries of the mind, the psyche, the spirit that cannot be probed by microscopes nor proved by chemical reactions. In time I'll know more. In time I'll understand.

As they still had two weeks before they were due to report for duty at the University of Colorado, they decided to drive on to Los Angeles to visit Manny's brother, Charles. Elisabeth was so enchanted by everything she saw that her mother laughingly charged her with being Americanized. No, she assured her mother, she had not forgotten her Swiss heritage. The next time Mrs. Kübler came to stay she would find the garden of the house in Denver full of Swiss flowers, the cellar full of preserves and the beds and tables covered with quilts and cloths embroidered like those they'd had in Meilen. And indeed, as soon as they arrived back in Denver after the unplanned extension of their vacation, Elisabeth set about the task of turning a suburban American home into a fragment of Switzerland. When she left to return to Zurich, Mrs. Kübler expressed her satisfaction.

Before long the family was settled. Kenneth toddled about in the yard lisping a few sentences, and Manny was enormously pleased with the first proper house he had ever lived in. Only Margrit, who had gotten used to New York and enjoyed the bigger city, was restless.

At the university, Manny made the satisfying discovery that he was a good lecturer. He had had some doubts about his capability at the podium, but he overcame initial auditorium nervousness through his painstaking preparation of lectures, and he soon learned to leaven with humor the gravity of his subject. As the medical center's neuropathologist, Manny's competence was immediately acknowledged.

However, Elisabeth was not so happy with her professional work. Her immediate superior was an inexperienced young man, a textbook psychiatrist who was ambivalent about listening to an older, female colleague who tried hard to introduce into the therapeutic community some of the techniques she had found so effective at Manhattan State. The therapeutic community was a comparatively new approach in psychiatric medicine, where patients were encouraged to have a say in the management of their communal living.

There were about thirty patients, most of them schizophrenics. Elisabeth believed that chemotherapy should play a role secondary to individual therapy, and she was convinced of the paramount importance of one-to-one encounter sessions. She argued the need to present patients with goals toward which they could strive.

Nurses and other members of the staff tried to form cooperative professional relationships in the wards, but they often expressed their feelings to Elisabeth of being caught between a maverick psychiatrist who claimed to be guided by her "gut-reaction" diagnoses and the rigidly orthodox and conservative "boss."

Hamstrung by procedures and regulations, Elisabeth found the therapeutic community work not only frustrating but boring. However, just as she had in Montefiore, so in Denver she found her work with psychotically disturbed children to be stimulating and rewarding. She conducted her child psychiatry clinic on most afternoons. Here she did not have to brook interference and was allowed virtually a free hand to employ her own techniques. There was no mystery about them, no secret formula. When the mental health of young patients improved and when impressed colleagues asked about her approaches, she talked about using her head and her heart, about intuition and common sense, about listening—and understanding, especially understanding family dynamics—for the clues to psychoses that were most often uncovered in the home and at the hearth. Only on the rarest occasions did she prescribe drugs.

245

While the children's clinic stimulated her mentally, it was the mountains that buoyed her spirit. Although Kenneth was too young for climbing or skiing, she often took him with her on hikes in the high trails. Even at a tender age her son seemed to have the same sense of wonder in the mountains that she had had as a child in Switzerland. Sometimes she took Margrit along for company, but she was never able to convert Manny to her passion for climbing. When she could persuade him to drive her to the foothills, he usually elected to sit in the car with a book or to listen to the radio while she scaled the rocks, often carrying Kenneth on her back.

Soon after her arrival in Denver, Elisabeth was fascinated by the pioneering work of Professor Sydney Margolin. A gray-haired, dignified giant of a man, a Vienna-born and -educated Jew, Dr. Margolin was widely regarded on the campus as an eccentric. His radically unconventional approaches to psychophysiological research and his absent-mindedness made him the butt of some faculty humor, but those who knew him recognized a genius, a man of culture and profound wisdom. He was a psychiatrist, as was his wife, who was the daughter of an associate of Sigmund Freud.

Elisabeth first saw him at one of his always crowded lectures and was immediately captured. She wrote in her journal, "He has the best mind I've ever encountered. . . . This is the man who is going to be my teacher. Dr. Margolin is surely the reason I'm in Denver!"

She went to see him in his cluttered, book-lined office at the university. They talked in German, and she was surprised by the breadth of his interests. Before referring to his academic work, he discussed Indian lore and culture. Without any sense of embarrassment, she found herself telling him of her remarkable experience in Monument Valley. He didn't laugh, as she had half expected he might, but listened intently without interrupting. When she finally asked him what he made of her experience, he offered no opinion beyond suggesting that she herself should seek the answers, and that she might be helped by participating in his laboratory seminars.

He anticipated the reason for her visit by suggesting that she join his staff as an assistant. He smiled at her elation, then warned that he was not known to be the easiest boss and that she might well be disillusioned when he put her to work. He gave her an outline of his re-

246

search. He had himself created his own department of psychophysiology, and the immediate focus of his research was in the field of psychosomatic medicine—the close relationship between pathology and the emotions.

Without her enthusiasm and regard for Dr. Margolin, the man, Elisabeth might well have been disenchanted when she reported to his laboratory in July 1963. He put her to work repairing and often completely rebuilding discarded polygraphs, popularly known as lie detectors, which he used for evaluating the role emotions play in causing physiological problems—in effect, the close links between the state of the mind and the state of the body.

In a typical demonstration—and one in which Elisabeth participated—a pathologically obese patient was sought out. Students were invited to question the woman on her symptoms and motivations. Then, to verify the theoretical framework of the "Pickwick" syndromes in which the case had been presented, the patient was hooked up to a polygraph and then left alone with a tray of food. Observers in an adjacent room watched the polygraph recordings of brain impulses, blood pressure, heart and breathing rates. These were then compared with readings given by a woman of average weight. Similar tests were made with the cooperation of asthmatic patients, arthritic patients and others.

Never satisfied with standard apparatus for measuring physiological responses, Dr. Margolin was always looking for more sensitive methods. One reason he was known on the campus as an eccentric was that he spent much time scouring the far corners of laboratory storage rooms, and even military junkyards, for discarded electronic apparatus and appliances which he cannibalized for the building of unique devices suited to his own research.

But Elisabeth would brook no criticism of the professor, even when he allocated her the task of cleaning up the junk. This menial work was her first job in Margolin's laboratory. It was a testing time for her, for she spent most of her first months squatting on the floor armed with brushes, rags and cleaning fluid, removing grime and rust from Dr. Margolin's latest treasure.

Included in the research of the Margolin laboratory was the exploration of altered states of consciousness—a term widely used today but

247

novel at that time. Central was the study of hypnosis. The professor gave a series of lectures on hypnosis and taught some simple techniques. He then asked Elisabeth and a dozen or so hand-picked students to work on different approaches to the study.

She found that she could as readily be hypnotized as hypnotize others. As a research group, they attempted to better understand their own behavior patterns through hypnotic reverie in which they were regressed to re-experience their earliest memories. When Elisabeth was regressed, she talked about living the life of an American Indian in the Southwest. Some time later, in a deep trance, she recorded a terrifying experience. In her reverie an Indian of another tribe attempted to drown her in a river. The man tumbled her out of a canoe and then forcibly held her head under water. She described into the tape recorder how she managed to escape and scramble up a bank to safety. Because of her obvious distress, the hypnotist quickly brought her out of her trance.

In an adjacent house one of the students in the research group was also being hypnotized. The following evening when the complete research team gathered at Dr. Margolin's house to evaluate their experiments, Elisabeth played the tape on which she had recorded the attempted drowning. The student who had been hypnotized at the same time leaped to his feet. In his own reverie he had been canoeing on a river and had encountered a woman of a different tribe. He had tipped over the woman's canoe and had tried to drown her by forcing her head under the water!

Elisabeth excitedly questioned Dr. Margolin on the meaning of this extraordinary "coincidence," but the professor smiled and declined to draw any conclusions. He wanted to know what Elisabeth herself thought of it and what her own attitude was toward the concept of reincarnation. In his lectures and in his workshops Dr. Margolin's approach to "teaching" the mysteries of the mind was invariably Socratic.

Elisabeth's relationship with Dr. Margolin was now similar to the rich relationship she had had with Dr. Amsler at the Zurich eye clinic. He was much more than her director. He was her beloved mentor and father figure—and she felt able at any time to share with him her hopes and dreams, her excitement and gratitude.

She and Manny were frequently invited to the Margolin home,

sometimes for a quiet dinner, when their host would show off his very large collection of rare Indian artifacts, sometimes in the company of the brilliant minds he always attracted—the university's intellectuals or visiting European philosophers, scientists and men of letters. Elisabeth had never felt more intellectually stimulated. The professor often deliberately provoked her to debate, perhaps on the theories of Freud, Einstein or Darwin or on various metaphysical concepts.

If Dr. Margolin had one passion outside his own research, it was for music. He was never happier, never a better host, than when he had invited to his gracious home a string quartet—or, on more than one occasion, half the Denver Symphony Orchestra—to play for his guests. Manny especially relished these musical evenings.

At the end of the academic year Dr. Margolin invited Elisabeth to stay on his staff with the title of instructor in psychiatry. He was often absent from the university—sometimes on his anthropological expeditions in the Southwest, and sometimes overseas—and he expected Elisabeth to run his laboratory without specifically instructing her what to do. He gave her the key to his filing cabinets, and in the folders she discovered such a wealth of material on psychophysiology and other scientific research that she could, as she told Manny, have happily spent a year doing nothing else but reading his papers.

In his lectures and seminars Dr. Margolin found it difficult to speak in terms comprehensible to his students, and one of Elisabeth's self-set tasks was to transcribe into understandable language what she referred to as the "Margolin pearls." In her journal she recorded, "He is the Moses and I am his Aaron. He is the super brain and I am the interpreter. I have found I have a surprising gift as a communicator. I can speak in down-to-earth language, even if the accent is an odd mixture of Swiss and Harlem! . . . The Margolin laboratory is the most creative and exciting corner of the campus. . . . Oh, how I love this man!"

Through her first year with Dr. Margolin, Elisabeth's lectures and seminars had been confined to the students working in the Margolin laboratory. Then on an autumn afternoon as she was cleaning up the latest junked polygraph, Dr. Margolin strolled into the laboratory and casually asked her how she was getting on. She reached for the cleaning fluid and murmured that she would soon have the apparatus sparkling clean. He watched her for a while in silence, and then mentioned that he would have to be out of town on Friday, when he was scheduled to give a lecture to eighty senior medical students. Would Elisabeth please fill in for him? He turned and sauntered toward his office.

Her heart missed a beat. Then she stammered her alarm. She had never spoken to a large group! Did he simply want her to read his prepared lecture? Over his shoulder he told her that he had no planned lecture. Elisabeth could talk on any subject she fancied. She got up from the floor, wiped the grease off her hands and followed him to the office. But the students wouldn't listen to her, she protested. They were expecting him to lecture and they would walk out of the auditorium as soon as she reached the podium. Dr. Margolin shrugged. She had time to prepare her lecture. He waved a hand behind him at the filing cabinet. There was plenty of material from which she could choose.

In her own encounters with medical students and at lectures given by other psychiatrists Elisabeth had observed that medical students had little time for psychiatry. Most of them planned to enter other specialties. Would-be surgeons and internists were bored by lectures on manic-depressive psychosis and the principles of schizophrenic therapy.

For the next two days she spent most of her time considering a suitable subject for her first lecture. Somehow she had to capture the interest of the students. Somehow she must demonstrate that psychiatry was relevant to all branches of medicine, that it was the science of understanding the human mind and the ways in which destructive forces of fear, guilt and shame could cause mental breakdown and sometimes even irreversible physical damage.

What she needed was a topic of universal interest, a subject that would stifle the usual yawns. She was in her garden on Sunday morning sweeping up fallen leaves and thinking about the approach of winter and how the first frost would soon kill off the last of the flowers when the idea came to her.

The thought matured slowly as if, she later recorded in her journal, it were "a photographic print developing in a darkroom," as if it were a topic impinged upon her mind.

Yes, of course, that was what she could lecture on! She would talk to the senior medical students about death.

250

23

The Measure of Their Worth

STILL CLUTCHING HER BROOM, Elisabeth ran to the back of the house, where Manny was occupied with setting up a toy train set for two-and-a-half-year-old Kenneth, to tell him the subject she had chosen. He looked up and laughingly told her that with her broomstick, a black cat, a conical hat and a topic like that she would at least be sure to amuse the medical students.

She took several minutes trying to convince him she was serious, but he continued to protest her decision. The medical profession was concerned with life, not death, he argued, and he reminded her of the old adage that physicians buried their mistakes. Death was surely the last subject anyone would want to discuss in the halls of healing.

She retorted that it was precisely because no one in medical schools ever talked about death that it was so important to air the subject. No one mentioned it because the medical profession was, she suspected, collectively afraid of death—probably more so than the public. Couldn't Manny understand how important it was to break the conspiracy of silence shrouding the terminal wards of hospitals? Couldn't he see that it was time to speak out on a topic that was usually whispered about behind the hand? When it came to the issue of death, America was surely the most primitive country in the world. In Switzerland and in most other countries death was more often accepted with quiet grace.

The very arguments that Manny raised reinforced her conviction that she had chosen the right subject for her lecture. She could help the students face their own fears of death. She could speak about death traditions and attitudes in other countries and cultures, and contrast these practices with the way Americans preserved and pampered their corpses, rouged their lips and cheeks to give mourners the illusion that the dead person was only sleeping, that death had not really happened. Above all, she could try to convince students that a dying person is still a human being in need of understanding and special care.

She spent the afternoon working out the form of her lecture. She would divide it into two parts. In the first half she would speak on the rituals and customs of other cultures, and on the American way of coping with death. Then in the second session, in the manner of Swiss medical schools, she would try to bring to the auditorium a person who was actually dying and give the students an opportunity to question the patient.

When she presented her ideas to Manny at supper that night, he was much more impressed with her concept. Her difficulty, he suggested, would likely be in finding a dying person who would volunteer to be questioned in public.

On the following Monday morning Elisabeth went straight to the medical center's library. In the volumes and journals of psychiatry and internal medicine she found no useful literature on thanatology (the study of death). Much was written on terminal ailments, the symptoms of physical decline and the like. Some of the books carried chapters on palliative treatments, such as pain-killing drugs. But nowhere could she find material on the emotional aspects of dying, on the fears of dying patients and their special needs. Apparently no one had written on the role of the physician or nurse in coping with the feelings of the dying patient.

In the university library she found more helpful literature. The anthropological and sociological sections had volumes on death rituals, explaining, for example, why black veils are worn by grieving widows and why stones are placed upon graves. She was fascinated to learn how much poetry and music had been inspired by death. She read about the death rituals of Confucians, Taoists, Buddhists, Hindus, the rituals of Alaskans and American Indians, the Jewish view of death and the customs and attitudes of other cultural and racial groups.

Then she went on a search for a dying patient. Eventually she found a lovely young sixteen-year-old girl suffering from leukemia. Linda's green eyes were flashing angrily as Elisabeth entered her room, and her clenched fists pounded a pile of a hundred or more letters. As Elisabeth approached she suddenly swept the letters across the blanket and onto the floor.

Without prompting, Linda explained the cause of her outburst. Almost all the envelopes contained "sweet sixteen" birthday cards, mostly pink, sentimentally promising a roseate future. A week or so earlier Linda's mother had advertised in a Denver newspaper that her daughter might not see another birthday, and had invited the public to send birthday and get-well cards.

The cards had had an effect opposite to that which the senders intended. Linda knew she was dying, and she bitterly resented this conspiracy of silence in her presence and the outpouring of sentimentality, the gaudy pictures of roses and sunrises and the gushing expressions of affection from total strangers.

In another bout of fury Linda raged that she was not the piously innocent sacrificial virgin that all these cards suggested. In fact, she hated everyone at the moment, her mother included, and God as well. Why should she have been picked out of the crowd to die? What had she done to deserve it? Pity from strangers and mushy good wishes were the last things she wanted. All she wanted was to scream and to hit out and to hate.

Elisabeth listened. Only when Linda lay back exhausted on her pillows did she speak. "It must be tough," she said softly. "It must be very tough."

For the first time the girl turned her head and looked at Elisabeth. Then she began to cry.

Elisabeth spent more than an hour at Linda's bedside, mostly in silence—a silence in which trust matured. Then she asked Linda if she would agree to help some young men and women training to be doctors to understand what it was really like to be so ill. She could greatly help these medical students to be the kind of doctors who would truly grasp what someone like her was thinking and feeling, hoping and hating. Would Linda consider helping the students become better doctors by talking to them and answering their questions? Linda nodded.

Elisabeth spent the next two days preparing her first major lecture. She felt confident about her material, but on Friday afternoon when she walked to the stage in front of eighty medical students, her knees felt as if they were made of rubber, and the palms of her hands were cold and sweaty.

The students yawned or chewed gum. She sensed their disappointment at the sight of her instead of the renowned Dr. Margolin. She announced the subject of her talk and with a throat constricted by nervousness, she spoke on the attitudes toward death of different races and cultures. She spoke of America being a death-denying society, of how death was hidden from sight behind the screens in sterile hospital wards, and how corpses were hustled away to morgues or funeral homes.

Ten minutes into her lecture she was gratified to see that the students were listening intently. The sprawlers were sitting forward in their seats. Her nervousness retreated and her throat relaxed. Toward the end of her survey of rituals and attitudes she spoke of how the conditioned and common fear of death tragically demeaned the care of the dying, of how members of the healing professions themselves resented and even denied death, and how, because of this fear and denial, doctors and nurses fell wretchedly short of giving the quality of care deserved and needed by their patients.

Then she announced that, after a break, they would have the opportunity to meet someone who was terminally ill, someone who would not play games with them but who would answer truthfully their questions on what it felt like to be dying.

Before the lecture, Elisabeth had arranged for Linda to be wheeled in an invalid chair from her room in the hospital to the auditorium. She met her at the back of the stage. The girl smiled, as if to an old friend. She had washed and set her hair and touched her high cheekbones with a little color. She had dressed in a white turtleneck sweater, a light green jacket and slacks closely matching the color of her eyes—clothing that disguised her painfully thin body. She looked, thought Elisabeth, quite lovely.

When the students had resettled in the horseshoe-shaped auditorium, Elisabeth pushed Linda's chair onto the stage. A collective indrawing of breath, a whispered sound of disbelief came from the audience. The students had expected, of course, an old man or an old woman, someone wizened with age, not, as some of them later admitted, a teenager, not this lovely girl within a few years of their own ages, not a girl whom they could have proudly taken to a campus dance, or skiing or, perhaps—if she had been a couple of years older—to bed.

Elisabeth introduced Linda and thanked her for volunteering to help make the lecture more graphic. The girl smiled shyly. Then Elisabeth invited a half-dozen of the students to come to the stage. None moved. The students seemed stunned and incredulous, these young men and women who ordinarily were so brash, assertive, confident, some cynical, some whom she knew to be conceitedly conscious of superior intellects—all of whom had chosen a profession dedicated to healing and giving solace.

Eventually Elisabeth was obliged to handpick the students to step up to the stage and to undertake the interrogating of Linda. They came slowly, reluctantly, and half surrounded the girl in the wheelchair. Elisabeth herself started the questioning. Would Linda like to talk about her illness? Would she speak about how it felt to lose the strength of her body? What did she feel when she had first been told she had leukemia? What did she feel about her family? Did her friends still come to see her? What were her hopes and dreams?

At first quietly, shyly, and then in a stronger and more confident voice, Linda answered these personal and intimate questions. The illness made her feel tired. She loved tennis, but then one day she found that she couldn't breathe properly and she had had to withdraw from a tournament, and this had upset her very much. She hadn't known anything about leukemia, but she had understood that there was something seriously wrong with her when her mother had uncharacteristically started buying her lots of clothes and other things. Her

255

mother had also suddenly started kissing and hugging her a lot. Her friends now rarely or never came to see her, and when they did most of them pretended nothing was wrong with her. She would rather they didn't come at all than that they should feel so awkward with her. Two or three of her special friends still came to see her. That was nice. What she hoped for most was that she would graduate from high school. She was trying to keep up with her school work, but it wasn't easy, because she always felt so tired.

With a flash of anger Linda referred again to her mother's advertising her birthday and sickness in the paper. Her mother hadn't even asked her for permission to do this! She hated the sickly pink "sweet sixteen" cards from all those strangers. It was all so phony!

Elisabeth drew away from the chair and invited the students on the stage to question Linda. At first they shuffled their feet. When they started to ask questions—mostly irrelevant clinical questions on symptoms—Elisabeth realized that they covered up their own discomfort, their own fears, with stiff attitudes and academic terms, maintaining an emotional distance between themselves and the girl. They sounded cold, aloof and uncaring. The students in the audience followed the demonstration in tense silence.

Elisabeth also observed that Linda seemed freer, vastly more at ease, than the healthy young men and women sitting around her. Clearly it wasn't Linda but the students who were deeply afraid of dying.

At the first sign of Linda's fatigue, Elisabeth sent the students to their seats and beckoned to the orderly to wheel the girl back to the hospital ward. She gave her a big hug and thanked her for so courageously sharing her feelings. Before she disappeared from sight, Linda turned and smiled and waved to the students.

When she had gone, the silence in the auditorium was absolute. Elisabeth gave this silence full play before she invited discussion. The students now dropped their masks of sophistication and professional aloofness. One student after another rose to speak. Some choked as they did so. They admitted, most of them, that they had never been more moved in their lives.

Moved by what? Elisabeth interjected sharply.

Moved by Linda's courage, said one student. Moved by her youth and her beauty and the denial of her hopes ever being fulfilled, said another.

Perhaps, suggested Elisabeth, what they—so healthy, so self-assured—were facing for the first time was their own mortality, the fact that they too could be struck down in the prime of their youth. If they could thus face and admit—and thus vanquish—their own fear of death, they would be vastly better able to understand what goes on in the minds of all terminally ill people. Through Linda's courage and selflessness in offering to come and speak to them, they would perhaps understand that the care of the terminally ill is not merely an intellectual challenge, but also a very human act calling upon the qualities of the heart. The full measure of their worth as physicians would be gauged not only by their scientific skills, but by their capacity for compassion.

Concluding her lecture, Elisabeth suggested to a completely silent auditorium that if Linda had helped the students break through the barrier of their greatest fear—the fear of death—and if she had helped them to understand that the art of healing is as much an art of the heart as of the head; if the young girl had given them a fresh, true and noble interpretation of love, then Linda's life—short though it seemed likely to be—would prove rich far, far beyond her present awareness.

═══24═══
The Three Wise Men

THE STUDENTS FILED OUT of the auditorium, and Elisabeth was left alone except for an aging janitor who was waiting to turn out the lights and lock up. She apologized to him for the lateness of the hour. So many students had remained behind to ask questions, to defend their behavior, to plead for a reprint of the lecture, that the session had taken considerably longer than she had anticipated.

She stuffed her notes into her tote bag, and instead of phoning Manny to pick her up in the car she decided to walk home. So many ideas were stirring in her mind. There was so much to think about.

It was one of those autumn twilights with the air crisping to a hard frost and holding the pungent smell of burning leaves and the more fragile scent of the bygone summer. Walking briskly through the campus and down streets of family homes, she absorbed the suburban serenity. Outside one home a family was packing a recreational vehicle, arguing good-naturedly about the hour at which they would set out for the mountains on the following day. Through the window of another house she observed a family seated at their dining-room table, and in the lighted garage of a third a man and his teenage son were working with a saw and lathe.

She should be satisfied with her own life in this safe and pleasant place. With their combined incomes, she and Manny now had no financial problems. Kenneth was healthy and growing apace. Her own home was comfortable, her kitchen and garden her delight. She had friends enough—warm-hearted neighbors and intellectual company. Her work was always stimulating, and doubtless when Dr. Margolin returned to Denver and was told of the success of her lecture he would give her more responsibilities, more chances to share her philosophy and experiences with medical students. Then too she had the mountains for her retreat, and opportunities to explore the Southwest, to re-experience perhaps those strange feelings of having lived before in this corner of the planet. Whence, then, came these abrasive thoughts that paradise had not been reached, that she was at a distance yet from her still-undefined life goals?

Turning into 17th Avenue, she saw the lights of her own home and reluctantly switched her thoughts from philosophical musings to domestic problems. She had just employed a new housekeeper after having hired and fired four in the six months since Margrit had left for Switzerland. She also had a visitor at home, her mother-in-law, who invariably created some tension. The elderly deaf-mute woman had an insatiable curiosity about family affairs. Only the previous evening Elisabeth had flared on discovering that her mother-in-law had poked about in the closets of the master bedroom. A few days earlier when there had been dinner guests there had been another row when Elisabeth had thrown out a vase of plastic flowers with which her mother-in-law had decorated the dining-room table and then awkwardly tried to explain that plastic flowers and plastic tablecloths, indeed almost everything plastic, were anathema to her.

Now as she paused on the path to the front door, Elisabeth wondered whether her own feelings of restlessness, her sense of being stalled in the pursuit of her goal, albeit still undefined, had caused her to overreact to comparatively trivial irritations. Indeed, the two or three needling issues, which should have been forgotten as soon as they were resolved, only stimulated her impatience to be on the move toward that special frontier which she had known since her childhood to be awaiting her. If there was one temptation to be avoided at all costs it was the possibility of being lulled into accepting the "good life" of the American suburbs. As she walked the lawn-flanked path to her own front door, she saw suddenly an image of the mountain men climbing the slopes in Switzerland—those tiny figures who clung to the distant rock face and pitted their strength and skill against the might of nature—men who had left behind the warmth and security of the cabin to test their courage, skill and resolve on frozen wind-swept peaks. Symbolically, this was what she wanted most to do—to quit the cushions and comforts, to feel the pain of stretched sinew and the knife edge of mountain wind.

That night after Manny was asleep, Elisabeth lay long awake, still troubled by feelings of non-fulfillment, by fears of being sidetracked or halted by cosseting. She urgently needed, she decided, help and advice. Her first thought was to seek out Dr. Margolin. She now felt as close to him as a daughter, yet the very closeness of her relationship with her mentor could, she considered, be a handicap to objective counseling. She thought then of two other men, Dr. René Spitz and Dr. John D. Benjamin, sages both, who might help her to understand her feelings of stagnation. Both men were associated with the university's department of psychiatry.

Dr. Spitz, a Swiss, the author of the internationally acclaimed work *The First Year of Life,* was a visiting professor of psychiatry at the University of Colorado. He lived six months of each year in Switzerland, and six months in Denver, where he maintained a gracious European-style home. She had recently attended a couple of his lectures and had been deeply impressed by the sagacity of the small white-bearded man who looked very much like pictures of Sigmund Freud. She wrote to him and asked for a consultation.

On a bitterly cold day in mid-January, Dr. Spitz received her warmly and took her to his library, a handsomely proportioned room, its walls lined with books from floor to ceiling. There was a crackling log fire in the ornate hearth. When she was comfortably seated in a cushioned chair, he removed his gold-rimmed spectacles and peered at her quizzically. His eyes were warm, his voice soft and very kind.

Partly perhaps because they communicated half in Swiss-German and half in English, she felt so much at home with the distinguished professor that she could have believed that she was back in Zurich. In fact, they began the session by talking of Zurich, of buildings, streets, restaurants and mountain scenery familiar to them both, of people they both knew, including Professor Bleuler, whom Dr. Spitz much admired.

It seemed to Elisabeth as if she had known Dr. Spitz for many years, and that in relating to him her life story, and then her present hopes and restlessness, she was reaching a deeply understanding heart. She remained closeted with him for seven hours, their dialogue interrupted only by a housekeeper bringing sandwiches and refills of the coffeepot.

He reminisced about his meetings with Freud, Jung, Adler. He, too, had struggled to find a satisfying philosophy: the search for life's meaning was an endless one. He cautioned her against firm conclusions. Had not the aging Freud himself recanted many of his earlier theories? He, Dr. Spitz, was constantly rethinking, even in his ninth decade, many concepts he had advanced vigorously in the prime of his life.

Elisabeth still had much to learn. She could study a thousand books and sit at the feet of a score of masters, but the most significant gap in her knowledge was in her understanding of herself—in comprehending what had created her personality, in understanding her motivations and reactions, her basic likes and dislikes, as well as her disquiet and her sense of harmony.

At this stage of her career what would prove most valuable to her was an examination of even the seemingly trivial experiences of her infancy and childhood out of which the tapestry of her personality had been fabricated. In short, Elisabeth's greatest gain could evolve from psychoanalysis, and he suggested the Chicago Psychoanalytic Institute, which was affiliated with the University of Colorado.

She was surprised and disappointed. Psychoanalysis was one area of psychiatry that she had never considered. She told Dr. Spitz that she was quite repelled by the idea of lying on a leather couch for hourly sessions four or five times a week for from three to five years. Couldn't she just as easily, conveniently and much more economically talk to her bedroom wall or to the flowers in her garden?

Dr. Spitz agreed that psychoanalysis was not for everyone, and indeed there were few who could afford the time or the money for it; but no matter her present prejudice against it, he believed that were Elisabeth to make the investment the profit would be more than worthwhile.

She looked up at the clock on the mantelpiece and gasped. She could recall, she told him, no occasion when time had passed more quickly. He bowed with old-fashioned courtesy, kissed her hand and smilingly assured her that when a young woman forgot the time while in his company his leathery old heart was more than gratified. (The leathery old heart was soon to stop beating. Elisabeth's consultation was the last of any length given by Dr. Spitz. She never saw him again. Some time later he returned to Switzerland, where he died.)

Dr. Benjamin was younger than Dr. Spitz by a decade. He was a thin, inconspicuous-looking man with tufts of gray hair at the temples of an otherwise bald head. He had gained fame as a writer and lecturer on a variety of psychiatric theories and procedures. When, ten days after seeing Dr. Spitz, she arrived at his office, she did not know that he too was close to death.

Once again she poured out her life story and confessed her feelings of restlessness. She told him how she had worked at a state hospital and coped with every variety of serious psychotic ailment. She had had experience with neurotic adults and mentally disturbed children in the sophisticated environment of Montefiore. She had worked with Dr. Margolin on his psychophysiological research. She had lectured on psychiatry to medical students. The idea of private practice had now faded from her mind, one reason being that she couldn't conceive of charging the standard fees of psychiatrists, nor could she see herself sitting in an office chair all day. Yet she would like, if possible, to be independent, to set her own rules, to be able to follow her own course without interference.

With all this experience, and perhaps some special gifts in the arts of healing and communicating, how, she asked him, should she now be employing her time and her energy?

Dr. Benjamin questioned her closely, first on her feelings of restlessness and then on her expressed hope that there was "a still misted horizon out there" waiting to be explored. She believed that her feelings and hopes were associated. The restlessness stemmed from her need to seek—but what was it that she should be seeking.

262

Just as Dr. Spitz had declined to do, so Dr. Benjamin refused to answer these direct questions; and like Dr. Spitz, Dr. Benjamin too concluded by urging her to undergo psychoanalysis at the Chicago Psychoanalytic Institute.

Still refusing to accept this advice, Elisabeth now sought out Dr. Margolin. She felt she had been foolish not to go to him with her problem in the first instance. He knew her as well as, perhaps better than, anybody. He would surely understand, would be bound to give her answers more palatable and practical.

Once again she related her life story—or at least those parts of it that he didn't know—and she told him that in spite of enormously enjoying her work with him, she knew that psychophysiological research was not meant to be her lifework.

Although she purposely did not tell him about her meetings with the other two eminent psychiatrists, Dr. Margolin used almost exactly their arguments in telling her that the time had arrived when she could profitably undergo psychoanalysis, and he too suggested the Chicago Psychoanalytic Institute as the only possible and most suitable place, since it had made special provision for non-resident clients. There was, he added, good airline service between Denver and Chicago. She could conveniently fly to Chicago twice a week.

In frustration Elisabeth threw up her hands. She acknowledged to him now her meetings with and the conclusions of Dr. Spitz and Dr. Benjamin. He laughed delightedly over this confession. The mule, he said, always needs three thwacks with a stick!

Elisabeth raised other arguments. The cost of psychoanalysis in Chicago would be appalling. She could not conceive of leaving her husband and child to fend for themselves through half of each week. She would have to curtail her work at his laboratory, and her salary was needed to pay off the mortgage.

Dr. Margolin shrugged away these objections. Surely they could be resolved if she had the will to resolve them. What Elisabeth didn't perhaps appreciate was what a privilege it would be to be accepted by the Chicago Psychoanalytic Institute. With recommendations from Dr. Spitz, Dr. Benjamin and himself, he believed Elisabeth might well succeed.

She talked over the proposition with Manny, and when they had totted up the figures of their family budget neither was very happy.

Manny agreed, however, that Elisabeth should go ahead with the Chicago venture if she wished, even if it meant returning to peanut butter and jelly.

Enclosing letters of high recommendation from her three advisers, she applied for admission to the Institute. She was invited for a series of interviews by a group of analysts who cross-examined her for hours on what she often felt were totally irrelevant matters. They asked her, for instance, to tell her favorite Bible story and the names of her favorite artists. They asked her technical questions on psychiatry and questioned her at length about her feelings on being a triplet. The only time she enjoyed herself was when she told the full group of a dozen analysts of her strong objections to psychoanalysis. Because it was so costly and time-consuming, she argued, it was out of reach of the masses, and her interest was in ordinary people, especially in the handicapped, psychotics and dying patients, none of whom were likely candidates for psychoanalysis.

On the journey back to Denver she had hopes of being turned down. Nothing felt right about the prospect of commuting to Chicago. She had a sense of struggling against the current instead of moving with it, as when she had applied for the job in India.

To her amazement, however, she was accepted. She would be expected to start her twice-weekly analysis in July. She would commute by air.

Since coming to Denver, during times of confusion she had sought out the one area where she could always find peace, the desert of the Southwest. Now whenever there was an opportunity, she drove out to the pueblos. In her journal she wrote:

Oh, this beautiful sense of timelessness, this feeling of belonging. These Indian people are my people, and when I'm with them it's like being home. I take within myself the beauty of the area, the changing colors, the vegetation, the scent of the air, the feel of the wind and the loneliness. I saw today two small Indian children sitting alongside the road—no sign of habitation, no adults. I could so easily have sat down with them and stayed with them forever. . . . Is this where I really belong?

It was in this period too that Elisabeth started to collect Indian artifacts. On one occasion in an Indian store she saw a woven basket on a shelf. She asked the Indian to show it to her, but knew before she took it in her hands that she had seen it before. It was as if she had found something she lost long ago. When Manny protested the price, Elisabeth didn't explain why she would have given three times its cost to possess it.

In spring Elisabeth found she was pregnant. She had badly wanted another child, but she had not been optimistic. Since the birth of Kenneth, when her cervix had been damaged, she had had three early miscarriages as well as corrective surgery. A new gynecologist warned her that she would have to take every precaution if she were to carry the baby to full term. At all costs she must avoid fatigue. Now at least she had a legitimate excuse to postpone the psychoanalysis in Chicago. She wrote to the Institute saying she was not prepared to risk the life of her baby by taking fatiguing air trips twice a week.

During her pregnancy Elisabeth enjoyed excellent health and continued to lecture medical students and work at the Margolin laboratory.

One lab project that created special interest sought evidence of physiological effects of pessimism and optimism. In the course of one of her lectures a student had asked if the rate of the growth of a cancerous tumor could be influenced by moods. Having no answer, she suggested that the student devise ways of measuring the growth rates of tissues of depressed and cheerful personalities. Results could be of far-reaching significance, Elisabeth suggested. It might be found, for instance, that a tumor in a depressed patient grew faster than a similar tumor in a person of cheerful disposition.

The group settled on measuring the growth rates of fingernails. By superimposing on each other photographs of fingernails taken each day over a period of many months, it was possible to obtain accurate measurements of growth. Comparing the growth rates of different personality types brought some interesting results, and an award for imaginative research for the student who was assigned the project. It was these kinds of experiments in the Margolin laboratory that fired extraordinary enthusiasm in the medical school.

Strangely, as Elisabeth now reflects, she did not give a sequel to her lecture on Death and Dying. The field of psychiatry was so broad that the topics of her subsequent lectures were necessarily limited to the curriculum, and ranged over the whole field of psychophysiology and psychopathology. She borrowed heavily from the "Margolin pearls" in his filing cabinets, interpreting the erudition of her mentor. Students were grateful for the teamwork which brought the genius of Dr. Margolin to a younger generation of physicians.

Whenever possible, Elisabeth tried to follow a lecture with a demonstration in the manner of Linda's participation in the lecture on death. To verify the theoretical framework of her lecture she invited students to question volunteer patients. She was surprised herself by the extraordinary popularity of this style of teaching—her laboratory courses were always oversubscribed—and she began to see that if teaching were both provocative and relevant, students had little difficulty absorbing essential data.

She continued to work through the beginning of her ninth month of pregnancy. On the first Friday of December she was concluding an auditorium lecture on psychosomatic asthma, and had just stretched out an arm to emphasize the salient issues written on the blackboard behind her, when she felt something give way in her abdomen. It was a few seconds before she realized that her amniotic membranes had ruptured and that her skirt was soaked.

She was sitting down when the mishap occurred, and the table in front of her saved her from embarrassment. She ended her remarks quickly and then called back the last of the students as he was leaving the auditorium. Without telling him the reason, she asked him to telephone her husband to call for her in the car immediately. It was rather urgent.

After Manny arrived, they called the office of her obstetrician, who reassured her that since she was not yet experiencing any labor pains, she could go home and take things quietly while he enjoyed a scheduled weekend of golf. Unless she developed a fever or other symptoms, he would not see her again until Monday. Elisabeth agreed, and looked forward to a weekend at home with Manny and Kenneth. She spent Saturday and Sunday cooking meals to be put in the freezer and eaten while she was confined to the hospital.

On Monday morning she awakened early, feeling wretched. She had no fever, but her abdomen was as tight as a board. Manny was

266

concerned and rushed her to the Catholic hospital at which she had been booked. Peritonitis was quickly diagnosed; because of the serious infection the chances of her baby's survival were now slender. Indeed, if there was to be any chance at all, she must on no account be given an anesthetic or any pain-killing drugs. Labor was immediately induced and for the next eighteen hours Elisabeth suffered what she describes as "a nightmare beyond description." Despite her constant pleading and screams, she was refused even the mildest analgesics. At times she couldn't breathe, and twice she had brief cardiac arrests. Crucifixes on the wall reminded her of the room in which Seppli had suffered and died, and there were moments when she too earnestly hoped to die. Her inflamed abdomen was so tender that even the gentlest touch set off a fresh spasm. Finally she was wheeled into a delivery room where attendants were constantly present.

From conversation around her bed she perceived that the Catholic medical staff appeared more interested in saving the life of her baby than her own life, and she convinced herself that she was compelled to suffer this intolerable pain because church dogma disallowed risking the life of a baby that was not yet ready to be born and yet could not survive much longer in the womb. As had happened at her first delivery, so now the opportunities for performing a caesarian section were allowed to pass.

Elisabeth believes today that under hypnosis she could have had a virtually painless delivery, and she still looks back upon the birth of Barbara as the "cruelest, most inhumane experience" she has ever had to endure.

The nightmare ended with Barbara's first cry. Weighing only three pounds and seven ounces, the infant was placed in an incubator.

All Elisabeth could now think about was leaving this hospital, with its appalling memories, and getting home to her garden and her family. Recalling how her own mother had in the face of strong medical opposition taken her triplets home where she could nurse them round the clock, Elisabeth decided that tiny Barbara's chances of surviving would rest on the kind of twenty-four-hour care that she alone could and would give her baby. Elisabeth herself left the hospital after three days, returning only to provide maternal milk. One week later, when Barbara had gained half an ounce above birth weight, Elisabeth put

267

on her white medical gown and went to the ward, where she personally authorized Barbara's immediate discharge from the hospital.

One day at home while she was breast-feeding Barbara, Manny told her for the first time of his desire to find another professional appointment. As the only neuropathologist in Denver, he was isolated from colleagues. Neuropathology was still a comparatively new science, and there were many times when he felt the need to consult and exchange ideas with other neuropathologists.

After some discussion she agreed that they should go. Perhaps, she thought, a move would be the answer to her own restlessness. They immediately set about the task of sending applications to a number of large medical schools, hoping that one among them might need both a neuropathologist and a psychiatrist.

It would be a month before they could expect replies from the dozen schools to which they had written, so Elisabeth impulsively decided to use up the remainder of her maternity leave by making a trip to Switzerland. Barbara, pink, almost bald, hazel-eyed and beautiful, now weighed about five pounds. Elisabeth was immensely proud of the baby, who had never had more than a 50 percent chance of surviving.

Manny drove Elisabeth, Kenneth and his new daughter to the Denver airport, where it was announced there would be a delay in departure because of bad weather in the vicinity of New York. The information made Elisabeth uneasy, with a sense of some danger ahead.

===== 25 =====

Nearer the Frontier

UNTIL THE STEWARDESSES started serving dinner, the flight to New York was unusually smooth. Barbara lay gurgling in a travel bed at Elisabeth's feet. Kenneth had wearied of toys and picture books and was restless. Stewardesses placed trays—the main course was a goulash—on folding tables.

Suddenly Elisabeth had a renewed sense of danger. Yet there appeared to be absolutely no cause for alarm. Stewardesses continued to push food trolleys down the aisle, and across the aisle two men in business suits who had clearly imbibed too much were laughing uproariously.

For a moment Elisabeth froze with fright. Then swiftly she pushed the food tray off Kenneth's table, and in spite of the boy's protests she fastened his seat belt. She also fastened her own seat belt and then picked up Barbara.

Within seconds and without any warning the plane hit an air pocket and dropped like a stone. The cabin filled with the screams of passengers, many of whom were hurled from their seats. Food trays and hand luggage were tossed about, and oxygen masks popped from their receptacles. A number of passengers were injured and burned by hot food. The stewardess who had served their meal had a badly lacerated face, and one of the half-drunk men appeared to be knocked out and was lying in the aisle.

Elisabeth and the children were unscathed, but the travel bed from which moments earlier she had snatched the baby was swamped with hot goulash. Had Barbara still been in it, she might have suffered burns, even if she had not been tossed violently out of it.

As she held Barbara to her breast and comforted Kenneth, Elisabeth searched her mind for an explanation of the premonition she had experienced. After Seppli's untimely death she had spent more time contemplating questions of life and death and the intuitive guidance given from time to time to individuals. Surely there had to be some caring force, some communication that could not be explained by science. For how else to interpret a clear warning of danger that could not be picked up by the aircraft's radar?

Busy now with the clean-up and Kenneth's tears, she pushed these thoughts to the back of her mind. Later there would be time to ponder these mysteries, perhaps to talk to people with more specific religious faiths.

She was met at La Guardia Airport by the courteous kindly officials of Swissair, who took immediate charge of everything, even providing clean bedding for Barbara. The remainder of the flight went without a hitch.

In Switzerland Elisabeth enjoyed seeing her mother again and catching up on the news. Erika proudly showed off her son, Thomas, Elisabeth's godson. No less proud was Elisabeth of Kenneth and her new baby daughter. Eva, whose second marriage was obviously happy, came to Zurich from her new home in Basel.

But Elisabeth wrote in her journal:

I love my sisters dearly and I know we would, were the need to arise, do all we could to help each other. But except for babies and backgrounds, our interests are now wide apart. I can raise little enthusiasm for discussion on domestic, parochial and even national issues. . . . I will always be grateful for my Swiss heritage, but emotionally my links to Switzerland have weakened to the point where I could snap them without tears. The fact is that I feel more at home in America than I do in the country of birth.

The weather contributed to dampening what she had hoped would be a rejuvenating holiday. Almost every day rain and bitter wind lashed Zurich, and the city that she had always thought of as being colorful and exciting now appeared cold and gray. The cold penetrated her marrow, and she was warm only under her featherbed. She shivered in her mother's home and in the stores, and found herself bickering with Mrs. Kübler and her sister over the low setting of thermostats. The controversy became absurdly important, and she blamed Swiss thriftiness for her discomfort. Then Barbara caught a cold and became very seriously ill. A pediatrician had to be called in. For two days her life hung in the balance. Elisabeth was obliged to stay at home, in a house that was cold in comparison with America's overheated ones, and worry about humidifiers, baby formulas and fevers when she longed to take Kenneth to the mountains. Her hopes that fresh Swiss air would enhance Barbara's growth were dashed.

So when she returned to America, she did so with a sense of relief and thankfulness, and a resolve that the next time she sang the American national anthem she would do so with special gusto.

Manny greeted her with the news that they had received affirmative replies to their applications for professional appointments from two cities: Albuquerque, New Mexico, and Chicago. Because of her love for the Southwest and Indian culture, Elisabeth's first choice was Albuquerque; but the better offer for Manny came from Chicago's Northwestern University Medical Center, which was associated with the Chicago Wesleyan Memorial Hospital. Elisabeth had the opportunity of an appointment at three places in Chicago, but none of them excited her.

Still steeped in the tradition that a wife should accede to her husband's preference, she agreed to go to Chicago, though she kept her options open on whether to join a university faculty at all. There would be non-teaching hospitals in Chicago, she pointed out, and other institutions as well that might need a psychiatrist. She also realized that Manny's choice would allow her conveniently to undergo psychoanalysis at the Chicago Psychoanalytic Institute.

Placing the children in the care of Margrit, who had returned from

271

Switzerland with her (Kenneth was now attending nursery school), Elisabeth and Manny flew to Chicago in early March for interviews and a scouting trip. The city overwhelmed her. How on earth, she asked Manny, could she ever get used to all the hustle and bustle and acclimatize herself to Chicago's weather after enjoying the clean and crisp air of Colorado?

They had taken a full week off work to allow time to explore the city, and perhaps to find a job for Elisabeth. They were anxious too to get the feel of the city and find the right place for a new home.

She called first at the Psychoanalytic Institute, where she was advised that she could start her analysis in July. Then, by appointment and on the recommendation of a Denver friend, she visited a center for retarded and handicapped children.

While touring the wards and dayrooms of the center, she had to force back tears. Even at Manhattan State Hospital she had not seen such tragedy and pathos. In one room she saw small patients of indefinable ages with old faces but whose physiques and behavior were infantile. In another room she met children with enormous hydrocephalic heads; and yet another room was filled with children who simply stared vacantly at the ceiling and were completely unresponsive to her touch, words or smile.

At the end of the tour, Elisabeth turned to the compassionate woman who had conducted her around the center and said that she was ready to hang up her coat and join the staff immediately. She longed, as she phrased it in her journal, "to help bring some of these children back to some sort of life."

But Manny, the pragmatist, cooled her ardor. At their hotel that evening he reminded her that the center was situated in a crime-infested area, difficult of access, and that sensibly they should first consider the welfare of their own children. What she should be contemplating was work not far from home, and the home should be in an area where they could raise Kenneth and Barbara without being constantly concerned about their safety and well-being.

After a visit and interview at the Michael Reese Hospital, she went to her last appointment, at the department of psychiatry of sprawling Billings Hospital on the campus of the University of Chicago. The head of the department had recently resigned, and the overworked deputy was clearly anxious to get through the formal interview as quickly as possible. Elisabeth was immediately impressed with the facilities. The job she had sought was either for in-patient service or to work for the consultation and liaison services. She was offered a position as assistant professor of psychiatry. Her full responsibilities would be explained to her should she accept the position. There would be opportunities to teach.

A special advantage of joining the faculty would be the priority given her children at the Laboratory School adjacent to the University of Chicago.

A possible new life pattern now began to emerge. From Billings Hospital it was only a fifteen-minute drive to Marynook, a small enclave of pleasant family homes inhabited largely by junior faculty and others associated with the University of Chicago. It was a racially mixed neighborhood in which whites and blacks seemed to live in harmony. Elisabeth and Manny parked their rented car and walked the tree-lined streets. They noticed approvingly many children on bicycles, toys on tidy lawns and swings in back yards. Marynook felt right, especially when a realtor took them to a fairly modern split-level three-bedroom dwelling. The house on Kimbark Avenue would be vacant for renting on June 1.

Quite confident that they were both going to be given the university positions for which they had been interviewed, they secured the house with a check for two months' rent.

Once more Elisabeth had a strong feeling of being on course, and in a letter to her sisters she wrote:

> I feel very strongly that there has to be a good reason, and one beyond the opportunity to go to the Psychoanalytic Institute, for our moving to Chicago. Of course, city-bred Manny is completely at home in this vast metropolis. If it were not for the way things have dovetailed together, including a super kindergarten for Kenneth, I'd be weeping for a home in the country. Perhaps some day ... I think what really clinched things for me is that we've already found a housekeeper. The people now occupying the house we'll be renting have this elderly black woman, Leola Ellis, who is going to stay with us and work for us. The present tenants describe her as a jewel, and I believe them. I always hoped that I would find a nanny like Leola for my children, for I want them to grow up really understanding black people.

Shortly after their return to Denver, Elisabeth and Manny were notified they had obtained the appointments in Chicago. At one of several farewell parties given in their honor, Dr. Margolin assured Elisabeth that so long as he was at the University of Colorado he would have a staff position for her should she ever want to return.

She wrote to Dr. Spitz to tell him of developments, of her new baby and of her intention to start her own psychoanalysis in July. In reply, Dr. Spitz expressed his delight. Though the Freudian technique would not necessarily work miracles, he felt confident that Elisabeth would gain a much better understanding of herself and her motives, and thus she would be a better teacher.

She pounced on the word. "Teacher!" she exclaimed aloud. Was that what she was meant to be?

She also went to see Dr. Benjamin, who was in a hospital and gravely ill. As a gift to him she conducted a vigorous campus campaign for blood donors and was chagrined to learn that she herself was prohibited from donating blood because her weight was only a hundred pounds.

On the day that the house on 17th Avenue was sold, Elisabeth stood meditatively at her living-room window overlooking the garden she had created, now abloom with Swiss flowers, including edelweiss and the blue wegwarte. After a moment, she shrugged and turned away. She deliberately curbed her thoughts whenever they seemed to be drawn toward sentimental nostalgia. She had learned long ago—at Meilen, Ecurcey, in Belgium and in Poland—that she could not afford the luxury of dwelling upon the past. She would think of her three years in Denver as good years—happy, exciting and rewarding years—and she would look back on them with gratitude but not with regret. She would, she decided, always live for the day—cheerfully if she could, painfully struggling if she must—and not long for her yesterdays.

Two weeks before they left Colorado, Elisabeth pressed Manny into taking her on a last drive into Indian territory. They did not drive as far as Monument Valley, where she had had the strange déjà vu experience, but once again she had the overwhelming conviction of having once lived among the Indians. This time she shared her thoughts with Manny. She was imagining things, he said. She confessed how difficult it was to reconcile her scientific mind with a deepening belief that there were factors, mysteries and other planes of consciousness beyond scientific explanation. How could science explain the intuition upon which she leaned heavily when treating patients? She related to him for the first time the extraordinary premonition of danger she had been given on the flight to New York. She was troubled by his skepticism, troubled that differences in their beliefs might cause a rift between them, a rift that could become unbridgeable.

They drove to Chicago by way of Yellowstone Park, fulfilling a promise to Kenneth that they would show him geysers and bears. After ten days of leisurely traveling, Manny pulled the car into the driveway of the rented house on Kimbark Avenue. With the assistance of Leola, whom the children immediately adored, unpacking and settling into the new home proved no hardship, and they quickly got to know their neighbors. They were due to report for duty on the first Monday of July.

On the evening of the last Friday in June Elisabeth answered the newly installed phone. In a gratingly harsh and authoritative voice, the caller introduced himself. He was, he said, to be her analyst at the Chicago Psychoanalytic Institute, and she must report to him at eleven o'clock on the following Monday. Elisabeth told him that that would be impossible as she would be starting her new job at Billings Hospital on that day.

His voice rose an octave. Did Elisabeth not understand the extraordinary privilege of being accepted by the Institute? Did she not appreciate the tightness of his own schedule? She would either report to his office at eleven o'clock on Monday or he would erase her name from his list of clients; and if he did that he doubted whether any other psychoanalyst at the Institute would take her on. He slammed down the phone in her ear.

Elisabeth was thunderstruck. She had never experienced such rudeness. Given her continuing ambivalence about undergoing psychoanalysis, had it not been for the caliber of the three men in Denver who had urged it upon her, she would probably have limited her knowledge of the analyst to the ugly sound of his voice. All that now intrigued her was to find out what was wrong with him!

On Monday she reported at Billings Hospital along with a dozen other newly appointed psychiatrists. Because the new head of the department had yet to be appointed, some organizational confusion continued and she felt sure her absence would not be noticed were she to slip away for a couple of hours.

Taking a cab, she arrived at the analyst's office five minutes early. Feeling some anxiety about her first encounter with what was obviously an aggressive personality, she lit up a cigarette. She was not aware of the door of the analyst's office opening until she heard an angry and familiar voice behind her ordering her to put it out.

Elisabeth admits to having a "Freudian forgetfulness" about the face of the man selected to be her analyst. She can say only that she believes he had "sort of dark hair and a reddish face."

Certainly the face was glowering at her when she turned toward him. He beckoned her to his office and then jerked a thumb toward a leather-cushioned chair. So far as she recalls, his first words to her were "Go ahead!" She raised a puzzled eyebrow. He instructed her to start talking about her life.

Hesitantly she began to speak about being a triplet, about her birth and early childhood, but less than three minutes into her monologue the red face seemed to be contorted by pain. Was there something wrong? she asked.

He threw down his pencil. Indeed there was something wrong! Elisabeth, he said, obviously had a speech impediment, because he was able to understand only one word in five of what she was uttering. There would be little purpose in starting years of analysis until she first underwent speech therapy and learned to articulate the English language.

She gaped at him, her own cheeks reddening with anger. While it was quite obvious, she replied, that she had a foreign accent, she had in fact been a lecturer at the University of Colorado for the past three years and no one had complained of failing to understand her.

She stood up, smoothed her skirt and told him icily that even if there were no problem of communication, she was not going to waste her own time and money on undergoing analysis with anyone so rude and aggressive. She sailed out of the office with as much dignity as she could muster.

At Billings Hospital no one seemed to have missed her; a senior member of the faculty told her that her main responsibilities would be lecturing medical students on psychiatry, and the care of patients on the psychiatric in-patient unit. (Later on she would take over this unit and eventually the psychiatric consultations of the medical-surgical units.) Her spirits lifted. She was to be a physician once again!

Manny, who had to drive considerably farther to Northwestern University, picked her up in the car at five o'clock. They exchanged stories of their first-day experiences, and she told him of her brief unpleasant session with the analyst. It seemed likely, she thought, that she had burned her bridges at the Psychoanalytic Institute, but she wasn't going to shed any tears.

To her surprise, the analyst telephoned her again that night. He asked her to come to his office once more. She reluctantly agreed, for the sole purpose of analyzing mutual feelings of dislike, and returned to his office on the following day. She told him at once that she had come to see him again only to terminate their relationship in a professional manner. As if she were a recalcitrant child, he completely ignored this remark and instructed her to continue speaking about her life. She shook her head, and realizing that she would gain nothing from long years of analysis with such an arrogant and uncaring man, she terminated the session, thanked him for his time and left his office, determined not to return.

Although she was glad to be free of him, she had pricklings of conscience about shelving the concerted advice of her three mentors in Denver. Thinking of them, she wrote to the Institute to ask for another analyst. In her letter she explained tactfully the mutual antipathy between herself and the man to whom she had been officially assigned.

She was still waiting for a reply from the Institute when she first heard the name of Dr. Helmut Baum. In the Billings Hospital cafeteria two of her colleagues spoke enthusiastically of undergoing analysis with Dr. Baum. She decided it could be no coincidence when later in the day a third colleague mentioned Dr. Baum's name. These were the "coincidences" that always alerted her, and when in the past she had heeded them she had moved profitably forward. She wrote to Dr. Baum at the Psychoanalytic Institute and asked for an interview.

From the first moment she set eyes on the short, elderly, soft-spoken analyst, she knew he would be important to her. An Austrian-born and -educated Jew, Dr. Baum reminded her of Dr. Margolin in his ability to listen and understand. His hair was gray, his eyes dark brown and his mouth straight and strong under an aquiline nose. As a well-trained analyst he was impersonal and unwilling until much later to share his own thoughts and personal life. Then she learned that he had lived in Switzerland, and that his home in Basel was almost next door to Eva's present home. Mountain climbing had been his youthful passion, and indeed he and Elisabeth had climbed the same peaks and crossed the same glaciers.

At the first interview she felt free to tell him why she had come to the Institute and of her reservations about psychoanalysis. After her experience with the first analyst assigned to her, had it not been for the strong recommendations of the three Denver psychiatrists she would have abandoned altogether the idea of undergoing analysis.

He nodded his understanding. He was ready to take her on as a client, but he assumed that Elisabeth, on her side, knew what she was undertaking. There would be four one-hour sessions each week and, depending on what progress they made together, these sessions could continue for four or five years.

Elisabeth vividly remembers experiencing a very special moment of intuitive thought at the conclusion of her first meeting with Dr. Baum. When he rose from his chair and put out his hand, she had to curb a temptation to tell him that she knew he would become her teacher, just as Professor Amsler and Dr. Margolin had been.

Elisabeth recalls feeling a surge of excitement, a certainty that she was very close to a frontier of knowledge and understanding which she had dreamed about since her childhood.

=26=

"The Dying Are My Teachers"

ONE AFTERNOON almost three months to the day after Elisabeth had started work at Billings Hospital, she was sitting in her office with the door closed. She rarely closed her office door, because on principle she encouraged anyone—particularly students and nurses—to drop in and talk about whatever was on their minds. However, on this particular afternoon she was concentrating on the preparation of a lecture on psychosomatic medicine she was due to give to medical students within the hour.

When there was a tap on the door, she frowned at the interruption but invited the caller to come in. There were actually four of them, all young men. The spokesman, lanky, fair-haired and dressed in a sport coat with leather at the elbows, caught her frown and apologized for intruding. He and his friends, he explained, were students at the nearby Chicago Theological Seminary. His brother, a medical student in Denver, had sent him a transcript of her Denver lecture on Death and Dying. He and his friends had been fascinated.

The spokesman said that though the seminary filled their heads with theology, they were aware of a serious gap in the syllabus. They were given too little training in counseling and none at all in the kinds of problems they were certain to face when eventually they graduated and were assigned to pastoral duties. What they could certainly expect as ministers was to spend a good deal of time at the bedsides of the gravely ill and the dying. They were convinced that simply reading passages from the Bible and reciting the prescribed prayers would not adequately meet the needs of the dying.

None of them, continued the spokesman, had ever encountered a person who was dying. Would Elisabeth perhaps consider allowing them to be observers next time she talked to a dying person? They were certain that such an experience would be vastly more profitable than anything they might learn from a textbook.

Elisabeth studied the earnest expressions of the four young men. She had never heard such an admission of inadequacy from her medical students. She was touched that they should have come to see her, and moved by their humility.

She agreed at once to try to help them. She asked them to return in one week, when she would have a dying patient for an interview.

After the students had left, she sat for some time thinking about her prejudice against the established churches and the clergy. She had seen too many priests, ministers and rabbis approach the bedsides of the very ill and then fail so dismally to reach them or give real comfort. She had seen and heard the clergy recite prayers straight out of a prayer book and hurry away, evidently feeling that their duties were done, yet leaving patients still yearning for real communication. For the most part, she guessed, the clergy were as frightened by the prospect of death as were the patients themselves. Yet how could she blame the clergy if they were not given an opportunity to find out what really went on in the minds and the hearts of the dying?

After her lecture that afternoon Elisabeth set about finding a suitable patient to interview in the presence of the theological students. Not one of the physicians she approached would admit that he had a single dying patient in his care. On the following day she tried again but with no more success. To a resident physician in charge of patients in terminal-illness wards she protested that in a hospital of six hundred beds there had to be some patients who were dying. The physician retorted angrily that he would not allow any of his gravely ill patients to be guinea pigs. He was appalled that Elisabeth could even consider the idea of "exploiting" such patients.

She denounced the exploitation charge. She wouldn't dream of interviewing a patient who didn't want to talk or who was too fatigued to do so. All she wanted to do was to find a patient who would be prepared to assist theology students to become better ministers through helping them to gain an understanding of the feelings of the terminally ill. The doctor turned on his heel.

She approached a senior nurse about a young male patient whom she had seen earlier because he had had some psychiatric problem. The nurse asked Elisabeth contemptuously whether it would give her "some sort of kick" to tell a twenty-year-old in front of visitors that he had only a couple of weeks to live. Residents and interns too were full of excuses. Either they had no patients at all who were dying or their patients were far too sick to participate in any kind of discussion about their feelings. One senior doctor said the whole idea was "rather sordid, if not sadistic."

The week had almost passed before Elisabeth made any progress at all. There was one physician she had not approached. She knew that he often came back late at night to check up on his most seriously ill patients. This physician, she felt, had to be a very unusual humanitarian. She returned to the hospital at night and waited at a nurses' station for the physician to complete his late round. When he came down the corridor, she had a cup of coffee for him. He accepted it gratefully and nodded when Elisabeth suggested that he had to be very tired at the end of such a long day. Then she presented him with her request for a dying patient whom she could interview in the presence of four seminary students. The physician seemed to understand her intention, and he granted her permission to see an elderly man dying of a respiratory ailment. The patient, added the doctor, was awake at the moment.

Excitedly Elisabeth went straight to the room of the old man, who lay in bed with an oxygen tube up his nose. She explained briefly what she hoped to do on the following day—how she would like to talk to him about his sickness and his feelings, and bring four seminary students to listen in to their dialogue. The patient listened thoughtfully, then beckoned Elisabeth to his bedside chair. He would rather that Elisabeth stay for a while because he would like to talk to her immediately.

In her enthusiasm over at long last finding a suitable patient, Elisabeth failed to recognize the urgency of the old man's plea. She shook her head and told him she would be back on the following afternoon.

Next day she called up the students and told them that she had found a cooperative patient. As soon as they arrived at the hospital she took them to the dying man's room. It was obvious, however, that the patient's condition had deteriorated. He could barely raise a hand in greeting. Elisabeth asked him how he was feeling, but his response was unintelligible. Just before she and the students left the room, the patient managed a wan, apologetic smile and whispered, "Thank you for trying." Elisabeth and the students had barely reached her office when her phone rang. A duty nurse reported that the old man had just died.

Elisabeth still thinks of this patient's death as one of the most painful lessons of her professional career, and she likens it to the time when, years earlier, she had failed to heed Seppli's deathbed plea that she be with him.

In her office she shared her sorrow and guilt with the students. She told them how on the previous day she had failed to respond to the old man's plea that she stay and talk with him immediately. Because she had been so preoccupied with her own plans and her own timetable, she had denied him this last request.

Two days later Elisabeth managed to find another patient—also an elderly man, as it happened—to whom she was able to take the four students. They stood against the walls of the small room and did not themselves participate in the interview. The patient's main concern was that he had not made peace with one of his sons, from whom he had been estranged many years earlier. Elisabeth promised that she would do her best to help him find his lost son.

Elisabeth had stepped into her hospital and university responsibilities and also into her new life in Chicago much more easily than she had anticipated. Although Leola did not cook or keep house, she more than compensated as a nursemaid. Simply knowing that her children

282

were in such good care freed Elisabeth of much concern, especially when she was late returning home. Kenneth had entered the Laboratory School and was obviously very happy, and Barbara thrived.

The Marynook community was outgoing and politically active. Elisabeth and Manny got to know many of their neighbors at community meetings and were confident that if ever there was any sudden crisis at home immediate assistance would be forthcoming. In any case, Elisabeth could if necessary reach home within minutes of a phone call.

She was also profiting from her psychoanalysis with Dr. Baum. With his help she began to understand where she had come from and what direction she was taking. She told her analyst everything—her hates and hopes, her dreams and fantasies. She began to find through psychoanalysis, even after a few sessions, an increasing self-confidence.

Early evidence of a new self-assurance, she told Dr. Baum with some pride, was her decision to drive a car through Chicago's downtown traffic. If this achievement sounded like a small victory, she said laughingly, then her analyst should visualize her Swiss country practice, when she drove her first car and the only obstacles were chickens and an occasional cyclist.

After the session with the dying patient and the four theology students, she confided to Dr. Baum how withering it had been to be snubbed and rejected by the physicians at the hospital. As she gained insight on the childhood origins of her shyness, she began to overcome her fear of rejection and was able to approach much more boldly the senior physicians of whom she had stood in awe. An increase in assertiveness was the first fruit of her psychoanalysis.

Her lectures on psychiatry were proving enormously popular. (At the end of each of the five academic years she was on the Chicago University faculty, the medical students gave her the "Most Popular Teacher" award.)

The students were fascinated by her unorthodox and uncomplicated approaches in both her teaching methods and her psychiatric techniques. Her language was always easy to understand, her lectures clear, and her students surprised themselves by their own successes when they began to practice what they learned. She relied heavily upon her own experiences, particularly at Manhattan State Hospital. She was totally opposed to electric shock treatment, which she said was barbaric and useless. Today Elisabeth prides herself that in a score of years of practice as a psychiatrist she never made use of such "treatment" and was able to prevent hundreds of patients from undergoing it.

In her lectures she constantly stressed the importance of consulting patients about their treatment, including psychotic patients who initially were seemingly incapable of communication.

Even a patient who was severely ill, she insisted, had the right to voice an opinion on his own treatment. What was often forgotten in a modern hospital was that every patient possessed feelings and had a right to be heard. In her lectures Elisabeth recalled the time when she was first hospitalized as a very young child and how she was "parceled and labeled like a package handed over a post office counter."

In the modern hospital the patient who cried out his fears or who pleaded for rest or dignity rarely found anyone to listen to him. He was likely to be surrounded by physicians, nurses and technicians giving him infusions, transfusions and sedatives, and wiring him up to electronic monitoring devices when his deepest need was to find a compassionate person to stop by his bed, perhaps simply to hold his hand.

To her students Elisabeth stressed her conviction that modern medical techniques and efficiency—necessary though they were—often smothered the true art of healing.

In her psychiatry classes she invited each of the students to find the most seriously ill psychiatric patient, and then challenged him to make a diagnosis. She helped the students to understand the patient's disconnected language, and demonstrated how apparently nonsensical responses and gestures could be correctly interpreted.

For these demonstrations she used what was known as a "screening room," a small auditorium which had a one-way glass screen between the stage and the seats. The glass screen permitted students to observe Elisabeth and the patient, but the patient could not see through the screen, and was thus not distracted by the audience.

Elisabeth did not immediately plan additional interviews with terminally ill patients after her visit from the theology students. Insofar as she was concerned, the time with them had been a response to a specific request. However, the four students widely discussed their terminal-ward experience with other students, and shortly before the Christmas vacation in 1966 Elisabeth was approached by more students from the seminary. Several medical students and two or three nurses also asked if they could sit in on a dialogue with someone who was dying.

It would obviously be awkward and, as she pointed out, probably unproductive to squeeze more than a half-dozen observers into one small room; so Elisabeth said she would make arrangements to take a terminally ill patient to the screening room. Once again she encountered resistance from physicians. Eventually the same physician who had previously assisted her gave permission for a cancer patient, the mother of nine children, to leave her bed for an hour, if she was willing, and be wheeled to the screening room.

Elisabeth went to the woman's ward and explained that she was working with some students and nurses who wanted to learn what it was really like to be so very sick. The woman complained about her pain and discomfort, and she expressed her anger about the way one of her nurses treated her. She spoke too about her concern for her children and how they were now going to be cared for. The patient agreed to Elisabeth's request that she speak about these kinds of things in front of the students and nurses.

In the screening-room interview, the patient admitted almost immediately that she was dying and that she would never again leave the hospital. She could not understand why the doctors and nurses "played games" with her. She wept as she spoke about her children and what would become of them.

As soon as the patient showed fatigue, Elisabeth concluded the interview and thanked her for being "such a very good teacher." The woman's face suddenly brightened. She could not believe, she said, that anyone would so compliment her. She had thought of herself as "just a useless old thing and very grumpy."

Elisabeth assured her that if ever she wanted anyone to talk to, she, Elisabeth, would be available day or night. The patient nodded her understanding of the implied promise: She would not be left to die alone.

After the woman had been wheeled back to her ward, Elisabeth and the small audience discussed their reactions to being confronted by someone who was dying and who had spoken so honestly about her feelings.

The screening-room interview and subsequent discussion set the pattern for Elisabeth's seminars on Death and Dying. The account of it was the topic of lively discussion in the hospital. Most of the faculty and consulting physicians were hostile. In the department of psychiatry, Elisabeth's unorthodox teaching methods and techniques had been received by most of her peers with ambivalence or jealousy. Some openly rejected her methods. So the news that she had interviewed a dying patient in front of an audience, some of whom were not even members of the medical school, sharpened criticism.

The popular judgment was that Elisabeth had grossly exploited a vulnerable patient. One of the medical professors told his residents, interns and nurses that anyone who permitted Dr. Kübler-Ross to talk in a public arena to any of his patients would jeopardize his or her career at Billings Hospital or the medical school. (Later Elisabeth was to take a tolerant view of the antagonism of the physicians. From their standpoint, she was a new and untried faculty member, and there was no assurance that their patients would not be traumatized by mention of the word death or the recognition of just how ill they really were.)

But in spite of the senior staff's opposition, which filtered down to nursing stations and to medical students, Elisabeth continued to receive requests to conduct interviews with the terminally ill. They now came not only from students at the seminary and medical school and from nurses, but from chaplains, therapists, social workers, even orderlies, all of whom wanted to learn how to cope better with the dying patient.

Through the first six months of 1967 she continued to conduct weekly screening-room interviews, with increasingly large audiences. There were more protests from the faculty and senior staff. One senior physician jeeringly referred to her as the "hospital vulture."

It was rarely a simple task to find a suitable patient. There were weeks when she spent up to twenty hours searching for one patient and seeking permission to talk to him in front of students. However—

sometimes at the very last moment—she always managed to locate one physician who seemed to understand what she was doing and who consented to the participation of a terminally ill patient. And some sympathetic supervisors made discreet arrangements to have duties covered while nurses in their charge were given time to attend the interviews and discussions.

Although the hostility, overt and covert, of the majority of physicians and faculty continued, Elisabeth began to win over the nursing staff, many of whom readily admitted their need for instruction in nursing the terminally ill. Typically, a nurse confessed to Elisabeth that she avoided entering the room of a dying patient whenever possible, because she couldn't bear to look at the nightstand photograph of the woman's young children. Other nurses admitted praying that their terminally ill patients would not die during their duty shifts. Nurses attending the screening-room interviews came to understand their fears and to recognize the great privilege that was theirs in giving professional support and humanitarian comfort to the dying.

Some of the clergy made confessions too. One chaplain spoke for others when, following a screening-room interview, he told a discussion group that he had used his prayer book as a defense against having to listen to questions about death—questions that he might not be able to answer.

Almost without exception, the participating patients themselves responded with gratitude and a great sense of relief. Those who had previously refused to admit the gravity of their illness and the likelihood of early death welcomed a breakthrough of their defenses, and the fact that they no longer needed to hide the truth from their families.

Elisabeth noted in her journal that every patient taught her something new. As time went on, she was to recognize and record five basic stages in the process of dying, which did not necessarily follow each other consecutively and often overlapped: denial, anger, bargaining, depression, and acceptance.

Denial, she noted, almost invariably followed the first advice of a fatal illness. It was "the first protective reaction to shock." Anger expressed itself in a number of ways, often as envy of healthy people, sometimes as bitterness toward God, who had "let them down." Bargaining often took the form of the patient promising God that he would lead a better life if he were cured. The depression phase was a period of self-mourning. The final stage, the acceptance of death, brought with it a sense of fulfillment and of peace.

As she had promised she would try to be, Elisabeth was at the bedside of the mother of nine children when she died. It was a very peaceful death, and that night when she returned home Elisabeth wrote about the experience in her journal. Then she added:

> Those who have the strength and the love to sit with a dying patient in the silence that goes beyond words will know that this moment is neither frightening nor painful, but a peaceful cessation of the functioning of the body. Watching a peaceful death of a human being reminds me of a falling star—one of the million lights in a vast sky that flares up for a brief moment only to disappear into the endless night. To be with a dying patient makes us conscious of the uniqueness of the individual in this vast sea of humanity, aware of our finiteness, our limited lifespan. Few of us live beyond our three score years and ten, yet in this brief time most of us create and live a unique biography, and weave ourselves into the fabric of history.*

She added, "I still have so much to learn from the dying, who have become my best teachers." One of these teachers had been her father. Her mother was now about to give her a very different kind of lesson.

---

* This passage was later published in *Death: The Final Stage of Growth* (Prentice-Hall, 1975).

27

To Live Until You Die

IN THE EARLY SUMMER of 1967 Elisabeth and Manny moved for the fifth time. They now felt comfortably settled in Chicago, and assuming they would be living and working there for the foreseeable future, they bought a home a few blocks away from the house they had been renting. The new house was similar to the one they were leaving: a split-level two-bedroom home with a spacious yard.

On a warm Sunday afternoon in June they were enjoying the yard, abloom with flowers. Their visitor was Uncle Anschel, Elisabeth's favorite in-law, now frailer than when she had first met him and suffering from a chronic bronchial ailment. She watched him affectionately as he struggled to breathe while reading a story to Kenneth, who sat astride the elderly man's knees. A few feet away Barbara was laughing and splashing in a small plastic pool.

She and Manny had decided to postpone their annual summer vacation and instead take a holiday at Christmas in order, as they had just explained to Kenneth, to give him and his sister "a real Swiss Christmas" with sleigh bells and festivals. At Christmastime Elisabeth still felt such a yearning for the country of her birth that it was almost a physical pain, and now that Kenneth was old enough to enjoy it she was especially eager to have him experience the happiest season of her childhood.

Suddenly, and apparently without stimulus or prompting, Elisabeth felt a deep and inexplicable concern about her mother's well-being. Before speaking of it to Manny, she tried to rationalize her persistent disquiet. A recent letter from her mother had stated how well and strong she was feeling, although she was in her seventies. Ernst and his family were shortly to fly home from India to vacation in a rented house in the mountain resort of Zermatt. Mrs. Kübler was to join them, as were Eva and her children. She was looking forward to long hikes, and perhaps even a little climbing. But for some reason Elisabeth sensed her mother needed her urgently.

She now turned to Manny and told him that she had to fly to Switzerland immediately—tomorrow, if they could get plane reservations. Manny threw up his hands. It was she, he reminded her, who had insisted on a Christmas vacation, and he was the one who had been ready to fall in with these plans. Without any valid reason, it would be awkward to make the necessary arrangements at his hospital.

Elisabeth admitted that her impulsive decision sounded crazy, but there was some very important reason—a purpose she didn't yet understand—why she should be with her mother as quickly as possible. She had learned in the past the price of ignoring an urgent inner prompting like the one she had just been given. A week later Elisabeth and the two children arrived in Zurich, where they boarded the train for Zermatt.

Zermatt was the ideal place for a restful vacation and for what Elisabeth called "a time for old-fashioned happiness." Mrs. Kübler looked in the pink of health and had on the day the Ross family arrived been on an eight-mile hike with Eva and Ernst. The family spent the evening reminiscing while the Kübler, Ross and Bacher children got to know each other again. Elisabeth gave no hint of the reason for her unexpected arrival.

The weather remained perfect and the week passed quickly. After a couple of days of aching muscles, Elisabeth rediscovered her mountain legs and did some climbing. Her children were introduced to the taste of wild berries and of milk still warm from the cow. Mrs. Kübler hiked each day with her children and grandchildren. Everyone glowed with health.

On the last evening at the resort, when the sun was setting over the peaks, Mrs. Kübler sat with Elisabeth on the balcony of her bedroom, where Kenneth and Barbara, exhausted after the day's outing, were fast asleep. Mother and daughter sat through a long silence and watched shadows move like ragged fingers across the green valleys far below. Then Mrs. Kübler turned to face Elisabeth and said, "I want your solemn promise that you'll do something for me. I want you to promise that when I become incapable, when I become a human vegetable, that you'll help me to die." She spoke with an uncharacteristic urgency.

Elisabeth was taken aback, both by the appeal and by its timing. She reacted not as an expert on dying, not as a teacher who instructed others to be alert for symbolic language, but as a shocked daughter. She replied too quickly, "What nonsense is this! A woman who is in her seventies and who can hike miles every day in the mountains is sure to die very suddenly. Mother, you're the last person to become a human vegetable."

Mrs. Kübler continued to speak as if she hadn't heard her. She again asked for a promise that when she became incapable of caring for herself Elisabeth would help her to die.

Elisabeth looked at her mother with astonishment and again protested that the question was purely hypothetical. In any case, she said firmly, she was totally opposed to mercy killing, if that was what her mother was talking about. In her opinion no physician had the right to give a patient an overdose to relieve the patient's suffering. She could not promise her mother—or, for that matter, anyone else—to expedite dying. In the unlikely event that her mother did in fact become physically incapable, all that she could promise was that she would help her to live until she died.

Mrs. Kübler began to cry softly. It was only the second time in her life that Elisabeth had seen her mother shed tears, the first being when she had gone to be a housekeeper at Romilly. It was a difficult, awkward moment, and Elisabeth turned the conversation aside by

291

suggesting that Mrs. Kübler visit them, perhaps in the fall. Chicago would be cool then. She would love the autumn colors.

Mrs. Kübler rose from her chair and went inside. For a while Elisabeth sat alone and thought about her mother's request, her own response to it and her attitude toward euthanasia. It was tempting to avoid the issue. She remembered some lines of Erich Fromm, the psychiatrist-philosopher: "There is no such thing as medical ethics. There are only universal human ethics applied to specific human situations." There were times, she was obliged to admit, when it was wrong to keep someone alive, but such a time would only occur when a patient was clearly beyond medical help, when organs were kept functioning only with machines. So long as there was a meaningful life, so long as a patient could express and receive feelings, it had to be wrong to "play God" and decide arbitrarily whether a patient should live or die.

Surely, though, it was not to answer this hypothetical question that she had changed the family's vacation plans and come to Switzerland.

Next day, when Mrs. Kübler accompanied Elisabeth and the children to the train station, both women were tense and uncomfortable. However, when the train came in, Elisabeth turned to her mother, hugged her and said, "All I can promise you is that I will do for you what I do for all my patients. I promise I will do my best to help you live until you die."

Mrs. Kübler appeared to understand now what Elisabeth was saying. She nodded, wiped her eyes, smiled and said, "Thank you."

Those were the last words Elisabeth heard her mother speak. Three days after the family arrived back in Chicago, a cable came from Eva. It read, "Mother has had a massive stroke."

By the weekend, Elisabeth was back in Switzerland. She learned from Eva how the mailman had found her mother paralyzed and sprawled in the passageway of her home. When Mrs. Kübler had not responded to his usual knock on the door, he had called for help. Later he accompanied the unconscious woman to the hospital.

At the hospital Elisabeth found her mother unable to speak, unable to move anything except her eyelids and, very feebly, her left hand. It was obvious, however, from the expression in her mother's eyes, that Mrs. Kübler clearly understood what was said to her.

292

Elisabeth and her mother devised a method of communicating. Her mother would use her eyelids and her slightly mobile left hand to indicate affirmative or negative answers to questions put to her. One blink of the eyelids or one squeeze of the hand would signify an affirmative, and two blinks or two squeezes would mean a negative response.

Using this form of communication, Mrs. Kübler made it very clear that she did not want to remain in the hospital. Elisabeth confronted her mother with the impossibility of her returning home, where she would require round-the-clock nursing attention. It was Eva who came up with the solution. She knew of an infirmary, more a rest home than a hospital, in Riehen, a few miles outside of Basel. Eva lived in Riehen, and Erika too would be within easy range. The infirmary was set in spacious well-tended grounds and was run by a dedicated group of Protestant nuns. There would be no respirators or other life-prolonging equipment. When the question was put to Mrs. Kübler, her eyes blinked once and her face lit up.

On the journey from Zurich to Riehen Elisabeth sat with Mrs. Kübler in the ambulance. She had made a complete list of her mother's relatives and friends, and also an inventory of her mother's possessions. During the journey Elisabeth named her mother's possessions one by one and then she ran through the list of friends and kin. By squeezing her left hand, Mrs. Kübler signified her bequests. She indicated, for example, that Eva was to be given her pearl necklace, Erika a ring, a bureau was to go to a certain neighbor and her mink cape was to be given to the wife of the mailman.

By the time the ambulance pulled into the driveway of the infirmary, Elisabeth possessed a detailed list of her mother's bequests.

Mrs. Kübler was clearly delighted with her large well-appointed room overlooking a garden. Photographs of her children and grandchildren, which Elisabeth had taken and enlarged to poster size in her improvised darkrooms in the Bronx and Denver, were hung on the walls.

Communication demanded much patience, for Mrs. Kübler could only make her wishes known through blinking her eyes or through rattling the side rails of her bed. On one of her later visits Elisabeth noticed her mother staring meaningfully at a closet. It was obvious that she wanted something. Elisabeth touched every garment in the closet but in each instance received a negative response. Suddenly Elisabeth had a vivid recollection of her mother years earlier and how when resting she liked to clasp a scented handkerchief. Taking a handkerchief from her own purse Elisabeth dabbed it with eau de cologne. Mrs. Kübler's eyes sparkled as soon as Elisabeth pressed the handkerchief into her hands.

Immediately after taking her mother to the infirmary, Elisabeth spent a couple of painful days quite alone at the Klosbachstrasse apartment. She sorted clothes, furniture and objets d'art; she took down pictures and curtains and labeled everything for subsequent distribution according to her mother's expressed wishes. When everything was distributed or packed away—including boxes of geraniums from the balcony which had been her mother's special pride and joy—she walked through the empty, echoing rooms. She was overwhelmed by feelings that, she realized later, followed the pattern of feelings she had observed in dying patients.

Her first thought was that the closing of the house was all a bad dream, that it wasn't really happening and that she would always have a home in Switzerland. The family would surely meet here again—she, her mother and sisters and brother. She even had a vision of her father presiding once more over the dining-room table. She could smell his cigar, hear his deep rich voice as he poured wine and called for a toast. She could see her mother, gracious and controlled, entering from the kitchen and carrying a steaming tureen; see Eva laughing and moving toward the piano; picture Erika speaking conspiratorially; hear Ernst talking about some sporting event.

The vision lasted only a few moments before she felt a surge of anger—anger because it was a condition of life that time could not be frozen, that the happiest moments could not be retrieved and relived.

Her anger grew as she thought how she had been obliged to close down the home alone. None had understood that she was burning the last of the bridges that linked her to her youth and young womanhood. From now on, when she visited Switzerland she would come as a visitor. She would have to stay in hotels or, at best, crowded into her sisters' homes.

The deepest sadness followed an almost desperate sense of loneliness and isolation. She walked to the balcony and listened to the rumble of a monorail train pulling up the hill. It was from this balcony that she had seen the body of her father taken away. Her heart ached as she thought of the many times she had run down this street for a trolleybus to take her to the hospital and the university.

Elisabeth remembers too recoiling momentarily from a vision of the work that lay ahead of her—or, as she put it, "the higher new mountain peak that I knew I must climb." In this moment she felt she would give anything for the chance to be a Swiss country practitioner.

All these feelings coursed through her within a short span, and then came acceptance of reality. The house was quite empty. A new family would move in shortly. She would never come home here again. She would no longer have a home in Switzerland. Life did move on. She would have to face the challenge of the new mountain. No amount of wishful thinking could recapture the past or change the now.

She re-entered the main bedroom, closed the french windows and looked one last time at the famous church whose bells she had heard ringing while keeping the last vigil at her father's side. Then she walked to the kitchen and took the keys from the hook where they had always hung, went through the front door, locked it and walked down Klosbachstrasse. She didn't look back.

Elisabeth now believes that in closing down the family home in Zurich she was given a new and important understanding about life and death. Life, she now sees, is a series of losses, and every loss is a "little death." In the hour or so before she finally left the home on Klosbachstrasse she had gone through the five identifiable stages of dying. Each "little death"—and this was one of hers—was a salutary and perhaps essential preparation for death itself. But every ending was also a new beginning.

Another lesson, long and difficult, now focused on the infirmary at Riehen. Mrs. Kübler, paralyzed and unable to speak, held on to life—not just for the few weeks that Elisabeth and her sisters had anticipated, not for months, but for four years. She had clearly foreseen the manner of her dying and, recoiling at the prospect, had pleaded with Elisabeth for mercy killing.

For Elisabeth, the issue of euthanasia was no longer a hypothetical one, no longer an intellectual debating point, but a question of the heart and conscience. There were times when she was ready to change

295

her views, moments when she wondered agonizingly whether she should have given her mother the promise she had asked for; but these doubts stalked her only when she was far away from Switzerland. For when she was with her mother—and Elisabeth flew the Atlantic many times to be at her bedside—her conviction remained that neither she nor anyone else had the right to take the life of someone who could still express and receive feelings. Mrs. Kübler was not a human vegetable. She needed no machines to keep her heart beating or her lungs breathing.

To every visitor, she expressed gratitude and love through her eyes. Eva visited her every day, and Erika, who was working, came every weekend. The family was especially touched by the number of friends who made the journey from Zurich, including the mailman and milkman, who saved up to buy train tickets and spend an hour or two at her bedside.

Following one transatlantic visit to her mother, Elisabeth reflected in her journal:

> I often find it so hard to understand why a good and selfless woman has had to face what she most feared—a long, drawn-out death. When I see her I wonder what meaning such an existence can have? . . . She well knows how much she is loved. . . . Yesterday, when Mr. and Mrs. P. came to see me to talk about their child who has been in a coma for three months, I was truthfully able to say that I understood their feelings. . . . Mother helps me to care more deeply, to understand more readily, helps me to be a better physician, a better teacher, surely a better human being.

28

The New Frontier

By 1966 Elisabeth's now scheduled Death and Dying seminars were receiving widening academic recognition. Clergy and other members of the helping professions were now coming from other states, for news of the uniqueness and effectiveness of the seminars had been spread by word of mouth. The room in which she held the seminars could seat fifty, but there was always standing room only by the time the seminars began.

If Elisabeth had not yet completely vanquished the conspiracy of silence surrounding the hospital's wards for the terminally ill, at least the shroud was now drawn back.

The principal gain of academic recognition was that students and staff who wanted to attend the seminars no longer had to make excuses and apologies to their superiors. However, the faculty's suspicion endured. One morning two medical professors cornered her in a hospital corridor and asked her to explain in a couple of minutes what her seminars were all about. Elisabeth replied that with the help of the terminally ill she was trying to encourage members of the healing professions and others such as chaplains and social workers not to shy away from having close relationships with the dying. Those who attended the seminars were learning a lot about the mind, the heart and the spirit, and also a lot about themselves. The seminars were helping to sensitize students, nurses and others to the needs of the critically ill—needs beyond those which could be met by technology. At the same time, the seminars were helping those who attended them to shed anxieties about their own mortality.

However, two minutes in a busy hospital corridor hardly permitted full clarification of what the seminars were all about. To attempt to explain her work was like trying to define such words as faith and love. She could only say that strong men wept and hard-shelled nurses were inspired to a new quality of care after attending the seminars. If the professors really wanted to know what they were all about, why didn't they come along at eleven o'clock on any Wednesday morning and join the other observers in the auditorium?

She warned them to come early if they wanted to get a seat—and told them that the volunteer patient was as likely to be a teenager as an octogenarian, a cleaning woman as a mogul of industry. But the professors never did turn up, nor did any other member of the faculty.

Academic respectability increased Elisabeth's work load. She continued to teach psychiatry in her unorthodox fashion to medical students, continued to be on call as consultant for patients needing psychiatric help, and she was also given a new title: acting chief of inpatient service.

She was surprised one afternoon to be asked to receive a delegation from the Lutheran Theological Seminary. After five minutes of beating around the bush, Elisabeth asked the delegation if they would state clearly the reason for their visit. The spokesman cleared his throat. They had come to ask, he said, if she would join the faculty of the seminary. She could hardly have been more astounded had a group of Catholics asked her to be the Church's first female priest, or a delegation from the local synagogue invited her to be its cantor. She appreciated the invitation, but, she told them, she was a wishy-washy Protestant whose views were highly unorthodox! And Lutherans were not known for their liberal views.

The spokesman hurriedly assured her that she would not be expected to teach theology or doctrine. They wanted her to teach what they called the "skills of ministry," especially how to conduct sickbed counseling. Elisabeth said lightly that she would seize the opportunity if only to avenge herself for all the preachy sermons she had had to listen to as a child! In fact, she drove a hard bargain. If she was to teach, she would have to have an absolutely free hand. She would teach only in the presence of theology professors who would instruct students in classical theoretical dogma. Then she would apply the theory of ministry in a practical way.

The professors agreed to this proposal, and the outcome was a new form of joint teaching of hospital pastoral work. Her lectures to the Lutheran students were often lively, always controversial. Sometimes she deliberately played the devil's advocate to professors or students, especially those who thundered fire and brimstone. In a memorable demonstration, she presented two patients, one a convicted felon who had spent most of his life in jail, and the other a psychotic who beat his breast over imagined heinous crimes.

She invited one of the students to come to the stage and counsel the two patients. By the time he had finished expounding on sin, hell and damnation, the observing students were squirming with embarrassment. Elisabeth then took over the counseling and within minutes elicited from the psychotic the fact that he was a potential suicide whose false sense of guilt had been increased by the previous questioning. The man with the criminal record showed warm and human qualities when he expressed concern not for the temperature of hell but for the welfare of his wife and children.

With student participation, the demonstration became a moving and heartwarming dialogue between two battered people in real need and a group of young men and women ready to dedicate their lives to the ministry. A fresh breeze of honesty and compassion soon swept away the smell of sulfur and brimstone.

Paradoxically, in acknowledging that she had an ability to wither opponents, Elisabeth learned to be more tolerant of those who espoused doctrines and philosophies opposed to her own, to, as she told herself in her journal, "challenge damaging attitudes and creeds rather than attack the people who held and advocated them."

Through psychoanalysis Dr. Baum continued to help her expose her weaknesses (for instance, a tendency to overreact to criticism) and to underscore her strengths (for example, her exceptional talent for communicating). In any case, she always found it refreshing to pour out her feelings in Dr. Baum's office—something she couldn't do with Manny or anyone else. From the start of her sessions with Dr. Baum, she tackled her psychoanalysis with such vigor and intensity that she completed in twenty-six months the full analytical course, which normally took four to five years.

While recognizing her own profit from psychoanalysis, Elisabeth is always quick to stress that the cost alone of one-to-one analysis puts it far beyond the reach of most people. As an economically feasible and effective alternative she extols psychodrama, which allows groups of up to twenty-five to externalize therapeutically their guilts, griefs, fears and anger.

Elisabeth thrived on work, and although her timetable was crammed, she took on still more extramural tasks. One afternoon a week she worked with the blind at an institution known as the Lighthouse; one evening a week she lectured residents and interns at the state mental hospital, and once a month she drove up to De Kalb, Illinois, to evaluate and screen Peace Corps volunteers.

The main thrust of her work at the Lighthouse was to convince the blind that they were capable of competing in the sighted world, that they could, if they had the will, be independent and prosperous. She remained associated long enough with the organization to see a number of young blind people, mostly blacks, move out of sheltered employment and into the workaday world. The paper she wrote on the effectiveness of the Lighthouse project was widely distributed, and the methods she used to convince the handicapped that "life is a challenge and not a threat" were, she was subsequently advised, successfully employed in other institutions for the blind.

She was less successful as a Peace Corps consultant. The candidates she endorsed most highly were almost invariably rejected by the conservative authorities who had the final say in choosing the volunteers. She selected what she called the "high risk, high gain" young men and women. Like herself, they held unorthodox views, but she believed that they were the ones who were most creative and inventive; and precisely because they were nonconformist, she believed they would fare best in more primitive societies and would give a better image of America in other nations.

When her candidates consistently fell by the way at their final interrogations, she made it a point to learn from a conservative psychologist the reasons for the failures. From then on she primed her unconventional volunteers on what to say in order to impress the selection board, and just when to hold their tongues. With this foreknowledge her "slate" of candidates (in her journal she referred to them as "these beautiful people so like the Volunteers with whom I worked in France, Belgium and Poland") started to gain approval.

With all her teaching and her other activities, Elisabeth filled every minute of every hour. She needed help, particularly with the main focus of her interest and work, the care of the dying. There was one responsibility she could not and would not hurry, and that was the time needed at the bedsides of the terminally ill. Unexpectedly, she found stalwart assistance.

One of the most difficult of her cancer patients was Miss Hettie Glenfib, a touchy, ill-tempered sixty-five-year-old woman who had been highly successful in business. Miss Glenfib, whose conversation was filled with the oaths of a dockworker, had alienated her family and she had no friends. Indeed, she was so abusive to nurses that they entered her room only on a bell summons or when they were compelled to attend to her basic needs. Elisabeth had herself been verbally abused by Miss Glenfib.

On one visit, Elisabeth found the woman screaming four-letter words at a hospital chaplain. What fascinated her was that the chaplain was not in the least disconcerted by the torrent of abuse. Elisabeth sat down in the second chair and listened to the dialogue. She was impressed by the cool and caring way the chaplain took advantage of the patient's pauses to speak simply of life's values.

This chaplain, Elisabeth decided immediately, was just the colleague she needed to help her counsel the hospital's terminally ill patients and their families.

She invited him to her office, where he introduced himself and told her something of his background. The Reverend Renford Gaines, a black Canadian in his early thirties, had given up a successful career as a printer to become a minister. It had not, he admitted, been easy to

301

sacrifice his expensive tastes, but he had done so because he could not resist a conviction that he was meant to give his life in service to others.

Elisabeth seemed to hear the echo of her own voice. She saw in the Reverend Renford Gaines a mirror of her own hopes, her own drive and her own concern for the lost and the lonely. While she found close philosophical affinity with the chaplain, she was also intrigued by the fact that they complemented each other in their culture, race, sex and, as she soon discovered, in their talents and skills.

Elisabeth had often been uncomfortably aware of a philosophical imbalance in her seminars, as well as in her bedside counseling and when talking to concerned and grieving relatives. Her patients and their kin frequently raised spiritual questions about life's meaning, the existence of God and whether there was life after death. She herself was still feeling her way toward spiritual truths and was often out of her depth when faced with such questions.

Now, she was persuaded, she had found in this articulate chaplain an answer to her dilemma. The Reverend Mr. Gaines enthusiastically accepted her invitation to be her working colleague. Their teamwork proved to be effective and harmonious. She and the chaplain made hospital rounds together and made themselves available, one or the other, day or night, to dying patients. The chaplain also joined Elisabeth at her seminars. When a patient raised religious questions, he answered them clearly and concisely. He was alongside Elisabeth when she wheeled into the auditorium the feisty Miss Glenfib. Owing in large measure to the spiritual counseling of Elisabeth's colleague, Miss Glenfib had broken through her rage to a plane of equanimity. Her body was now emaciated, for she was within two weeks of her death, but the former shrew and terror of the wards looked directly at the invisible audience and said with poised, dry-eyed conviction, "I've lived more in the past three months than I have in all my adult life." The nurses who had once done their best to keep out of her way broke down in sobs.

Elisabeth's invitation to her seminars was an open one, for it was her often stated belief that everyone, even young children, could profit from the teaching of the dying. (Three years later Elisabeth took the dying Uncle Anschel into her home, not only as an act of mercy and

302

because he was beloved, but because she was convinced that her children would gain immeasurably from someone whose life was drawing to its close.) She saw her own work essentially as that of a catalyst—the one who brought together the dying "mentor" and those people ready to learn critical truths about life.

She sought no publicity for herself or for her seminars. She thought she didn't need any, because her lecture room was always filled to overflowing. But except for some clergy scattered across the country who had been told of the seminars by their friends in Chicago, and a small group of physicians and students in Denver, few people knew about her work. In the new year of 1969 almost nobody beyond the campus of the University of Chicago even knew her name.

Then in 1969 there occurred two closely timed and linked events which were to end her virtual anonymity. The first was a request from the Chicago Theological Seminary for a few paragraphs about the purpose of her seminars to be published in the school's journal. She scribbled off a short article over the signature "Elisabeth Kübler-Ross"—a name she sometimes used in order to avoid confusion with Manny. In her covering letter to the journal she asked that her rough English be polished, reminding the editors that she was still writing in a foreign tongue. To her amazement the piece was printed exactly as she had written it, even to the split infinitives and dangling participles! Except for a short piece she had written for a house journal on helping the blind and otherwise handicapped to gain dignified employment and thus self-worth, it was the first time she had been in public print.

Although the seminary's journal had a very limited circulation, a copy of it reached the desk of one of the editors of the Macmillan publishing company in New York. Shortly she was approached by a representative of the company who asked her whether, with the promise of a modest advance on royalties, she would consider writing a book—say, 50,000 words—on what she had learned from her work with the terminally ill.

Taken aback, she protested that the thought of writing a book had never crossed her mind, and again cautioned that in writing English she would be writing in a foreign tongue. She was assured that her editors at Macmillan would correct her English where necessary. Casually mentioning the fact of the invitation to Manny, and without consulting a lawyer, Elisabeth signed a contract.

For many weeks it weighed heavily upon her. How, she asked herself, could she possibly find the time to write 50,000 words? When she received the small check from Macmillan, she set aside hours each day, usually from midnight until 3:00 A.M., for writing. She was a two-finger typist, and her machine was an old one, but she persevered. She had promised Macmillan a manuscript within six months, but she surprised herself with the way the typed pages increased. She rarely revised, writing largely from her own case histories and from transcriptions of her interviews in the lecture room. She started off with the common fear of death, and went on to speak of attitudes toward death and dying. Then in consecutive chapters she discussed the five stages of death.

Her last chapters dealt with the problems facing the family of a terminally ill patient and the reactions of the students and others to her seminars. She concluded with a chapter on therapy with the terminally ill.

She wanted the simplest of titles, and eventually settled for *On Death and Dying*. The last words that she typed were the dedication. She thought of the two men who had most influenced her, and after a thoughtful pause her small hands moved to the typewriter, and she wrote, "To the memory of my father and of Seppli Bucher."

It had taken her a few days more than three months to write the book. She first sent the manuscript to two friends, Edgar Draper and Jane Kennedy, asking them to check for repetitions and any outrageous syntax. Three other friends took turns typing a clean copy. In May she sent the manuscript to Macmillan, grateful for the extra hour or two of sleep she could now have at night. She had almost forgotten about her literary endeavors when in the fall of 1969 she recieved the first copy of a book that was to become one of the biggest nonfiction best-sellers of all time. Indeed, a decade after she "put down on paper just the kind of sentences and words I use when talking to my students" (as she wrote to Erika) the book was still on the best-seller lists.

It was not, however, the volume titled *On Death and Dying* that was to make Elisabeth's name a household phrase. In the first week of

November 1969 she received a telephone call from *Life* magazine. An editor told her that her short piece in the Chicago Theological Seminary's journal had reached his desk. Elisabeth was in her office talking to a group of student chaplains when the call came through, and it took her a few moments to collect her thoughts. The *Life* editor asked if she would give permission for a writer and a photographer from the magazine to attend one of her seminars. The editor misunderstood her silence and went on to say that *Life* had an international circulation of millions, and that the magazine's readers could only profit from learning that dying patients should be encouraged to speak about their pain and predicaments. Elisabeth replied simply that everyone was welcome at her seminars and she suggested that the following Wednesday's seminar would be suitable.

The day of *Life*'s phone call was a particularly busy one, and she gave the request so little thought that she failed to mention it to Manny that evening. However, on Monday, in consideration of the fact that a reporter would be present at the next seminar, she selected an articulate, elderly man to be the interview patient. The man had been in the hospital for some months, and she had grown very fond of him. He didn't mind in the least that a reporter and a photographer would be on the other side of the glass screen.

However, when she arrived at the hospital early on Wednesday Elisabeth was told by a senior nurse that the elderly patient had died during the night. She was meditating sadly about the old man when the *Life* editor, Loudon Wainwright, and the photographer, Leonard McCombe, arrived.

Without telling the *Life* visitors that there was no patient for interview, she directed them to the auditorium so that they could set up their cameras and recording equipment on the observers' side of the glass screen well in advance of the arrival of the spectators. She then went to the cancer wards of the hospital in search of a substitute patient.

She glanced into a semi-private room and saw, as she noted in her journal, "one of the loveliest human beings I have ever set eyes upon." Eva was sitting up against the pillows, and her burnished long hair framed a sculptured high-cheekboned face of exceptional beauty that challenged the fact that the girl's life was gravely threatened. Sitting

305

at the foot of her bed, Elisabeth introduced herself. Eva, she learned, was twenty-two years old and had been admitted to the hospital a week earlier because she had acute leukemia.

Elisabeth still vividly recalls her first meeting with Eva. She remembers the feelings of trust, love and sorrow that at once seemed to connect the two of them and to hold them in a bond of special intimacy. Eva was full of feelings and ready to pour them out. Elisabeth reached forward to hold her hand and to explain the immediate need.

Would she on short notice, today, be prepared to share how she felt about her sickness with fifty or more people who were eager to learn how to be better physicians, nurses, therapists, social workers, priests, ministers and rabbis?

Eva's lovely dark eyes widened. What could *she* say to help anyone? She would like to share feelings, but she needed someone to help her by asking the right questions. Elisabeth promised to do exactly that, and added that she believed the others would learn from Eva much that was critically important to their work. There was one other thing, however, that Eva should know. In the audience on the other side of the screen there would be a writer and a photographer from *Life* magazine. Would Eva give them permission to write about her and to take pictures?

Eva's eyes grew rounder still as she threw back her head on the pillows and laughed excitedly. "Me in *Life!*" she exclaimed. "Am I really that important? No one at home would ever believe it!"

As at all the seminars, the interview room on the observers' side of the one-way glass was filled to standing room well before Elisabeth and Eva arrived on the illuminated side of the partition. Loudon Wainwright wrote in *Life* that many of the observers showed anxiety in their faces, and the few who talked did so in whispers. Then suddenly on the other side of the screen—the only area now lighted—a door opened.

Wainwright wrote, "A gasp of shock jumped through the watchers ... Eva's bearing and beauty flew against the truth that the young woman was terribly ill."

Most had probably expected a patient frail and bent, old and tired, certainly not this young woman who could have been an ingénue playing a role on a film set. Eva had dressed carefully in a soft white blouse and tweed slacks. Sitting back comfortably in an office chair, she exhibited no sign of nervousness. Elisabeth indicated the two microphones on the table that separated the two women. Eva smiled her understanding that every word she uttered—her laughter too and tears—would be heard by the invisible audience.

That this was no theatrical performance was soon made clear as the dialogue began—a dialogue that ranged through hope, anger, bitterness, denial, near despair, through sudden unexpected merriment, and dreams and hope once more.

During most of the interview, Elisabeth and Eva maintained eye-to-eye contact, both so absorbed in their intimate exchange that they seemed to be alone.

Eva spoke wistfully about her illness and about the boy friend she had hoped to marry in the new year. She also talked about God. "When I was little, I always believed in God, and I still want to . . . but I don't know. Sometimes when I talk to somebody and we talk about not believing in God, I'll sort of look up and think—well, you know—don't believe me. I'm just kidding You if You're there."

In reply to a question about the sort of help she would most like in the hospital, she replied with determination, "Oh, just come in and tell me when you find out about somebody that wasn't supposed to make it—and did."

With candor, Eva spoke of the middle-aged woman with breast cancer who was her roommate. The woman, she said, cried day and night, and Eva described how she herself felt when surgeons told the roommate that her mastectomy had been successful. "I know nobody's coming to tell me that I have even a fifty-fifty chance," she said. "It was when I heard about my roommate's successful surgery that I ran into the hall and cried, and felt that nobody could possibly understand what I was feeling. I thought, I'll gladly give my own breasts to my roommate if only I can live."

Buffeted by the crests and troughs of her own emotions, by sudden hopes that an answer would be found to the relentless advance of her own dread disease, and then by recognition of reality—an acknowledgment that her brave youth and striking beauty would soon vanish—Eva sometimes sparkled, sometimes wept.

Photographer McCombe captured her changing moods—the gaiety

of her laughter, the agonizing moments when she pressed her hands to her face and the long tresses of dark hair fell forward to conceal her sorrow.

A week later, on November 21, 1969, Loudon Wainwright's sensitively written story and McCombe's dramatic pictures were published in *Life* magazine. Eva's beautiful face was suddenly known to millions—her hopes, pain, fears and valor too.

Also, overnight, the name of Elisabeth Kübler-Ross was known worldwide.

Elisabeth's only concern was how Eva would react to the story and to the pictures. It was very important, she felt, to be with Eva when she opened the pages of the magazine. On the day of publication, Elisabeth went to the hospital early, arriving a few minutes before the magazine stand opened. She bought the top issue on the rack and rushed to Eva's ward.

The young woman turned the pages, and on seeing the pictures, exclaimed ingenuously, "Oh, they're not very good of me, are they?" Elisabeth sat silently as Eva read Wainwright's text. When she had finished, Eva looked up, smiled and said, "It's so beautifully written, isn't it!" It was just what Elisabeth had hoped to hear. Her patient was excited and moved by the story, not depressed or angry.

Copies of the magazine sold out quickly and before long Elisabeth came up against a very different reaction. The feature enraged most of the faculty and attending physicians.

Articulating the mood of his colleagues, one doctor stormed into the office of a chaplain who had worked with Elisabeth and bellowed, "We have tried for years to make this hospital famous for our excellent cancer care. Now this woman comes along and makes us famous for our dying patients!"

The accusation was only the first skirmish in a bitter new attack upon Elisabeth. She was now the hospital's pariah. In the wards, in the corridors, in the cafeteria, members of the faculty and physicians turned their backs on her.

The Reverend Renford Gaines, upon whom she had been leaning for support, had just left to take over a parish. Except for the nursing staff that she had trained in caring for the dying, some medical students, and some of the student chaplains—all of whom whispered their encouragement, for they were all intimidated—she was alone once more, more alone perhaps than she had ever been.

She approached one chaplain whom she believed to be sympathetic. He told her that it had been made clear to him and to his colleagues that they had to make a choice between the hospital's physicians and "that Death and Dying woman." Elisabeth, he added as he glanced furtively about him, would surely understand that in order to keep his own post and to do his work he could no longer be associated with her. Another chaplain told her that he had been hailed that morning on the ward by a senior physician who had sarcastically asked, "Are you looking for another dying patient for publicity?"

An order went out from some senior professors to residents, interns and nurses that Elisabeth Kübler-Ross was on no account to be given permission to take any terminal patients from the wards. No TV or newspaper interviews would be allowed, and all requests from the news media were to be channeled through the public relations department.

In the course of the next few days Elisabeth visited the wards to try to find another patient, but the boycott was total. Nurses, residents and interns who had previously been cooperative and were still supportive were forced to deny Elisabeth any more patients. Some expressed their anger over the order, but it meant more than their jobs were they to defy it.

On the next Wednesday morning she went to the auditorium without a patient. For the first time in two years most seats were empty. Word that the Kübler-Ross seminars had been terminated had spread through the hospital. The only people who turned up were students from the seminary, together with a few of those members of the clergy who had previously attended. Elisabeth had given them an ultimatum: to come to one more seminar to analyze and begin to understand their own fears and reactions. Those who did not show up would be excluded from any of her future courses.

With her back to the chairs where two weeks earlier she and Eva had sat for their intimate dialogue, Elisabeth faced the small audience. She recalled how the seminars had been started at the request of four theology students who had wanted to learn how to minister to the very sick and the dying. She had often thought of those students with gratitude. In the early days there had been strong opposition to allowing students even to listen to dialogues between herself and the terminally ill. It now seemed as if the seminars on Death and Dying had come full cycle.

The high and the mighty were aligned against her once more. However, with the help of the theology students, she told her listeners, the prejudice could again be broken down. If the hospital continued to prohibit the participation of patients, then she would bring in patients from outside the hospital. Neither prejudice nor misunderstanding would stop the seminars. That she promised.

A young hospital chaplain stood up. He was a thin, nervous man who, in a high-pitched voice accompanied by emphatic gestures, said that he and his colleagues had been advised that they should not continue to attend the Death and Dying seminars. In fact they had come that day only to say goodbye to Elisabeth. He was sorry, but even though he would like to lend his support he could not take the risk of alienating the physicians.

Elisabeth's eyes glinted as they swept the faces in front of her. She spoke witheringly. If this was the decision of all the chaplains and theology students, then they should all re-examine their motives for being ministers or training for the ministry. If they could not stand up for what they believed to be right, then how could they be of any real help to anyone? She was not a theologian herself, but she remembered enough of the Bible to recall how Daniel had stood alone for the right and how he had faced the lions in their den. Didn't they claim to follow the Great Teacher who in Jerusalem 2,000 years ago had stood up for his convictions at the cost of his life?

No one replied. After a charged silence she challenged the chaplains and students to consider what their response might be were they to be sent as missionaries to a jungle where yellow fever raged. Would their fears prevent them from going? It was now so quiet in the auditorium that she could hear the thumping of her own heart. She knew that she was isolated, as isolated from support as she had been when she had traveled alone across Europe and been obliged for her own safety to sleep on a tombstone; as isolated as when her father had closed the front door in her face. Dismissing the class, she challenged each of them to search his conscience and to think about what she called "this landmark decision in your lives."

When they had left, she remained for a few minutes in the deserted room. Dark, predatory thoughts assailed her. Perhaps, after all, she should give up the work on Death and Dying. Why should she have to tolerate any longer the cynicism, abuse, misunderstanding and epithets? In the pocket of her dress was a note, anonymously written, that had been placed on her desk. She now reread it. It began, "To the Vulture, who hovers over the dying and who exploits the emotions of the gravely ill."

Perhaps, after all, it was impossible to end the taboo surrounding the subject of death. How could she have ever believed that she, a small woman from a faraway country, could take on the establishment that had created this death-denying society? Perhaps her dream was too idealistic and unrealistic. Would it not be better to resign from the hospital? Should she become a full-time mother and housewife? Perhaps she could persuade Manny to buy a house in the country, a house with a yard where she could grow vegetables and fruit, and a kitchen and a cellar big enough for bottling and canning. To justify her training, her professional experience, and to ease her conscience, she could have a few patients, preferably children. Or she could adopt a dozen babies, one of each race, color and creed. Together they could demonstrate how people could grow up and live in harmony. It was something she had often thought about.

Even as she raised these options, however, Elisabeth knew she would reject them, knew that it would be totally out of character for her meekly to withdraw from opposition and settle for a life of comfort in the suburbs. She knew that once having set her face toward a mountain, no matter how high, she could not look back.

But as she left the empty auditorium, the main issue was still unresolved. What should she do now? Where should she go? She walked down the corridor toward her office not knowing that the answers were close at hand.

On her desk was a pile of mail forwarded from the New York offices of *Life* magazine—letters and requests written in response to her interview with Eva. They were letters of tribute from the dying, of gratitude from the grief-stricken, letters extolling Eva's courage and honesty and thanking Elisabeth for bringing the subject of death out of the shadows and into the spotlight.

"Never have I been more deeply touched," wrote a recently widowed woman from Texas. "Eva's beauty and integrity have just filled my morning with song," wrote a male cancer patient from California. "Thank you, I've been trying to tell my mom all the things that you said," wrote Tommy, a thirteen-year-old leukemia victim in Atlanta, Georgia. "At last there are people saying it the way it is," wrote a dying man from a New York hospital.

A twenty-five-year-old Minneapolis woman suffering from a terminal disease noted, "When I read the *Life* article, I saw myself as a young child standing on the side of a pool and hearing a veteran swimmer in the deep end shouting, 'Jump in. It's not so bad. Jump in and learn to swim!'"

With the letters—the first trickle of a deluge to follow—came invitations to lecture and to conduct seminars. They came from medical schools, from nursing and other professional associations, from service clubs and churches, and were soon followed by invitations from overseas, from Europe, South America, Australia, Japan.

When she had read all the mail, Elisabeth cupped her chin in her hands. She recalled the essay she had written as a twelve-year-old in a classroom in Switzerland. I want to be "a researcher and explorer of unknown frontiers of human knowledge. I want to study life. I want to study the nature of man. . . . Above everything else in the world I would like to be a physician. . . . this is what I most want to do."

Elisabeth gathered up all the letters from her desk and took them to Eva, for she needed someone immediately with whom she could share the restoration of her childhood vision, her new sense of excitement, and her joy in finding her purpose once again.

29

A Contemporary Portrait

IN THE INTRODUCTION to this biography I described my driving Elisabeth from a small community in Wisconsin to her home at Flossmoor, south of Chicago—a six-hour journey on a winter's night. It was on this drive that she spoke to me about her psychic and mystical experiences.

Since that night she has spoken about these experiences from many public platforms as well as through the media; in doing so she has split the camp of her huge following like a lightning bolt. In shifting from the language of science to the language of mysticism, Elisabeth has lost the company of a number of her peers.

When I first met her, she was entering this arena of high controversy; but characteristically she was not disturbed by the prospect. She had been commissioned, she felt, to use her renown to declare to anyone who would listen that man indeed possessed a spirit and that his spirit survived death—which she now refers to as the "transition." The possibility of nuclear war gives urgency to Elisabeth's propagation of her gospel that the existence of an afterlife has been validated by her scientific research and personal experiences.

Today she sees her prime task as helping people to live a full life without being burdened by their "negativities," helping people to take care of "unfinished business" before they die.

She claims that the evidence of patients who have had near-death encounters with spiritual guides and relatives who have predeceased them supports her belief that physical existence, with all its pain, stress, struggle and challenge, is, in effect, "a learning experience and a growth period" for an ongoing journey.

She is convinced that the only thing of value that man carries with him through the "transition" is the record of how much he contributed to the commonweal—"how much he cared and how much he loved."

Following the feature story in *Life* magazine and the publication of her book *On Death and Dying,* subsequent articles in many other journals and innumerable newspapers, and her personal appearances on national television, Elisabeth was catapulted into fame as the leading authority on the care of the dying.

Her own life changed radically. Having found that a prophet is not accepted in his own country, she resigned from the University of Chicago at the end of the last seminar of 1969 and accepted invitations to lecture and to conduct workshops.

Shortly before Christmas 1969 she and her family moved to a Frank Lloyd Wright–designed home in Flossmoor. At last she had found the big house she had yearned for since leaving Meilen. The temptation to retire from public life was very strong, and she seriously thought about working out of her new home, caring for a manageable number of terminally ill patients.

But when the letters and appeals for lectures and help continued to pour in from across the world, she smothered thoughts of retiring and began a lecture schedule so demanding that before long it permitted her only weekends with her family.

Soon she was traveling in excess of a quarter of a million miles a year to her lectures and workshops, and her Flossmoor home became less a refuge than a communications center requiring two full-time secretaries to handle an average of 3,000 letters each month.

An image of Elisabeth that comes readily to my mind is of a tiny figure in the foyer of a small airport, a tiny figure jostled by the press of Friday evening commuters. I see her with her shoulders bent under the weight of two large suitcases, her salt-and-pepper hair clinging damply to her temples. We had arranged to meet for further taping of her story.

My mind retains this image, I think, because it seems symbolic of the loneliness of most of her days. The thousands who see her on public platforms hold to the misconception that Elisabeth is always surrounded by friends. In fact most of her life is spent alone in impersonal airports and bleak hotel rooms.

Of course, I've seen her many times with throngs acclaiming her, seen huge audiences clapping and stomping their feet, seen medical students at Stanford University line up to kiss her hand. Yet even amid the thunder of applause in these moments of adoration she seems to be isolated, lonely.

I once heard her say poignantly, "They put me on a pedestal, then treat me as a sort of demigod, yet all I want of people—of someone—is for them to say, 'Come on in and have a cup of tea with me, and kick off your shoes—or may I give you a back rub, or a big hug, or let me hold your hand for a while, or here is a shoulder to cry upon.' "

Lonely in a crowd, she revels in real solitude. Just as she did as a child when she sought out the secret Sundance Rock in Meilen, so now she seizes every opportunity for "space," as she calls it—the slopes and peaks of mountains when within any sort of range, or the quiet of an empty church when in a city.

To help me understand her work, Elisabeth invited me within a few weeks of meeting her to attend one of her Death and Dying workshops. It was held at a retreat in the hills of Virginia, where I observed her, a skilled physician of the soul, with sixty-five people of diverse backgrounds and ranging in age from twenty to eighty. The majority of those in the workshop had confronted death directly or indirectly. Perhaps a dozen were terminally ill; as many more were unable to shake off their grief over having lost a spouse, child or someone else very close to them. The remainder were mostly physicians, nurses, therapists, social workers and members of the clergy—professionals obliged to cope almost daily with the dying and the grief-stricken.

On the first day of the five-day workshop, Elisabeth asked everyone individually why he or she was there. The answers were mostly pat and cerebral. A bearded psychologist spoke in professional terms of his need to communicate more effectively with terminally ill and grieving clients. A middle-aged Canadian nun spoke piously and, in the context of the question, irrelevantly of her faith. More pertinently, an oncologist admitted his discomfort when telling patients of poor prognoses. A tense young Jewish woman, thin, pale and obviously desperately ill, spoke almost flippantly of her lethal malady and atheism. She had come to the workshop, she claimed, to learn how to deal with a distraught family. Others talked in clichés of seeking truth and expertise.

Working sessions lasted into the small hours, with the group mostly sitting on throw cushions in a half-circle. Elisabeth perched on a stool in front of a huge stone fireplace. She favored ankle-length skirts and, when seated hugging her knees to her chest—a favorite posture—she looked young and deceptively vulnerable. As she probed for abscesses of the psyche, for the roots of fear and for traumas concealed, her warm brown eyes were acutely observant as they swept faces for nuances of expression and for gestures indicative of camouflaged bitterness, guilt and fear.

Suddenly on the third day the abscesses were lanced and the poison erupted. The Canadian nun screamed her rage over being denied authority to perform her church's religious rites. The psychologist broke down and sobbed out his unresolved grief over the death of his mother. Flushed and sweating, the oncologist confessed his own terror of cancer and of death. The Jewish woman talked of a loveless childhood and of her fear of hell. The night was filled with the sounds of screaming and weeping.

Once the poison was drained—guilts confessed, rage externalized and fears expressed—unpressured hours were given to cleansing and to healing. Those who had come to the workshop, for whatever reason, began to see that in boldly facing their own fears, guilts and unresolved griefs they could better minister to their fellow men, to their clients, patients, families, neighbors and congregations. On the last evening all seemed to be imbued by a new hope and sense of purpose.

Elisabeth herself appeared to drink from some secret well of energy. After the scheduled sessions, she continued counseling on an individual basis, sometimes until dawn. Her obvious physical fatigue seemed to heighten the impact of her teaching. At times she was so weary that she looked to me to be almost translucent, a figure seen by candlelight. Her words appeared to acquire the property of floating, as if tangibly hovering like a dragonfly over a pond.

This illusion may have been caused by her audience's intensified receptivity, a receptivity created by the buoyancy that follows the lifting of long-carried burdens.

Almost as vividly as I can recall any spoken words I remember Elisabeth saying on the last night of the workshop, "People are like stained-glass windows. The true beauty can be seen only when there is light from within. The darker the night, the brighter the windows."

In uttering this reflection, Elisabeth turned her head and looked directly at the dying Jewish woman, whose expression had now totally changed. Although her face was still marked by lines of suffering, there was now a radiance about her. The sunken dark eyes had lost their bitterness and fear, and they shone.

The workshop engendered a spirit of fellowship among disparate personalities. In drawing upon their courage to be completely honest about their feelings, and in sharing their fears and pain, the group found that they were united by tribulation, by their struggles and hopes.

After a euphoric valedictory ceremony, which included a possibly unique ecumenical communion service at which the Jewish woman assisted a Catholic priest and a Protestant pastor in administering sacramental bread and wine, Elisabeth laughed at suggestions that she was a miracle worker. She was, she insisted, simply a catalyst; if miracles had been wrought then they had stemmed from the fortitude needed for absolute self-honesty.

Immediately following the workshop I spent three days keeping up with Elisabeth's frenzied pace. She flew directly from Virginia to Indianapolis to speak that night to a group of hospital chaplains. She urged them to sleep by day and to work at night. Most people died, she pointed out, in the small hours of the morning. Ten minutes at a bedside between midnight and four o'clock, when fear, pain and loneliness stalked the wards, were likely to prove vastly more profitable than two hours at a bedside in the hurly-burly of a hospital's workday.

The following day had been proclaimed by the city's mayor "Indianapolis Kübler-Ross Day." At a convention organized by a group called People Helping People, Elisabeth was scheduled to speak in a 15,000-seat auditorium. In the greenroom behind the stage she slumped into a chair and held her head. I asked whether fatigue had overtaken her. She spread her hands in a gesture of despair. No, it wasn't tiredness. Her mind was a complete blank, she protested, and she had no idea what to talk about. She had taken one look at the carnival-type lights on the stage and the group of dancing girls "warming up" the audience. The atmosphere was burlesque, she said, not the atmosphere in which to share thoughts on the subject of death and the care of the dying. I was amazed that after having given a thousand lectures, Elisabeth seemed to be as nervous as a curate preparing his first sermon. She asked me to leave the room for a few minutes, as she needed to seek "guidance."

Five minutes later a distraught middle-aged woman appeared at the back of the stage and demanded to see Elisabeth. I overheard snatches of the dialogue as the woman related with a sense of total despair and hopelessness how her three teenage sons had recently been murdered, execution style. The boys had been shot in the back of the neck by robbers. Elisabeth thanked her for bringing her an answer to her prayer and urged her to listen carefully to the lecture, as it would be given for her alone. She hoped to meet her again later.

In her lecture Elisabeth spoke almost exclusively to the grieving woman, somewhere in the darkness of the cavernous auditorium—spoke intimately of her evidence for the existence of life after death and of her conviction that a life's purpose could be fulfilled even when death came in childhood.

After the lecture the mother came backstage again to see Elisabeth and thank her. Tears coursed down her cheeks as she said simply, "If my three boys have helped all these people to understand death—and to understand that they should live, as you urged them to do, each day as if it were their last—then my children surely have not died in vain."

On the following day we were in Weston, Massachusetts, where Elisabeth made the commencement speech at Regis College and received an honorary doctorate of science degree (one of her twenty honorary degrees). The title of her address was "Love and Hate." Under

318

a striped marquee stretched over flowerbeds ablaze with color, she spoke about Hitler and about the symbolic meaning of the butterflies scratched onto the walls at Maidanek. She spoke too of the work of her "dear friend and personal heroine" Mother Teresa, in the slums of Calcutta. She spoke of the potential to love and the potential to hate in the heart of every human being. She was given a ten-minute standing ovation from students and faculty.

That night we flew to Washington, D.C., and drove to the famous Ford's Theater, where Abraham Lincoln was assassinated. Here Elisabeth received the Woman of the Year Award (in science and research) bestowed annually by the *Ladies' Home Journal*. The theater was crowded with celebrities. Manny had bought Elisabeth a tangerine chiffon dress, an Yves St. Laurent original. Kenneth and Barbara flew in from Chicago to see their mother introduced by former First Lady Lady Bird Johnson. (In 1979, according to the votes of its readers, the *Ladies' Home Journal* named Elisabeth one of its Ten Women of the Decade.)

Following the Ford's Theater ceremony, a celebration party was held in Elisabeth's honor at a gracious home in Virginia. Although she had not slept more than forty hours in a full week, Elisabeth danced into the dawn. Her hostess that night, Mrs. Ann Dailey, was subsequently instrumental in establishing the first American hospice for dying children. Mrs. Dailey says that the idea was first raised when Elisabeth took time out between a waltz and a fox trot! The child of Meilen was never far removed from the eminent psychiatrist.

The first modern hospice for the care of those approaching death was established in England, but Elisabeth is widely given credit for importing the concept to America. An alternative to the often coldly aseptic and dehumanized care given in hospitals, a hospice is a facility which provides sensitive and personalized care by those involved in the healing ministry, particularly physicians, nurses and clergy equipped by personality and training to meet the needs of the terminally ill. Hospices, with their more homelike environment, are now being established all across America, and in a sense each one is a monument to Elisabeth. She herself is on the boards of a dozen hospices.

In spite of her schedule of lectures (immediately after the Washing-

319

ton visit she flew to Europe for a series of lectures in Switzerland, Austria and Germany) Elisabeth always finds or makes time to see dying patients. Six weeks later, on her birthday, I caught up with her again in northern California. After a morning lecture to five hundred health professionals she received an urgent message from a dying physician in a town a hundred miles away. Although she was due to give a lecture that evening, and all three thousand seats had long been sold out, she decided that with fast driving she could spend an hour with him.

We skipped lunch, and two hours later we were at the patient's bedside. He was thirty-five years old and had played football for his Ivy League college. Now he was emaciated and ravaged by cancer. "Dr. Kübler-Ross," he pleaded through quivering lips, "I don't want to die." His expression suggested that by simply touching her hand he would be healed.

Elisabeth held on to the hand and said gently, "I've come to you because I'm specially interested in your living." The doctor's brow furrowed, and she added, "I mean living each minute to the full, whether you have five days to live or five months or five years." She paused and then asked, "When did you last talk to your children?"

We had seen a frightened boy and girl, perhaps seven and eight years old, in the yard as we had entered the house. The doctor's wife, elegantly dressed, stood tensely at the door of the bedroom.

The doctor let go of Elisabeth's hand in protest. Had he not played checkers with his children the previous evening?

Elisabeth nodded. "Yes. But wasn't that just to salve your conscience? What I'm asking is when did you really talk to them, really share with your family the wisdom that you now possess and have found through your illness?"

There was more to the dialogue than that, though not much more, because a hundred miles away three thousand people would soon be filling a lecture hall. Elisabeth did have the time, though, to meet the dying man's children, who spoke resentfully of having always to tiptoe through their home. They were not allowed to have their friends in the house, they told her, "all because of Daddy's sickness."

We left the house to the sound of children's laughter. We had seen them excitedly bring their Crayola drawings to their father's bedside

320

for his appreciation. For the next two months I kept in touch with the young doctor and his wife by phone. Two nights before he died his voice was firm when he said, "I'm not sure that the past few weeks haven't been the richest of my life. My family now finds more happiness in one hour spent together than we used to find in a month."

Elisabeth arrived at the lecture hall that evening with five minutes to spare. Fire marshals had to turn hundreds away at the door. At midnight she had the first chance to blow out the candles on her birthday cake.

My notebook is full of similar examples of her care. Typically, a physical therapist from California, a woman in her mid-forties, told me how Elisabeth had prevented her suicide. The therapist, suffering from multiple sclerosis, had been deserted by her husband. One evening she decided life was not worth living. She had already swallowed a quarter of a bottle of barbiturates and was beginning to feel drowsy when she suddenly felt a desperate need to tell at least one person the reason why she was taking her life.

When she removed the bottle of pills from her purse, Elisabeth's business card had fallen onto the bed. The therapist's now befuddled mind tried to put a context to the name of Kübler-Ross. Finally she recalled sitting alongside Elisabeth on a plane and how, before parting, Elisabeth had invited her to phone an Illinois number if she were ever in grave need.

The therapist told me, "It seemed to take just short of forever to get to the phone, and when I dialed the Flossmoor number I must have sounded so crazy that I'm surprised Elisabeth even bothered to listen. I told her how many pills I had swallowed and that I was about to finish off the bottle. I had expected Elisabeth to plead with me. I'd thought she would tell me she was getting in touch with the local police or the paramedics. Instead, all she said was 'I'll meet you on the steps of the Santa Barbara [California] Mission at sunset tomorrow.'"

The therapist continued: "If in the next half-hour or so I'd heard anyone knock on my door, I would certainly have taken a lethal dose. But when neither police nor paramedics arrived, all I could think about was whether Elisabeth would keep her promise."

Next evening when the therapist had hobbled up the steps of the Santa Barbara Mission, she found a very small figure wearing a peasant blouse and corduroy slacks sitting at the top—and she was smiling broadly.

Elisabeth would not allow the therapist to contribute to the price of the costly air ticket from Chicago. She has not, in fact, ever charged any of her threatened or dying patients a penny.

Once when I asked her about fees for her services, she replied, "How can I charge? It would be like a minister or a rabbi saying, 'For consolation—that will be twenty dollars'! How can I spend the night with a dying child and then tell the mother the next day, 'That's six hours at fifty dollars an hour—three hundred dollars, please'!"

The money she receives from her lecturing finances her practice and her secretarial staff, and contributes substantially to her healing center, called Shanti Nilaya.

I was with her one warm afternoon in June when she stopped to pick wildflowers in a meadow in the hills above Escondido, California. A butterfly circled her head and came to rest upon the fingers of her outstretched hand. She looked up delightedly. "That's confirmation," she laughed. "Here is where we are going to build our healing center."

The center's forty acres, nestling within a rampart of hills and enormous granite rocks that look as if they have tumbled from the moon, is, she says, the fulfillment of her hopes to find a geographical focus for her work. All her staff training for workshops is now done at Shanti Nilaya—the Sanskrit words for Home of Peace, and a name she was given in one of her cosmic consciousness experiences.

The winds of controversy that have swept around Elisabeth Kübler-Ross since she first proclaimed her conviction that death is man's final stage of growth have now become a whirlwind as she moves ever more deeply into the frontier of mysticism.

One tranquil evening we were sitting watching the sunset from the patio outside her office at Shanti Nilaya. Elisabeth pointed across the now half-shadowed meadow to where she planned, as funds became available, to build a children's center, a chapel, a lecture hall and the like. I tried to picture the completed healing center of her dreams, and felt some of the excitement she was now feeling. In a long and comfortable silence, I thought about her life: about Meilen and Mai-

322

danek, about her student days, her arrival in America. I thought about her struggle to bring into the open the taboo subject of death.

Turning toward her, I asked what she would change were she to live her life over again and whether there were some things she regretted.

She was about to reply, but suddenly rose from her chair and went into her office close by. Returning a minute later, she waved a piece of paper at me. "Here's your answer," she said, smiling. "It's a letter from an eighty-five-year-old woman."

The last paragraph of the letter read, ". . . and if I had to live my life over again I would dare to make more mistakes and take more risks. I would climb more mountains and swim more rivers. I would eat fewer beans and more ice cream. If I had my life to live over again I would certainly pick more daisies."

═══ Epilogue ═══
by Elizabeth Kübler-Ross

I WANT TO SAY a few words in epilogue to Derek Gill's biography of my life through 1969. For many years people had approached me asking that a book be written about my developing years, and I always declined such invitations out of the strong belief that biographies should not be written during a person's lifetime. Rather, I felt they should be seen as a gift of sharing and information *after* death has occurred—a means to better understanding, for those who are interested, of the commitment of the person whose life has been described. To read one's own biography in one's own lifetime prompts mixed emotions; and there is, as well, the uneasiness of sharing incidents in one's life which were precipitated or determined by the actions and feelings of people still alive and often easily identifiable.

Then Derek Gill crossed my path and, with a very great enthusiasm, devotion and appreciation of my life's work, offered to write my story. Impulsive as always, I said yes; and during a drive from a memorable lecture in Wisconsin to my home in Flossmoor we discussed this joint undertaking. It has taken nearly three years, and dur-

324

ing that time much has altered in his life and in mine. Yet though motivations have changed, interests have changed, people have changed, the story recounted here remains the same: my early upbringing, the school years, the years of wandering through postwar Europe, my move to the United States (and my response to this culture shock), and my work as a physician in this country, so different from my life as a country doctor in Switzerland. When Derek Gill approached me, I was ready at last to share this life story, because my work in the last few years has led me not only to a greater understanding of life and death but to a deeper realization of the significance of our early years. Research in the process of time, in death itself, and especially in life after death, has revealed insights that are very important in the bringing up of children, for the way in which we are going to raise our next generations.

This book becomes important only when we have a full understanding of the purpose of life, the significance of our relationships, and the awareness of the extraordinary guidance and help that we receive from an invisible world which very few people perceive. We must also realize the fact that in our lives there are no coincidences. Even the parents we choose do not become ours by coincidence. They, and our siblings, our teachers, the friends who share parts of our life, are all determined by our own choices and are part of the overall plan that directs our life—a plan that will reveal itself only at the end, at that final transition into another existence: the moment we call death.

I believe this book will be seen as even more significant when the story of my later years, and of our research into life after death, is published in the future, and it is seen why that which happened to me *had* to happen. It will become obvious why I had to be born a triplet, had to share every doll, every dress, my teachers, my mother and my father, had to experience a total lack of individual identity in a grown-up world that was unable to differentiate between my sister and myself. This early loneliness and, at times, self-chosen isolation were preparation for the years to come. I had to find my love objects in birds and animals, in meadows and among hills and trees and wildflowers rather than among individuals. I had to leave home before I was sixteen, had to work through years of hardship and physical deprivation. Thereby I was blessed with experiences I would never otherwise have had. Those years in the French part of Switzerland, in Poland, France, Germany, Belgium and Italy were gifts of awareness, gifts of sharing with other human beings who had survived the war but lost many loved ones under the most tragic of circumstances. By viewing the gas chambers, the concentration camps, the train filled with the baby shoes of murdered children in Maidanek, by talking with the Jewish girl who had lived through the nightmare of seeing her family march to their deaths, I learned that it is our choice, our own personal choice, whether we want to continue living as victims of resentment, negativity, the need for revenge; or whether we elect to leave the negativity behind and view such tragedies as the windstorms of life which can both strengthen us and help us to grow. Such experiences can help others shed their negativity as well, leaving them stronger and more polished and more beautiful, like a rock that has gone through the tumbler. The woman who had lost her entire family and twelve of her thirteen children at Maidanek taught me the lesson of unconditional love, of faith and of trust.

In those years of wandering I encountered not only the devastating consequences of Nazism, of a Hitler, a Goebbels, a Ribbentrop, but the unconditional love of Quakers from all over the world, and members of the International Voluntary Service for Peace, mainly from Switzerland, who spent years of their lives helping others. It was these Volunteers in the work camps of postwar Europe who showed me what love truly means, love given when we have no expectation of reward and are recompensed "only" by the fruits of our labors.

In those years I worked unremittingly under the most primitive conditions, labors that prepared me for the life of a workaholic. I never really learned to take time off, to dance, to giggle or laugh, perhaps even to be a child or an adolescent. I never dated or went to dances (and therefore never learned what it meant to sit on a bench waiting for a partner who never came!), and I was deprived in many respects of personal one-to-one relationships. Yet in those years I felt a sense of total contentment and happiness. There were always rewards from the work and service, pain and suffering. And I had as well my family, memories of hiking and climbing in the Swiss mountains, strolling through moors and forests, collecting rocks—memories of what I call

326

old-fashioned happiness. These have stayed with me always. Without them I would probably not have survived and achieved as I have.

My years in the United States were difficult at first, for I had a tendency to compare my life here with my independent status as a country doctor in Switzerland, where monetary rewards were few but the gratitude and love of the villagers more than compensated for this lack. Here I found a society that allows for an incredible freedom far beyond anything I could have experienced in Switzerland. My destiny had to be the United States, where I was free to pursue my own work, my own research and my own form of teaching, none of which would have been possible in any other nation in this world.

Here, through this teaching, through my own methods and my own enthusiasm and belief in my work, not only with the dying but with so-called hopeless chronic schizophrenics and with blind and retarded children, I finally found a home. My support always came from the patients and their families, and from the students who filled my classrooms to standing room only—and not from the medical establishment. A black cleaning woman at the University of Chicago became my teacher. A dying child showed me the wonderful ways in which children communicate their awareness. The mother of a dying child who shared with me her agony and despair taught me that human beings have the ability to grow out of terrible experiences and become able to help others in similar pain. And most of all Eva—who shared with me in interviews (and then in a *Life* magazine article) what it was like to have leukemia, to be twenty-two years old and to have to die with very little time to prepare—demonstrated by her courage and dignity and love an incredible lesson about life.

By drawing worldwide attention to our work, the *Life* article made it possible for more and more people to share the lessons we learn from the dying. As a result of this work, more than a hundred thousand courses on death and dying are now offered in the United States alone. Hundreds of hospices are being created here. And Shanti Nilaya, our Home of Peace, a retreat and workshop place in the mountains of Escondido, is beginning to be filled with the requests of children and adults who seek a place where people can grow. They come to get rid of their negativities and the negatively conditioned learning that prevent them from living fully and from dying in the awareness of having truly lived, not merely been alive. Here they come to the realization that life can be simple and meaningful if we will face the reality that fear and guilt are our only enemies.

To do this, we must have the courage and honesty to look within ourselves, to identify our fears, greed, guilt and shame, whatever prevents us from using our energy positively. If we are able to follow our own intuition and not be concerned about what others may say or think about us; if we listen to our inner voice and to our fellow human being who is suffering; if we share our love without expectation of reward, we will realize that each of us is student as well as teacher, teacher as well as student, and our rewards will be manifold and come when we least expect them.

It is from dying patients and from research into life after death that we have learned how to deal with people's unfinished business—their guilt, shame, fear. It is from them that we have learned how to externalize these guilts and leave them behind, learned how to exchange pity and sympathy, which belittle man, for true understanding and compassion.

I have had many wonderful mystical experiences, from cosmic consciousness to the awareness and ability to be in touch with my own guides, although I come from a conservative Protestant, authoritarian European background and I have never sought or previously understood the concept of "higher consciousness." I have never been able to meditate regularly; activities of this nature do not accord with my personality. I have never had a guru; I have never been able to visit India, though I have dreamed of it for many years. I have lived a life of unremitting work; leisure has never had much part in it. Yet despite all this, I have had, very possibly, every mystical experience that human beings are capable of having. I have experienced the greatest highs without ever having taken any drugs. I have been able to see the light that my patients see in their near-death experiences, and I have been surrounded by that incredible unconditional love that all of us experience when we make the transition called death.

I hope that this book will help others to realize the beauty, intricacy and magnitude of the threads necessary to weave the fabric of a life that has, I hope, touched others and attempted to make the world a better place. I hope it offers readers the realization that there are dimensions of understanding they too can reach, experiences they too will be able to have.

Derek's biography ends on November 21, 1969, because this date marked the end of one part of my life and the beginning of a new part. Its true dedication should be to Eva, the dying young woman who taught me so much, and whose story, published in *Life* on that date, changed my life overnight. From an inconspicuous existence in which I did my own thing, my own work, shared what I had learned with theology students and with the medical students, nurses and social workers at the university hospital, I found myself featured in headlines all over the world, and the recipient of a flood of mail that has not ceased since then. After Eva made the world aware of a physician who had spent much of her life listening to dying patients and asking them to be our teachers, I lost the privacy to which I was accustomed. But Eva's sharing made it possible for me and others to reach millions of people throughout the world through our books, our teaching tapes, our lectures, seminars and workshops, and share with them the lessons we learn from dying patients.

I thank her for that great gift, and I hope that her parents will realize that more than ten years after her death she is still touching the lives of thousands and thousands of people every week. Perhaps they will be enabled to understand that there is purpose and meaning in everything that happens, and that in our most anguished moments may reside the greatest of gifts, not only for ourselves but for the world.

I am grateful to Derek for his labors and his patience, and to my publishers for their help and support. But most of all I thank my young dying patient and her parents for what they have given us by their sharing.